FROMMER'S

D0000651

COMPREHENSIVE
TRAVEL GUIDE

Athens
10th Edition

by John Macneill
Assisted by Sheila Keenan

MACMILLAN • USA

MACMILLAN TRAVEL

A Prentice Hall Macmillan Company
15 Columbus Circle
New York, NY 10023

ISBN 0-02-860058-4

ISSN 0899-2924

Design by Michele Laseau
Maps by Geografix Inc. and Ortelius Design

SPECIAL SALES

Bulk purchases (10+ copies) of Frommer's Travel Guides are available to corporations at special discounts. The Special Sales Department can produce custom editions to be used as premiums and/or for sales promotion to suit individual needs. Existing editions can be produced with custom cover imprints such as corporate logos. For more information write to: Special Sales, Macmillan, 15 Columbus Circle, New York, NY 10023.

Manufactured in the United States of America

Contents

Appendix   194

Index   201

List of Maps

What the Symbols Mean

 Frommer's Favorites Hotels, restaurants, attractions, and entertainments you should not miss.

$ Super-Special Values Really exceptional values.

Abbreviations in Hotel and Other Listings

The following symbols refer to the standard amenities available in all rooms:

A/C   air conditioning
MINIBAR   refrigerator stocked with beverages and snacks
TEL   telephone
TV   television

The following abbreviations are used for credit cards:

AE   American Express
CB   Carte Blanche
DC   Diners Club
DISC   Discover
EC   Eurocard
ER   enRoute
JCB   (Japan)
MC   MasterCard
V   Visa

Trip Planning with This Guide

USE THE FOLLOWING FEATURES:

What Things Cost   To help you plan your daily budget

Calendar of Events   To plan for or avoid

What's Special About Checklist   A summary of each region's highlights

Suggested Itineraries   For seeing the regions or cities

Easy-to-Read Maps   Walking tours, city sights, hotel and restaurant locations—all referring to or keyed to the text

Fast Facts   All the essentials at a glance: currency, embassies, emergencies, safety, taxes, tipping, and more

Smart Traveler Tips   Hints on how to secure the best value for your money

OTHER SPECIAL FROMMER FEATURES

Did You Know?   Offbeat, fun facts

Impressions   What others have said

Inivitation to the Reader

In this guide to Athens, I have selected what I consider to be the best of the many fine establishments I came across while conducting my research. You, too, in the course of your visit to Athens and some of the excursion sites, may come across a hotel, restaurant, shop, or attraction that you feel should be included here; or you may find that a place I have selected has since changed for the worse. In either case, let me know of your discovery. Address your comments to:

John Macneill
Frommer's Athens
c/o Macmillan Travel
15 Columbus Circle
New York, NY 10023

Disclaimers

I have made every effort to ensure the accuracy of the prices as well as of the other information contained in this guide. Yet I advise you to keep in mind that prices fluctuate over time and that some of the other information herein may also change as a result of the various volatile factors affecting the travel industry.

Neither the author nor the publisher can be held responsible for the experiences of the reader while traveling.

Safety Advisory

Whenever you are traveling in an unfamiliar country, stay alert. Be aware of your immediate surroundings. Wear a moneybelt and keep a close eye on your possessions. *Be especially careful with cameras, purses, and wallets*—all favorite targets of thieves and pickpockets. Although Greece is comparatively safe, you should nevertheless bear in mind that every society has its criminals. It is therefore your responsibility to exercise caution at all times, in heavily touristed areas no less than in secluded areas (which you should avoid, particularly after dark).

Accent Marks

To aid the reader in the pronunciation of Greek street names, which sometimes can be quite long, I have added an accent mark indicating where you should put the stress. Thus, for example, in Leofóros Vassiléos Konstantínou (King Constantine Avenue), one of the main thoroughfares in Athens, the accents tell you that the words should be pronounced Leh-oh-*FOH*-rohs Vah-ssee-*LEH*-ohs Kohn-stahn-*TEE*-noo (easy enough if you repeat the words a few times).

1

Introducing Athens

Greece is the cradle of Western civilization, the origin of the drama and history and philosophy, the birthplace of democracy . . . et cetera, et cetera. That gets the clichés out of the way. Nevertheless, it's hard to imagine what civilized life would be like today without the influence of ancient Greece. The Greeks did indeed invent drama, and amphitheaters to perform it in. They also invented the Olympic Games. Euclid and Pythagoras formulated the theories that geometry students slave over to this day. And there isn't a computer programmer who hasn't studied the logic of Aristotle. Ancient Greece created a style of architecture that was the model for the White House, the Lincoln Memorial, and state capitols all across the United States. Doctors still take the Hippocratic oath, named for the father of medicine, Hippocrates—a Greek, of course. Children learn about the ant and the grasshopper and other characters from the fables of Aesop. And Greek myths have become so interwoven with our civilized consciousness that we sometimes forget where they came from. Oedipus, after all, was a Greek, not a character living in Freud's Vienna.

And then there's the Greek language. It doesn't exactly sound like poetry when spoken in the streets of Athens (ancient Greek, however, did), but what a debt we owe to it! *Sophisticated, metropolitan, aristocratic, philanthropy, gymnastics, pornographic*—they are all words from the Greek. Even a "modern" word such as *ecology* is derived from the Greek words *oíkos,* meaning "house," and *lógos,* meaning "word" or "thought."

The mighty Romans, conquerors of almost the entire ancient world, were so awed by the accomplishments of ancient Greece that they copied its art and its architecture and in general acted as if they had been conquered by the Greeks rather than the other way around. Perhaps in a way they were. Perhaps in a way we *all* were.

1 History & Background

Geography & People

GEOGRAPHY

On a map, Greece looks almost like an inkblot that landed in one large glob and burst into a score of splotches. The glob is the mainland, and the splotches are the islands. The total land area of Greece is 51,182 square miles—roughly the size of Louisiana. One-quarter of this area is islands, and the remainder is mountains. The island quarter I leave to Chapter 10; right now I'll examine the three-quarters that make up the landmass.

It's a complicated land, so I'll begin by dividing it, like Gaul, into three parts: the Olympian north, central Greece, and the Peloponnese.

THE OLYMPIAN NORTH This region includes Epirus, Thessaly, Macedonia, and Thrace. Mount Olympus, the dwelling

What's Special About Athens

Architectural Highlights
- The Parthenon, one of the world's most famous architectural wonders.
- The temple of Olympian Zeus, which took 700 years to complete.

Churches
- Ághios Gheórghios, the tiny white church that crowns Mt. Lycabettus (Lykavittós).
- Metropolitan Cathedral (Naós Mitropóleos), the grand Byzantine church that dominates the plaza midway between Sýntagma Square and Pláka.

After Dark
- Strolling down Kydathinéon Street in Pláka, listening to the hurdy-gurdy man, checking out the tavernas, stopping for a cup of Greek coffee.

Natural Spectacles
- The Acropolis, the spectacular rock rising over 500 feet above sea level in the heart of Athens.

Literary Shrines
- The ruins of the Theater of Dionysus, where works by Sophocles, Aristophanes, and Euripides, as well as other classical greats, were first performed.

Museums
- The National Archeological Museum, where history is housed; look for the not-to-be missed frescoes from the island of Santoríni (Thíra).
- The Museum of Cycladic Art's unparalleled collections.

Parks & Gardens
- The National Garden (Ethnikós Kípos), which has all matter of flora and a bit of fauna in a small zoo.
- The winding road to Ághios Gheórghios (see above), which cuts through a lovely park with a grand view of the city.

Ace Attractions
- The changing of the guard at the Tomb of the Unknown Soldier, in front of the Parliament Building.

Sunday Selections
- Picking up a few bargains from the flea market's colorful pushcarts, in Monastiráki, near Omónia Square.

Film Locations
- *Never on Sunday* at the port of Pireaus.

Festivals
- The summertime Athens Festival of theater, dance, opera.

place of the gods, is up there; so is Mt. Áthos, with its famous monastery. Thessaly is considered the breadbasket of Greece, because it supplies most of Greece's wheat, corn, barley, and cotton.

CENTRAL GREECE   This region can be subdivided into six areas—Aetolia, Acarnania, Phthiotis, Phocis, Boeotia, and Attica. The first four names you can forget for the moment, but Attica is the land around Athens (you'll probably be seeing quite a bit of it), and Boeotia (pronounced Bee-*oh*-sha) is where you'll find Delphi of oracle fame.

THE PELOPONNESE   To the southwest is a peninsula known as the Peloponnese, which can almost be considered an island since the completion of the Corinth canal, which separates the Peloponnese from central Greece. The canal, incidentally, was begun by Nero but was not completed in its present form until 1893. It's a spectacular tourist sight in its own right.

The Peloponnese is where you find such haunts of the ancient Greeks as Corinth, Mycenae, Epidaurus, Olympia, and Sparta; some 4,000 years of history; and mountains rising to almost 8,000 feet.

THE COUNTRYSIDE   Greece is a land of bleached limestone ridges, brown hills, olive groves, and an incredible collection of bays and coves lapped by green and turquoise seas. In the north, Greece is cut off from Albania, Yugoslavia (or what used to be Yugoslavia), and Bulgaria by mountains; in the west, it's isolated by the Ionian Sea; in the south, it's cut off by the Mediterranean; and in the east, it's isolated by the Aegean. Because of the mountains and valleys, communities have historically been isolated and have tended to retain their own individual characteristics; Greeks still tend to identify themselves as Cretans, Athenians, Rhodians, and so forth. This individuality has helped make the country's folk art and folklore so varied and fascinating.

All the groups still retain their rivalries, as you'll find out if you go to a taverna and the singer announces a song from "beautiful Thessaloníki" (*cheers!*), then a song from "beautiful Rhodes" (*bravos!*), and then a song from "historic Macedonia" (*whistles!*). The most reliable, charming, tolerant, and intelligent of these groups is the one that you happen to be talking to at a particular time.

PEOPLE

Overall the Greeks are a lively, friendly, fun-loving, and sometimes exuberant people. And Greek is the only language in the world in which the word for stranger is also the word for guest—*xénos.* Greeks take a great delight in the fact that so many tourists appreciate their country, and they also have a great pride in their country, its heritage, and its ruined symbols of glory.

IMPRESSIONS

Let there be light! said Liberty,
And like sunrise from the sea, Athens arose.
—Shelley (1792–1822), *Hellas*

Hospitality (*philoxenia*, "love of strangers") has always been an admirable Greek trait. From the fishing families who open their homes to tourists on the islands (it's more than that they can use the money) to the hotel clerks who act as if they've always known you, the Greeks actually seem to like visitors.

Greek is the only language in which the word for stranger is also the word for guest—xénos.

Perhaps it's because Herodotus, one of the first world travelers, was so tolerant of other races and because for centuries Greeks have roamed the world and come back home to settle, with a view of things that is less insular than the views of many other nations. (In many a small village, there's a local Greek-American—an older man who spent his youth in the United States, made his "fortune," and came back to settle and be the ultimate arbiter of all arguments about that country and its doings. Sometimes he's living on monthly Social Security checks.)

But perhaps it's nothing more than the innate native sense of drama—the opportunity to take the stage at somebody else's prompting. To any Greek, all the world's a stage, just as it always has been—especially the marketplace, the main square, and the cafés along the harbor.

Stop and ask for directions in the street and all the nearby people gather around and put in their two-bits' worth. At last, weary of making yourself understood or of trying to get any uniformity out of the replies, you walk away and leave the discussion. When you look back, they're still arguing.

Friendliness, in short, is a national characteristic, and you'll often encounter the all-purpose greeting *Yiássou!* ("Your health!") spoken by people you don't know. *Kaliméra* ("Good morning") and *Kalispéra* ("Good evening") are useful greetings to sprinkle around, too.

History & Politics

HISTORY

ANCIENT GREECE, RATHER THAN modern Greece, is what brings most visitors to Athens (the Greek islands are something else again); and since you're going to be looking at quite a lot of ruins, you may as well take a quick refresher course in the Minoans, Mycenaeans, and Macedonians. After all, the more you remember, the more you'll enjoy.

The Bull Dancers

Around 3000 B.C., the most ancient civilization of Greece began to flourish. Known as the **Minoan,** this civilization, with Crete at its center, lasted almost 2,000 years.

Dateline

- **3000–1400 B.C.** King Mimos and the Cretans build Knossós.
- **1400–1150 B.C.** Agamemnon rules; Jason and the Argonauts sail; the Trojan War, is fought.
- **1200–1100 B.C.** Dark ages descend.
- **800–600 B.C.** Athens unites with towns of Attica; ➤

Dateline

Draco proclaims severe laws; Solon reforms constitution; Homer composes the *Iliad* and the *Odyssey*.

- **520–480 B.C.** Themistocles fortifies Piraeus; Greeks win at Marathon and Salamis; Aeschylus wins Athens drama festival.
- **480–430 B.C.** The Parthenon is built; Pericles is in power; Aeschylus, Sophocles, and Euripides are at work.
- **430–400 B.C.** Naval battle of Syracuse; the Erechtheum on the Acropolis is completed; Aristophanes writes comedies, Pericles dies, Socrates drinks hemlock; Sparta triumphs.
- **360–300 B.C.** Alexander the Great's conquests, Aristotle founds school.
- **200 B.C.–A.D. 300** Rome sacks Corinth.
- **A.D.. 300–1200** Constantine builds Constantinople; Crusaders build forts and sack Constantinople.
- **1453** Constantinople falls to the Ottoman Turks.

The Minoans were generally peace-loving people. They lived in cities without protective walls, and they were never invaded. They were an artistic people but didn't develop a script until sometime around 1700 B.C. The art, which you can still see in some of the ruins at Knossós in Crete, was colorful and sunny—red columns and sky blue temple walls.

One of their favorite pastimes was bull jumping (the bull dancers would grab the bull's horns and flip themselves over its back), a sport that makes today's bullfighting look like a sheepdog trial. Bulls, in fact, were a key part of the culture and were worshipped by the Minoans. The most famous bull of all, the Minotaur, was a creature with a bull head and a human body, the mythological offspring of a bull sent from the sea as a sign of King Minos's right to the throne of Crete. Unfortunately, when the king refused to sacrifice the bull from the sea to the god Poseidon, his queen was cursed with a passion for it. Her child, the Minotaur, was imprisoned by King Minos in the center of the Labyrinth, a maze so convoluted that no one could reach the center to kill the Minotaur and thus free the people from the influence of the monster. Except the great Theseus, of course, but even he couldn't kill the Minotaur without the help of Minos's daughter, Ariadne. We'll come back to Theseus in a minute.

The Family That Slays Together . . .

On mainland Greece, the first civilization you have to contend with is the **Mycenaean,** which started to make its presence felt about 1400 B.C. It was focused on the city of Mycenae, about 25 miles from Corinth in the Peloponnese. Mycenae was the home of that happy family headed by Agamemnon, king and Trojan War hero, who was put to death by his wife, Clytemnestra, and her lover, who in turn were wiped out by her son, Orestes, at the instigation of his sister Electra.

About 1100 B.C., a people called the Dorians invaded Mycenae and other cities of Greece and crushed them. Almost overnight, the great "palace bureaucracies" disappeared, and the Greeks were reduced to living in small, illiterate communities. This was the Dark Age of Greece.

The Yarn Spinners

Throughout history, the Greeks have been nothing if not hardy, and at this time they began to develop the *polis,* or what we call the city-state, which was to become the central political unit in the upcoming classical period. The *polis* was a cluster of houses around a "palace" that stood on a safe hill, called an *akrópolis,* and its inhabitants usually had a common family relationship. Apart from that, they had nothing—no culture and no literature, only memories of past glories. So they got together on their *akrópolis* and consoled themselves by singing songs and reciting poetry extolling the heroism of their ancestors. Two of these songs were the *Iliad* and the *Odyssey.* No one knows for sure in what form Homer learned the legends he wrote about in the *Iliad;* but no matter how he received them, he handed the legends along in a great new art form that excites scholars to this day.

Around this time, 800 B.C., the Greeks came into contact with the Phoenicians, who had a system of writing; so the Greeks adapted their alphabet, just in time for Homer to polish up his spoken poetry and get it down on stone.

The Spartans

Slowly, aristocracy began replacing monarchy (except in Sparta and Macedonia); trade was flourishing, slavery was increasing, and coined money was introduced to simplify trading throughout the Mediterranean. Revolutionaries came along, roused the slaves, and overthrew governments—except in Sparta, where two kings ruled and reared their people to live frugally (hence the word *spartan*) and to cultivate physical discipline. Spartan youths were given military training from the age of seven; and all men of military age lived in barracks until they were 30, even if they were married. Thus, when any revolutionary tried to start

Dateline

- **1450s–1820s** Most of Greece is ruled by the Ottoman Empire.
- **1821** Greek War of Independence.
- **1830** Part of Greece is recognized as a sovereign state, as the struggle to free the rest of the country continues.
- **1832** Prince Otto of Bavaria is installed by the Great Powers (Britain, France, and Russia) as King Othon I of Greece.
- **1863** Othon, grown unpopular, is replaced by a Danish prince as King George I.
- **1909** Military summons Elefthérios Venizélos from Crete to head a government of national reform in Athens.
- **1912–13** Balkan Wars. Greece regains territory from Turks in the northern part of the country.
- **1917** Greece joins Allies in World War I.
- **1923–36** Period of political instability as Venizelists battle royalists for control of the government.
- **1936** Gen. Ioánnis Metaxás establishes a dictatorship friendly to the monarchy.
- **1940** Italian invasion across Albanian frontier; it is quickly repulsed.

➤

Dateline

- **1941–44** German occupation of Greece.
- **1945–49** Greek Civil War between Communists and pro-monarchy government forces.
- **1950s** Period of national reconstruction.
- **1967** Military junta seizes power, abolishing the constitution; the king flees.
- **1974** Democratic rule returns.
- **1975** New constitution is promulgated; Greece is declared a republic.
- **1981** Greece becomes 10th member of the European Community (now Union).
- **1991** Official celebration of 2,500 years of democracy.

anything in Sparta, he was quickly put down by the militaristic establishment.

Theseus Rides Again

The scene now shifts to Attica, which is the part of mainland Greece where Athens and several other small independent cities were located. These city-states were being united by King Theseus. (This is the same Theseus who penetrated the Labyrinth and killed the Minotaur—the Minoan civilization was still there all this time.) No sooner had Theseus finished with the Minotaur than he was off battling the Centaurs. Somewhere along the way, he became king of Athens, married an Amazon, conquered Thebes, and united Attica.

Throughout history, the Greeks have been nothing if not hardy.

Sometime around 621 B.C., a legislator named Draco appeared on the Athenian scene and codified laws that substituted public justice for personal revenge and thus outlawed the feuds that were a popular Greek pastime. His laws were so severe that the legislator has been immortalized by the word *draconian.* The laws were said to be written in blood rather than in ink, because he awarded the death penalty for many crimes, from murder to stealing a cabbage! These laws held for only a quarter of a century until Solon, who came to be called the founder of Athenian democracy, abolished the death penalty for everything but murder. Solon also instituted constitutional reforms that set up free elections and brought all classes (except slaves) into the process of government. And so democracy began.

Marathon and Salamis

A hundred years later, democracy and everything else that Greece had built up were threatened by Persia. The first of Persia's expeditions took place in 490 B.C., when its army arrived at Marathon. This was the event after which a Greek solider ran the 26 miles back to Athens, gasping "We have won!" before he collapsed and died. In their second expedition, the Persians were matched by the genius of Themistocles, an Athenian leader who made his people nervous by

IMPRESSIONS

There is no end to it in this city; wherever you set your foot, you encounter some memory of the past.
—Cicero (106–43 B.C.), on the Athens of his day

going out and building a huge fleet rather than an army. However, he turned out to be right: The Persians were blasted off the sea at the battle of Salamis. When the Greeks and their Spartan allies turned to the attack on land at the Pass of Thermopylae, they trapped the Persians for four days. But the Persians eventually gained the upper hand, and the Spartans, rather than retreat, remained and died to the last man. A Greek poet composed one of history's most famous epitaphs for them: "Stranger, go tell the Spartans that here we lie in obedience to their wishes."

The Golden Age

Athens, now a naval power, was headed for its golden age. Its ruler at this time (the middle of the 5th century B.C.) was **Pericles,** the most dazzling orator in a city of dazzling orators. He practiced democracy at home but imperialism abroad. One of his wisest decisions was to pay jurors, so that even the poorest citizens could sit on juries. One of his not-so-smart decisions was to restrict Athenian citizenship to people whose mother and father were both Athenians. This would have been fine if he hadn't at that time fallen under the spell of Aspasia.

Aspasia had been born in Mileta but had migrated to Athens, because that was where the action was in those days; she quickly established herself as a beautiful and intelligent courtesan, who taught rhetoric on the side. One of her students was Socrates and another was Pericles. Pericles took her as his mistress and promptly divorced his wife, but he couldn't marry Aspasia because of the new law he himself had brought into being. So they lived together. Aspasia became the uncrowned queen of Athens, and their son was honored with citizenship by a special act of the Athenians. Aspasia was later condemned to death for impiety, a trumped-up charge, and Pericles had to muster all his dazzling oratory to save her.

It was Pericles who built the Parthenon, the Propylaea, the long walls to Piraeus, and many of the temples you'll see on your strolls around town. This was quite a time in Athens. Aspasia was right—Athens was *the* place. While Pericles was building his Parthenon, Aeschylus, Sophocles, and Euripides were writing their plays, and Socrates and Plato were teaching. But Sparta was smoldering with jealousy and became increasingly worried about Athens's imperialistic policies.

Now we get involved with a long, lingering, 27-year war—the **Peloponnesian War.** Pericles led Athens, avoiding battles on land and attacking the Peloponnese from the sea, because Athens ruled

IMPRESSIONS

As a city, we are the school of Hellas.
—Pericles (495–429 B.C.)

So far has our city surpassed the rest of mankind in the field of thinking and speaking that her pupils have become the teachers of other men.
—Isocrates (Greek Orator, 436–388 B.C.)

the waves. Unfortunately, however, Pericles saw only two years of the war—he died of a plague that struck Athens in 429 B.C. A host of demagogues and lesser leaders followed, and they eventually brought Athens to defeat in 404 B.C. But victorious Sparta's influence lasted only 30 years; Sparta was then superseded as the leading power by Macedonia, a kingdom in the north of Greece.

The Prince and the Horse

Macedonia's ambitious king, **Philip II,** sought to unify all of Greece, restore Greek culture to Macedonia, and eliminate Persia as a lingering threat. But before he could do that, he divorced his wife, who thereupon hatched a plot and had him assassinated because she was jealous of his new consort. His nephew was next in line to the throne, but the crown went instead to his first wife's son, **Alexander.** One of the earliest legends about Alexander arose when he fulfilled an oracle's prediction by successfully mounting a high-spirited horse named Bucephalus. Philip had intended to destroy this horse because he was unmountable, but the clever Alexander noticed that the problem with Bucephalus was that he was literally afraid of his own shadow; so Alexander turned the horse's eyes into the sun and mounted. At the age of 20, Alexander became king, and Bucephalus would soon carry him across an empire.

Alexander the Great

Alexander subdued Greece and united it against Persia; then he marched his armies across Asia Minor, Syria, Egypt, Babylon, Susa, and Persepolis, conquering each. He was on his way to conquer India when his troops finally became so exhausted that they compelled him to return to Macedonia. He was a humane man (he had studied under Aristotle) who maintained the civil liberties of all the peoples he conquered and honored their gods and their customs. He even went so far as to adopt one Asian custom for himself and married several Eastern princesses. In 323 B.C., Alexander caught a fever and died. He had lived an extraordinary life and died when only in his early 30s.

Alexander the Great's death marked the end of the classical period of Greece, whose achievements in literature, philosophy, and art remained unrivaled. The city-states withered, the upper classes took over, and there was constant bickering and battling until 146 B.C., when Greece was conquered by the powerful and indomitable armies of Rome.

Centurions and Christians

Although the Romans, as I noted earlier, admired the art and culture of Greece, they had no respect at all for its countryside. Rather than fight all their battles on Roman soil, they tended to move them to neutral territory. Mark Antony and Octavius fought it out with Brutus and Cassius in Greece, at Philippi; Octavius then routed Antony and turned back Cleopatra's ships in Greek waters.

For 500 years, right through the early era of Christianity, Greece was subject to the power of Rome. It also became a stronghold of

Christianity. St. Paul preached in Greek, and his famous epistles were written to the Greek communities of Corinth, Thessaloníki, and Ephesus.

Many tourists travel to Greece mainly to see the classical ruins—but there's much more by way of history.

For most practical purposes, the history of classical Greece ends at this point. Tourists travel to Greece mainly to see the remains of the classical ruins and to relive the days of glory of Pericles and the Athenians. That's what Greece is all about. Obviously, though, its history continues, and there are many people who want to see the country's examples of Byzantine art and culture (which you'll read about next)—but that's not the essential Greece. From the time of St. Paul and the Apostles, the history of Greece is a chronicle of sieges, battles, and struggles to regain independence. The struggle was heroic enough, but it lacked the grandeur of the times in ancient Greece. Or maybe the later Greeks just didn't have a Homer to glorify it.

Byzantium

In A.D. 330, the Roman emperor Constantine chose a fishing village on the Bosporus, the channel leading to the Black Sea, to be his eastern capital. He named it Constantinople (Constantine's City). Eventually it became the capital of its own empire, the Byzantine, and managed to resist invasions and maintain its hold on the Balkan Peninsula, Asia Minor, Cyprus, the Middle East, and Egypt. Rome at the time was slowly succumbing to invasions of barbarians. Greece was a mere province.

For many hundreds of years, Byzantium was the only civilized part of Europe. Art, especially religious art, flourished, and churches, monasteries, and palaces went up everywhere. Then the Eastern and Western churches separated; Venetians, Franks, and soldiers from other countries in Western Europe formed their crusades and pillaged Constantinople. The city eventually fell to the Ottoman Turks (in 1453), Greece was reduced to an even more insignificant province, and Athens became a small town. The Parthenon was turned into a Turkish mosque.

For the next 400 years, Greece remained under Turkish rule. In the early 1600s, Venice tried to move in but without success (although you can still see the Venetian influence in a place such as Corfu). In the early 1800s the Greeks started to muster groups of revolutionaries, and on March 25, 1821, they formally began their struggle for independence when an archbishop raised a new blue-and-white flag at a monastery near Pátra. (The date is now Greek Independence Day.)

This was the period when Lord Byron and other volunteers rallied to the Greek cause. In the end, with the help of Great Britain, Russia, and France (already after Byron's death at Messolónghi in 1824), Greece finally defeated the Turks in a spectacular sea battle off the Bay of Navarino—spectacular and extraordinary because the Turks lost 53 ships with 6,000 men on board, but the allied fleet didn't lose a single vessel.

Independence, Defeat, and Independence Again

In 1829 the "protecting powers" declared Greece an independent nation. Unfortunately, they couldn't agree among themselves on territorial and legal conditions. (Some of these problems remain undecided to this day.) A year later, Greece became a kingdom; and in 1832 a 17-year-old Bavarian prince, Otto (or Othon in Greek), was named to the throne. He lasted until 1862 and was then replaced by a member of the Danish ruling house, King George I. Thessaly, Macedonia, and Thrace remained under Ottoman rule, but after the Balkan Wars of 1912–13 they became part of Greece, leaving Turkey with only the eastern half of Thrace, including Constantinople (which was then renamed Istanbul).

Meanwhile, political and social instability in Greece had forced the military to intervene in 1909 and summon to Athens as prime minister a hero from Crete, Elefthérios Venizélos. Venizélos sought to modernize Greece, but in doing so came into conflict with the king. The two also disagreed about which side Greece should take in World War I; Venizélos, favoring the Allies, prevailed, and King Constantine I abdicated (he was succeeded by his son, Alexander).

Conflicts between Venizelists and royalists marked the period between the end of World War I and the beginning of World War II. One battle royal was over Greece's failed military campaign in 1922 to regain territories in western Turkey. The royalists finally won out when, in 1936, Gen. Ioánnis Metaxás established a pro-monarchy dictatorship.

At the start of World War II, Greece declared its neutrality. But on October 28, 1940, the Italian ambassador paid a predawn visit to Metaxas and handed him an ultimatum from Rome: Open the Greek-Albanian border to Italian troops or else. (Italy had seized Albania a year earlier.) Metaxas replied with a firm "*Óchi!*" (no). (*Óchi* Day is now a national holiday.) The Italians then invaded through Epirus but were quickly repulsed. In early 1941, however, their allies, the Germans, came down through Yugoslavia and drove all the way to Athens; they stayed until 1944, experiencing the reverse of Greek hospitality.

The anti-German resistance movement was dominated by Communists, who after 1944 turned to fighting with government forces for control of Greece. The Greek government received the support first of the British and then of the Americans (under the Truman Doctrine, 1947) in what became a bitter civil war lasting until the defeat of the insurgents in 1949.

A period of political stability and economic recovery followed under conservative prime ministers. But in the early 1960s an old Venizelist, George Papandréou, won the elections and a tug-of-war between him and the young king, Constantine II, led again to political unrest. In 1967 a military junta seized power, forcing the king into exile; it ruled until 1974, when democracy was restored under a former premier, Constantine Caramanlís. Then, in a referendum, the Greek people voted to reject the monarchy.

In 1981, Greece became a full member of the European Community, now called European Union. Later that year elections gave the country its first Socialist government, under Andréas Papandréou, American-educated son of George Papandreou. By 1989, however, charges of corruption had so undermined the Socialists that they lost the elections to an odd coalition of conservatives and Communists.

In 1990 the right-of-center New Democracy party, under Constantine Mitsotákis, won a majority in Parliament. Caramanlis, for the second time since 1980, was elected president of the republic.

In 1993, however, the Mitsotakis government lost its majority and new elections were called. The Socialists, under Papandreou, returned to power. They moderated their socialist program but exacerbated a foreign-policy issue that had brought down the previous government—namely, the dispute with the neighboring Former Yugoslav Republic of Macedonia (FYROM) over that state's adopted name, "Macedonia," and national symbols (among them the star of Vergina, identified with Alexander the Great), which Greece regards as inherently Greek. The Papandreou government imposed an economic embargo on FYROM until the two sides resolved their dispute. Meanwhile, the New Democracy party chose a new leader, Miltiádes Evert, former mayor of Athens, who represented a younger generation of Greek politicians.

POLITICS & ECONOMY

Today, Greece is a republic, with a democratically elected parliament, prime minister, and president. It is a full-fledged member of the North Atlantic Treaty Organization and the European Union (EU).

Membership in the EU has led to an expected increase in prices, but the increase has been contained, in part because of government efforts to keep inflation relatively low (at press time it hovered around 12%). While Athens is still less expensive than Paris or London (the U.S. State Department, in fact, currently rates Athens as one of the most affordable cities in the world), it's no longer the delectable bargain it was only a few years ago. And while visitors may find a mediocre taverna meal acceptable when it costs only a few bucks, they'll want more than slapdash service and food when the prices get up around $15 and $20.

Regardless of the outcome of inflation, there is no question that the Acropolis and Delphi, Epidaurus and Mycenae, Corfu and Crete will continue to exert their mystical pull on the rest of the world. And in a world where tourists constantly have to worry about mayhem and muggings, Greece is refreshing because it's a country where you rarely have to worry about crime—maybe a little fiddling with a bill now and again or an improperly adjusted taxi meter, but nothing that's going to cause you to waste half your vacation sitting in the American consulate's office or a police station.

■ *Athens is one of the most affordable—and safest—cities in the world.*

The EU's integration into a single-market economy has brought about significant changes. For example, European airlines are now able to bypass Athens and fly directly to the islands, a blessing for anyone who doesn't want to tangle with the hassle of twin airports;

chefs from other countries are moving into the city's kitchens or opening their own restaurants, broadening the choices for local and visiting gourmands; in hotels, amenities, facilities, and services are likely to edge slowly up to the standards prevailing in the United Kingdom, Germany, and France (but so, too, will the rates). One of the most onerous changes may be the creation of standard work hours throughout the EC, which might mean the elimination of the siesta to coincide with the schedule of more mundane northern climes. (It might be better for Europe if the bureaucrats in Brussels were to do an about-face and impose siestas on northerners.)

However, bureaucrats may come and go and regimes may triumph and founder, but the glory that was Greece will remain. Or as Pericles once said, "Future ages will wonder at us, as the present age wonders at us now."

2   Food & Drink

Meals & Dining Customs

Lunch is closer to 2pm than to noon, and nobody thinks of starting dinner before 9 in the evening (even later in summer). If you have a date, arrange to meet for drinks at 9pm, then go on from there. If you're accustomed to eating earlier, you'll have problems. Most restaurants don't start serving dinner until at least 8pm, but a few (mostly in the budget category, which are probably accustomed to serving tourists from the United States or Northern Europe) will serve you a meal as early as 6 or 7pm. Now you know why there are so many snack bars in Athens!

It's a Greek custom to smoke—*a lot* and at *any point*—during the meal. You won't find NO SMOKING sections in Greek restaurants; so if smoking really bothers you, avoid small, intimate restaurants—or better yet, ask for a table outside.

Cuisine

You may have heard some people say that Greek food is dull. Dull? Try this for starters: *karavídes*—fried crayfish with Russian dressing; *kochéli*—lobster, mussels, crab, shrimp, or red snapper baked in a shell with cognac; *moussaká*—chopped meat with eggplant, cheese, and béchamel sauce; *tyrópita*—a delicious little cheese puff filled with feta; *yígantes*—white lima beans in tomato sauce; and *dolmadákia*—grape leaves stuffed with meat, onions, and spices and served with lemon sauce.

That's not a random selection from many menus. It's not even a random selection from one menu. It's only the start of a recent meal I had, and represents what the Greeks call *mezédes*, or hors d'oeuvres. The meal then proceeded to a mixed grill of lamb chop, veal, and kidney, with tomato and spring onions; it was followed by a deep-fried fritter served in a hot sugar sauce, followed by apple spiced in honey.

So let's straighten out some of the facts about dining in Athens. Greek food is *not* dull. Maybe if you stay there for a week or longer, your palate will lose its enthusiasm for more Greek food because so much of it is cooked in oil and flavored with lemon, or because so often it's lukewarm when served (on the theory that hot food is not good for you). But for the average visit of two or three days, you won't have time to sample all the dishes that you're going to want to sample. If you do stay longer and you want a change of pace, you can always go to one of the restaurants serving American or continental cuisine in their infinite variety.

Athens is becoming more cosmopolitan in its culinary choices.

Most Greek restaurants also serve a few dishes that are popular in Greece but are not Greek dishes. Most of the inexpensive restaurants feature spaghetti, cannelloni, wienerschnitzels, omelets, and steaks. Remember that Greeks have been entertaining tourists from other European countries for a long time now and try to cater to them. Each year Athens is becoming more and more cosmopolitan; and although you're probably not coming to the land of olives and feta cheese to eat pizza and tempura, you may like to know that they are available—together with the cuisines of Lebanon, Spain, Korea, Mexico, and Cyprus; there's even Polynesian at the Ledra Marriott's Kona Kai and Asian barbecues at the Inter-Continental's Kublai Khan. There always has been a choice of French and Turkish eating places, but now Athens has acquired Chinese and Japanese restaurants and even an English pub or two.

The other rumor you hear about Greek food is that it contains some unsavory ingredients. This is sometimes true in the country, and in the lambing season it is partially true in Athens. If anyone ever asks you if you'd like to try *amelétita,* just smile and say no thank you. Even in Greek it means "unmentionables." Or if someone suggests *kokorétsi,* you may want to decline; it's second cousin to Scottish haggis, and we all know what a yummy that is.

If you're tentative about what you eat (and when you're traveling, changing time zones, and generally rushing around, you have every right to be), stick to basic dishes such as roast lamb and veal. They're cooked on the spit, with only a whisper of spices.

Drinks

COFFEE

Ordering a cup of coffee for the first time in Athens is almost as bewildering as trying to order a sandwich in New York if you're a stranger (with the choice of white, whole-wheat, rye, pumpernickel, toast, and so on). The list of coffees on café menus in Athens goes roughly as follows—espresso, cappuccino, French, Nescafé, and Greek (or Turkish coffee, as it's known outside Greece). If you just say coffee, you get either Greek (if the waiter thinks you look Greek) or Nescafé (if he thinks you look American). What you probably want is, in fact, French. Nescafé is instant coffee brought to you with a cup and some hot water and you mix your own. Cappuccino comes from those hissing Italian coffee machines and is a combination of coffee and cocoa with a white froth of steamed milk on top, sometimes served with a pinch of nutmeg or cinnamon. Coffee for the Greeks comes in three degrees of sweetness: *métrios*—medium in strength and sweetness; *varýs-glykós*—strong and sweet; *skétos*—plain, or without sugar. Most Greeks seem to drink it *métrios*, and that's the way you'll probably prefer it. Besides, it's the easiest to say.

WINES & OTHER LIQUID REFRESHMENTS

You can't *not* drink wine in the land of Bacchus. Most people think of *retsina* when they think of Greek wine, but there's more to it than that. Retsina is resinated wine. Originally the resin was added to preserve the wine, then everyone liked it so much that the resin stayed there. However, it's an acquired taste. Most visitors prefer the regular Greek wines, from the bottle rather than from the barrel. There are hundreds of them, some good, some okay, and some *yugggh*. Order the following and you won't go far wrong:

Reds *Demestica* or robust *Castel Danielis*, both from the Peloponnese; *Caviros* or *Cellar* from Attica (the closest thing to a local Athenian wine); *Naoussa* from Macedonia; or *Chevalier de Rhodes* from Rhodes. Of these, Demestica is the least expensive, and Caviros is the most expensive. *Porto Carras* is a sturdy wine from new vineyards associated with a new resort in the north.

Whites Again, *Demestica, Santa Helena,* or the Muscatel-like but light *Santa Laura,* all from the Peloponnese; *Robola* from Cephalonia; *Pallini* or the pricey *Cava Cambas* and *Elissar* from Attica; and *Domaine Carras* blanc de blanc from Porto Carras.

Rosés *Roditis, Cimarosa, King,* and *Cellar.*

Be adventurous and ask for half a kilo (yes, wine is measured by the kilo, or about 1 quart) of the open wine if they have it. This will be the local wine—the white will probably be resinated, the red will probably not be. Although retsina is an acquired taste, it's surprising how fast many foreigners do acquire the taste, and at prices around 570 Drs ($3) a kilo, who can blame them? Obviously you take potluck, but the wine from Attica, the region behind Athens, is usually good.

The main Greek apéritif is *ouzo,* a clear anise drink that turns misty gray when you add water. *Mastic* is a thick white gum from a tree that grows only on the island of Ios—it's dropped into a glass of water still clinging to the spoon, and it's stickier and sweeter than anything in the world.

There seem to be no Greek beers these days, so the most popular brews are the Dutch Amstel and Heineken, both of which are brewed in Greece. Beer is sold in two sizes—550 grams (19 oz.) and 330 grams (11 1/2 oz.); remember to ask for a small beer (330 grams), about the size that you're accustomed to back home (although many places seem to stock only the larger bottles).

A popular Greek refresher is lemonade—fresh lemon juice, the real kind, squeezed into a glass, and usually served with a separate glass of water so that you can mix to your own taste. You can spend an entire afternoon in a café nursing one glass of lemon juice. Two other popular Greek refreshers, on sale almost everywhere, are Coke and tonic water.

WATER

It's one of the most refreshing drinks in Athens and comes automatically to the table—even when you order coffee—but without ice. If you prefer bottled water, carbonated water is more reliable than the still variety; but if you order the latter at the table, you'll probably get a large $1^1/_2$-liter (about $1^1/_2$ qt.) bottle. It's perfectly acceptable in most tavernas or budget restaurants to take the bottle away with you if you can't manage to drink the whole thing. In the country, never drink water that has come straight from a well.

3 Recommended Books & Films

Books

Finding books on Greece is not difficult; choosing from among them is. The suggested list of books below is meant to alleviate the problem of selection for the traveler who is interested in learning something about the history, life, and culture of the Greek people but doesn't have the time to delve into thick scholarly tomes. Some of the books are thin enough to be taken along as companions.

CULTURE & RELIGION

Boardman, John. *Greek Art* (New York: Thames & Hudson, 1985).

Dinsmoor, William B. *Architecture of Ancient Greece* (New York: Norton, 1975).

Burkert, Walter. *Greek Religion* (Cambridge, Mass.: Harvard Univ. Press, 1987).

Dickinson, G. Lowes. *The Greek View of Life* (London: Collier, 1967).

Graves, Robert. *Greek Myths* (New York: Penguin, 1955).

Hamilton, Edith. *Mythology* (New York: New American Library, 1971).

Papaioannou, Kostas. *The Art of Greece* (New York: Abrams, 1988).

Schwab, Gustav. *Gods and Heroes: Myths and Epics of Ancient Greece* (New York: Pantheon, 1977).

Woodford, Susan. *An Introduction to Greek Art* (Ithaca, N.Y.: Cornell Univ. Press, 1988); *The Parthenon* (Lerner, 1983).

HISTORY

Bury, J.B., and Russell, Meiggs. *A History of Greece: To the Death of Alexander the Great* (New York: St. Martin's Press, 1977).

Campbell, John, and Philip Sherrard. *Modern Greece* (New York: Praeger, 1968).

Clogg, Richard. *A Social History of Modern Greece* (New York: Cambridge Univ. Press, 1986).

Woodhouse, C.M. *Modern Greece: A Short History* (London: Faber & Faber, 1986).

LITERATURE

Delillo, Don. *The Names* (New York: Knopf, 1982).

Dimaras, C.T. *A History of Modern Greek Literature* (New York: New York Univ. Press, 1972).

Fowles, John. *The Magus* (New York: Dell, 1985).

Homer. *Iliad* (New York: Penguin, 1950) and *Odyssey* (New York: Penguin, 1950).

Kazantzakis, Nikos. *The Greek Passion* (New York: Touchstone, 1971); *Odyssey: A Modern Sequel* (New York: Touchstone, 1969); *Report to Greco* (New York: Touchstone, 1975); *Zorba the Greek* (New York: Touchstone, 1971).

Renault, Mary. *The Bull from the Sea* (Pantheon, 1959); *Fire from Heaven* (New York: Pantheon, 1969); *The King Must Die* (New York: 1988); *The Mask of Apollo* (New York: Pantheon, 1988).

TRAVEL

In Athens you'll find a variety of good specialized English-language guides to the city and its historic districts (Pláka, Monastiráki), as well as to the many ancient sites nearby (Delphi, Mycenae).

Durrell, Lawrence. *The Greek Islands* (New York: Penguin, 1980).

Gage, Nicholas. *Hellas: A Portrait of Greece* (New York: Random House, 1987).

Geldard, Richard G. *The Traveler's Key to Ancient Greece: A Guide to the Sacred Places of Ancient Greece* (New York: Knopf, 1989).

Miller, Henry. *The Colossus of Maroussi* (New York: New Directions, 1958).

Sicilianos, Demetrios. *Old and New Athens* (London: Putnam, 1960).

Films

Greece is a popular location for film makers. The Aegean islands especially have served as the backdrop for several cinematic hits (and misses): *The Guns of Navarone* (1961), an action film about the Allied resistance to the German occupation of Rhodes during World War II; *The Greek Tycoon* (1978), a thinly veiled rendering of the Aristotle Onassis and Jackie Kennedy story; *Shirley Valentine* (1989), a poignant comedy about a British tourist who finds romance, along with plenty of sun and sand, on Mykonos; and *Mediterraneo* (1991), an Italian film set in the Dodecanese during World War II.

Two Greek literary works brought to the screen are *Zorba the Greek*, the novel by Níkos Kazantzákis, and *Z*, the fictionalized account of an actual event by Vassílis Vassilikós. In *Zorba the Greek* (1964), we see depicted the ever-recurring conflict between the Apollonian and the Dionysian elements in Greek culture, as personified, respectively, by the reticent young intellectual Alan Bates and the older, passionate, life-seizing Anthony Quinn. *Z* (1969), directed by Costa-Gavras, relates the circumstances of a politically inspired murder that had taken place in Thessaloníki a few years earlier and the efforts by the authorities to cover it up. The setting of the story, however, is not specified, for the point of the film is that such political crimes occur with impunity in any society in which the law can be easily bent to the will of those in power. Incidentally, the courageous prosecutor, played by Yves Montand, who tries to uncover the conspiracy, despite attempts to thwart him, was in real life Chrístos Sartzetákis, who later (1985–90) served as president of the republic of Greece.

Z, viewed as an attack on the right, was banned in Greece during the military dictatorship (1967–74). Also politically sensitive, for assailing the left and its role in the Greek Civil War, was *Eleni* (1985), based on a book by Nicholas Gage. Eleni, portrayed by Kate Nelligan, is the author's mother, who in 1949 was summarily tried and executed by Greek insurgents because she had helped her children flee from Communist-held territory to join their father in the United States.

Also drawing inspiration from literature are the films *Trojan Women* (1972), based on Euripides' tragedy, with Katharine Hepburn, Vanessa Redgrave, and Irene Pappas; and *Tempest* (1982), a comedy, after Shakespeare's play, about a middle-aged New York architect (John Cassavetes) who abandons his work and wife (Gena Rowlands), moves with his teenage daughter to Greece, and there finds romance with a carefree young woman (Susan Sarandon).

Three other well-known movies shot in Greece are *Boy on a Dolphin* (1957), about the search for ancient treasures off the coast of Hydra, starring Sophia Loren and Alan Ladd; *Never on Sunday* (1959), about a popular Piraeus *fille de joie*, played exuberantly by Melina Mercouri, who resists the efforts of an American tourist (Jules Dassin) to "reform" her; and *For Your Eyes Only* (1981), a James Bond thriller offering spectacular views of Corfu and the monasteries of Metéora, in central Greece.

2

Planning a Trip to Athens

WHETHER YOU INTEND ATHENS TO BE YOUR MAIN DESTINATION IN GREECE or simply a stopover on your way to the Greek isles, you'll find the information in this chapter invaluable as you make your travel plans. The chapter contains useful pointers on when to go, how much to budget, and how to get there. However, when you get right down to the detailed planning, you ought to check in with your travel agent for the latest updates on rates and fares.

1 Information, Entry Requirements & Money

Sources of Information

Before you go to Greece, you can obtain travel information as well as basic information about Athens and the rest of the country from the *Greek National Tourist Organization (GNTO).* The GNTO has offices in the following major cities:

UNITED STATES *New York:* 645 Fifth Ave., 5th Floor, New York, NY 10022 (☎ **212/421-5777,** fax 212/826-6940. *Chicago:* 168 N. Michigan Ave., 4th Floor, Chicago, IL 60601 (☎ **312/782-1084,** fax 312/782-1091). *Los Angeles:* 611 W. 6th St., Suite 1998, Los Angeles, CA 90017 (☎ **213/626-6696,** fax 213/489-9744).

CANADA *Toronto:* 2 Bloor St. West, Cumberland Terrace, Toronto, ON M4W 3E2 (☎ **416/968-2220,** fax 416/968-6533). *Montréal:* 1233 Rue de la Montagne, Suite 101, Montréal, QC H3G 1Z2 (☎ **514/871-1535,** fax 514/871-1498).

UNITED KINGDOM *London:* 195–197 Regent St., London WIR 8DC (☎ **071/734-5997,** fax 071/287-1369).

AUSTRALIA *Sydney:* 51–57 Pitt St., Sydney, NSW 2000 (☎ **2/241-1663,** fax 2/235-2174).

GREECE *Athens:* In Greece the GNTO is known simply as the Greek Tourist Organization, or *Ellinikós Organismós Tourismoú (EOT).* Its information office in Athens (☎ **322-2545** or **323-4130**) is right on Sýntagma Square, the city's main quadrangle, at Odós Karagheórghi tís Servías 2 (2 Karageorges of Serbia Street), in the National Bank of Greece. The head administrative office (☎ **322-3111**) is a few blocks away, at Odós Amerikís 2 (2 America Street).

Entry Requirements

PASSPORTS A valid passport is all that an American, a British, a Canadian, or a New Zealand citizen needs to enter Greece. You don't need an international driver's license if you're renting a car; your local license from back home should suffice.

VISAS For visits to Greece of less than three months, visas are not required by citizens of the United States, Canada, the United Kingdom, and New Zealand.

CUSTOMS   Greece permits you to bring in most personal effects and the following items duty free: two still cameras with 10 rolls of film each, one movie or video camera, tobacco for personal use, one bottle of wine and one bottle of liquor per person, a portable radio, a tape recorder, a typewriter, a bicycle, golf clubs, tennis racquets, fishing gear, skis, and other sports equipment.

There's no restriction on the number or value of traveler's checks on either entry or exit. Be very careful about antiques that you buy in Greece; the laws protecting Greek antiquities are very strict, and no genuine antiquities may be taken out of the country without prior special permission from the Archeological Service, at Odós Polygnótou 3 (3 Polygnotus Street), in Athens.

In the U.S.   Returning to the United States from Greece, American citizens may bring in $400 worth of merchandise duty free, provided they have not made a similar claim within the past 30 days. Remember to keep receipts for purchases made in Greece. For more specific guidance, request the free pamphlet "Know Before You Go" by writing to the U.S. Customs Service, P.O. Box 7407, Washington, DC 20044.

In Canada   For total clarification, Canadians can write for the booklet "I Declare," issued by Revenue Canada Customs Department, Communications Branch, Mackenzie Avenue, Ottawa, ON K1A OL5. Canada allows its citizens a Can$300 exemption, and they can bring back duty free 200 cigarettes, 2.2 pounds of tobacco, 40 ounces of liquor, and 50 cigars. In addition, they are allowed to mail unsolicited gifts (but *not* alcohol or tobacco) into Canada from abroad at the rate of Can$40 a day. On the package, mark "UNSOLICITED GIFT, UNDER $40 VALUE." All valuables you own and take with you should be declared before departure from Canada on the Y-38 form, including serial numbers. **Note:** The $300 exemption can be used only once a year and then only after an absence of seven days.

In the U.K. & Ireland   Members of European Union countries do not necessarily have to go through Customs when returning home, providing all their travel was within EU countries. Of course, Customs agents reserve the right to search if they are suspicious. However, there are certain EU guidelines for returning passengers, who can bring in 400 cigarillos, 200 cigars, 800 cigarettes, and 1 kilogram of smoking tobacco. They can also bring in 20 liters of fortified wine, 90 liters of wine, and 110 liters of beer. Persons exceeding these limits may be asked to prove that the excess is either for one's personal use or gifts for friends. For further details, contact **HM Customs and Excise,** Excise and Inland Customs Advice Centre, Dorset House, Stamford Street, London SE1 9NG (☎ **071/202-4227**).

In Australia   The duty-free allowance in Australia is Aus$400 or Aus$200 for those under 18. Personal property mailed back from Spain should be marked "AUSTRALIAN GOODS RETURNED" to avoid payment of duty. Upon returning to Australia, citizens can bring in 200 cigarettes or 250 grams of loose tobacco and 1 liter of alcohol. If you're returning with valuable goods you already own, such as foreign-made cameras, you should file form B263. A helpful brochure, available from Australian consulates or Customs offices, is *Customs Information for All Travellers.*

In New Zealand The duty-free allowance is NZ$500. Citizens over 16 can bring in 200 cigarettes or 250 grams of loose tobacco or 50 cigars, 4.5 liters of wine or beer, or 1.125 liters of liquor. New Zealand currency does not carry restrictions regarding import or export. A Certificate of Export listing valuables taken out of the country allows you to bring them back without paying duty. Most questions are answered in a free pamphlet, *New Zealand Customs Guide for Travellers,* available at New Zealand Consulates and Customs offices.

Money

CASH & CURRENCY

The unit of currency in Greece is the **drachma (Dr),** in the form of a coin or bill. (The drachma—called *drachmí,* plural *drachmaí* or *drachmés,* in Greek—was also in use in ancient Athens; see the coin exhibits in the city's Numismatic Museum.) As of this writing, US$1 = 250 Drs. Because of constant fluctuations in the exchange rate, however, and also because of possible increase in prices since the European Union inaugurated a single market, you should *use the figures in these pages as a guide only.*

The drachma is made up of 100 **leptá;** a single *leptó* is worth less than a penny. There is a new gold coin for 100 Drs, and coins for 1, 2, 5, 10, and 20 Drs. Bills are worth 50 Drs (blue), 100 Drs (red), 500 Drs (green), 1,000 Drs (brown), and 5,000 Drs (blue). There always seems to be a shortage of (or a reluctance to make) change in many places. If you know that you're going to be making inexpensive purchases or paying low tabs, ask for 1,000 Dr bills when you exchange currency.

Some coins may seem to be worth peanuts, but you'll need them for tipping, telephones, and trolleys.

Note: In the following pages, the dollar equivalents have been rounded off to the nearest dollar for the sake of simplicity.

TRAVELER'S CHECKS Traveler's checks are the safest way to carry cash while traveling. Before leaving home, purchase traveler's checks and arrange to carry some ready cash (usually about $250, depending on your habits and needs). In the event of theft, if the checks are properly documented, the value of your checks will be refunded. Most large banks sell traveler's checks, charging fees that average between 1% and 2% of the value of the checks you buy, although some out-of-the-way banks, in rare instances, charge as much as 7%. If your bank wants more than a 2% commission, it sometimes pays to call the traveler's check issuers directly for the address of outlets where this commission will be less.

Issuers sometimes have agreements with groups to sell checks commission free. For example, the Automobile Association of

America (AAA) sells American Express checks in several currencies without commission.

American Express (☎ toll free **800/221-7282** in the U.S. and Canada) is one of the largest and most immediately recognized issuers of traveler's checks. No commission is charged, as mentioned above, to **AAA** members and holders of certain types of American Express charge cards. The company issues checks denominated in U.S. or Canadian dollars, British pounds sterling, Swiss or French francs, German marks, and Japanese yen. The vast majority of checks sold in North America are denominated in U.S. dollars. For

The Greek Drachma

For U.S. Readers At this writing, $1 = 250 Drs (or 1 Dr = $0.004). This was the rate of exchange used to calculate the dollar values given in the table below and throughout this edition.

For U.K. Readers At this writing, £1 = 370 Drs (or 1 Dr = £0.002). This was the rate of exchange used to calculate the pound values in the table below.

Note International exchange rates fluctuate from time to time and may not be the same when you travel to Greece. Therefore, this table should be used as a guide for *approximate* values only.

Drs	US$	UK£
5	0.02	0.01
10	0.04	0.03
25	0.10	0.07
50	0.20	0.14
75	0.30	0.20
100	0.40	0.27
125	0.50	0.34
250	1.00	0.68
1,250	5.00	3.38
2,500	10.00	6.76
5,000	20.00	13.51
7,500	30.00	20.28
10,000	40.00	27.02
12,500	50.00	33.78
15,000	60.00	40.54
17,500	70.00	47.30
20,000	80.00	54.05
22,500	90.00	60.80
25,000	100.00	67.57

questions or problems that arise outside the U.S. or Canada, contact any of the company's many regional representatives.

Citicorp (☎ toll free **800/645-6556** in the U.S. and Canada, or **813/623-1709,** collect, from anywhere else), issues checks in U.S. dollars, British pounds, German marks, and Japanese yen.

Thomas Cook (☎ toll free **800/223-9920** in the U.S., or **609/987-7300,** collect, from anywhere else) issues MasterCard traveler's checks denominated in U.S. dollars, French francs, German marks, Dutch guilders, Spanish pesetas, Australian dollars, Japanese yen, and Hong Kong dollars. Depending on individual banking laws in each of the various states, some of the above-mentioned currencies might not be available in every outlet.

Interpayment Services (☎ toll free **800/221-2426** in the U.S. or Canada, or **800/453-4284** from most anywhere else) sells Visa checks sponsored by Barclays Bank and/or Bank of America at selected branches around North America. Traveler's checks are denominated in U.S. or Canadian dollars, British pounds, Swiss or French francs, German marks, and Japanese yen.

CREDIT & CHARGE CARDS   You'll find that carrying credit and charge cards is useful in Greece. **American Express, Visa,** and **Diners Club** are widely recognized. If you see the Eurocard or Access sign on an establishment, that means it accepts **MasterCard.**

Credit and charge cards can save your life when you're abroad. With American Express and Visa, for example, not only can you charge purchases in shops and restaurants that take the card, but you can also withdraw drachmas from bank cash machines at many locations in Greece. Check with your card company before leaving home.

Keep in mind that the price of purchases is not converted into your national currency until notification is received in your home country, so the price is subject to fluctuation. If your national currency—be it dollars, pounds, or whatever—declines by the time your bill arrives, you'll pay more for an item than you expected. But those are the rules of the game. It can also work in your favor if your national currency should rise, against the drachma.

CURRENCY EXCHANGE   Many Athens hotels will simply not accept a dollar- or pound-denominated check, and if they do, they'll almost certainly charge for the conversion. In some cases, they'll accept countersigned traveler's checks or a credit card, but if you're prepaying a deposit on hotel reservations, it's cheaper and easier to pay with a check drawn on a Greek bank.

This can be arranged by a large commercial bank or by a specialist such as **Ruesch International**, 825 14th St. NW, Washington, DC 20005 (☎ **202/408-1200,** or toll free **800/424-2923**), which performs a wide variety of conversion-related tasks, usually for only $2 U.S. per transaction.

If you need a check payable in drachmas, call Ruesch's toll-free number, describe what you need, and note the transaction number given to you. Mail your dollar-denominated personal check (payable to Ruesch International) to the office in Washington, DC. Upon receiving this, the company will mail a check denominated in drachmas for the financial equivalent, minus the $2 charge. The company can also help you with many kinds of wire transfers and conversions of VAT (value-added tax, which is known as IVA in Greece), refund checks, and also will mail brochures and information packets on request. Britishers can go to Ruesch International Ltd., 18 Saville Row, London W1X 2AD (☎ **0171/734-2300**).

Mutual of Omaha/Travelex, 1225 Franklin Ave., Garden City, NY 11530 (☎ toll free **800/377-0051** in the U.S.) provides foreign currency exchange at 30 U.S. airport locations or through the mail. With exchanges of $500 or more, they will guarantee to exchange back up to 30% at the same rate you originally exchanged with no service fee. Annual or short-term flight insurance policies are available starting at $5.

Traveler's Checks

Traveler's checks are accepted in major hotels, shops, and restaurants throughout Athens. Small establishments, however, such as neighborhood tavernas and snack bars and corner grocery stores, will more likely than not refuse to take them.

Credit Cards

American Express, Diners Club, Eurocard, MasterCard, and Visa are honored in Athens and major tourist centers throughout Greece. Prominently displayed decals identify cooperating merchants, but verify beforehand that the contracts are still in existence.

2 When to Go—Climate, Holidays & Events

Come to Athens as soon as you can get away—now, if you can. From the point of view of things to see and do, any time of the year is fine.

What Things Cost in Athens	US $
Taxi from airport to city center	6.00
Subway to Piraeus	.75
Local telephone call	.05
Double at NJV Meridien Hotel (deluxe)	225.00
Double at Astor Hotel (moderate)	64.00
Double at YWCA (budget)	25.00
Lunch for one at Ideal (moderate)	7.00
Lunch for one at Yalí Kafinés ouzerí (budget)	5.00
Dinner for one, without wine, at L'Abreuvoir (deluxe)	18.00
Dinner for one, without wine, at Taverna Strofí (moderate)	11.00
Dinner for one, without wine, at Eden (budget)	6.00

For dogged sightseeing, in fact, winter might even be best. On the whole, the best months are April, May, June, September, October, and November. The weather then is gentlest and the ruins are not swamped by tourists. You'll have a better choice of hotels then also. Avoid the Greek Easter unless you want to stay in Athens: It's a weeklong celebration, and everyone heads for the countryside and islands; the airport is a mob scene of people trying to get on overbooked flights. (Remember that I'm talking here only about Athens; some of the islands, particularly Crete and Rhodes, are also *winter* tourism destinations.) If you're on a tight budget, you'll find at least one advantage in coming in winter: Many hotels lower their rates from November through April.

Climate

Athens is roughly on the same latitude as Louisville, Ky., San Francisco, and Tokyo. Its climate is considered mild and probably is, except when you're trudging around town looking for a hotel at high noon in August. Rainfall is a skimpy 15 inches a year, most of it in short showers in winter. (If it rains in summer before the last week of August, it's news.) June, July, August, and September are hot but bearable because the air is so dry. On the other hand, don't try to fit in half a dozen temples between noon and 2pm; try to confine your sightseeing to the early morning or late afternoon. In winter, specifically in January and February, things can get a little chilly. The cafés and tavernas move indoors, and occasionally you may have to hold on tight for fear of being blown off the Acropolis.

But all the statistics in the weather bureau will never do justice to the Athenian evenings. The air is soft, scented, seductive, and scintillating—even alliteration doesn't do it justice. Yet one must admit that in recent years the air has become less seductive because of the noxious cloud of pollution, or *néfos,* that hangs increasingly over the city, particularly during the summer months. Government efforts to alleviate the problem—for a while by limiting the number of automobiles in Athens—have had little effect. As a result, the problem has become political and, as such, a frequent topic of discussion in the cafés.

Summers are dry and hot, with temperatures hovering around 90°F. It's cooler, of course, along the coasts and in the mountains to the north. In winter the temperature can go down to 40° in some areas (Athens has an average temperature of 55° in January), and rain can also be expected 12 or 13 days a month from October through April. But the sun shines some 300 days a year.

Athens's Average Monthly Temperatures (°F)

	Jan	Feb	Mar	Apr	May	June	July	Aug	Sept	Oct	Nov	Dec
Low	45.0	44.6	47.7	53.4	60.8	68.5	73.6	73.8	68.0	60.6	52.0	48.2
High	56.3	57.7	61.9	68.7	75.9	84.2	90.1	90.1	83.8	75.4	66.6	59.5

Holidays

The following are legal national holidays in Greece:

New Year's Day   January 1
Epiphany   January 6
Shrove Monday   Occurs 41 days before Easter
Independence Day   March 25
Good Friday through Easter Monday
May Day   May 1 (Labor Day)
Pentecost *or* **Whitsunday**   Occurs 50 days after Easter
Assumption of the Virgin   August 15
***Óchi* Day**   October 28 (see page 12)
Christmas   December 25–26

On these days, government offices, banks, post offices, and most stores are closed. Various museums and attractions, however, may be open to the public. Some restaurants also remain open. For further information, inquire at your hotel or consult the English-language publications, such as *The Athenian,* a monthly magazine, available at newsstands.

Athens Calendar of Events

The following is only a sample of the hundreds of special events—folkloric, religious, festive, and cultural—that take place throughout the year in Athens and elsewhere in Greece. For a complete list, contact the Greek National Tourist Organization (see "Sources of Information," above).

January

- **St. Basil's Day.** A legal as well as religious holiday, celebrated with the serving of a special New Year's pie (*vassilópita*) in which, traditionally, a coin is concealed; whoever finds it may look forward, it is said, to a year of good fortune. (Christmas gifts are exchanged on this day rather than December 25.) January 1.

⭐ **Epiphany**

Commemorating the baptism of Christ, this holiday is celebrated throughout Greece with a "Blessing of the Waters" ceremony. During the ceremony, the priest throws a cross into the water and then blesses the water as well as those who are about to dive into it to retrieve the cross. The most spectacular ceremony takes place in Piraeus. **Where:** Port of Piraeus. **When:** January 6. **How:** From Athens by subway from Omónia Square or by green bus no. 40 from Sýntagma Square.

February

- **Carnival (*Apókries*).** A time of fun and merriment during the period before Lent, with parades and masked celebrations (and in some places, especially villages, with bonfires and dancing). Date varies.

March

⭐ Independence Day

The national holiday of Greece, honoring the 1821 War of Independence, with military parades throughout the country. The big parade, of course, is held in Athens, with all the country's leaders in attendance.
Where: Sýntagma Square. **When:** March 25. **How:** Line up along Leofóros Amalías (Amalía Avenue) to view the parade. The official viewing stand is in front of the Parliament Building. **Note:** March 25 is also a religious holiday, the Feast of the Annunciation.

April

- **Easter Sunday.** The most holy day on the Greek Orthodox calendar. Date varies.

⭐ Acropolis Son-et-Lumière Show

Sound-and-light performances—in several languages, including English—dealing with the history and architecture of the Acropolis. Similar shows are given at other major archeological sites in Greece.
Where: Pnyx Hill, west of the Acropolis. **When:** April through October. **How:** Performances begin at 9pm. Purchase tickets before then at the Athens Festival Box Office, Odós Stadíou 4 (4 Stadium Street).

May

- **May Day (*Protomaghiá*).** Greece's Labor Day, marked with flower festivals and family picnics. May 1.

June

⭐ Athens Festival

A summerlong cultural festival—the major such event in Greece—featuring performances of drama, music, and dance, with the appearance of world-famous artists and orchestras.
Where: The 1,800-year-old Herod Atticus Odeum, at the foot of the Acropolis. **When:** Mid-June to the end of September. **How:** Purchase tickets—well in advance of a performance, if you want good seats—at the festival box office, Odós Stadíou 4 (4 Stadium Street).

- **Wine Festival.** Annual festival at Dafní, 11km (6½ miles) from Athens. Free wine tasting, with tavernas and dancing nearby. Similar festivals take place at other locations in Greece. Mid-June.

July

- **Epidaurus Festival.** Performances of ancient Greek drama in the amphitheater at Epidaurus (Epídavros), in the Peloponnese—the largest and best-preserved such amphitheater in Greece, July through August.

August

- **Olympus Theater Festival.** Ancient Greek dramas performed in the open-air theater at Díou, near Mt. Olympus. Mid-August.
- **Pilgrimage to Tínos.** Annual pilgrimage to the island of Tínos, in the Cyclades, where the ill and infirm, and their relatives, go to pray to the Virgin Mary for a cure at the church of Panaghía Evanghelístria (Our Lady of Good Tidings). August 15 (Feast of the Assumption).

October

- **Athens Marathon.** Annual race from the village of Marathon to the Panathenaic Stadium in Athens, a course of 42.2 km (26.2 miles). The race commemorates the run that Pheidippides, a courier, made in 490 B.C. to announce to the Athenians that their outnumbered forces had just defeated the Persians at the Battle of Marathon. Exclaiming "*Nenikíkamen!*" ("We have won!"), he collapsed and died. Undaunted applicants may contact SEGAS, Leofóros Syngroú 137 (137 Syngroú Avenue), 17121 Athens (☎ **01/932-0636**), for information. Mid-October.
- *Óchi* **Day.** A national holiday, honoring Greece's refusal in 1940 to accept an ultimatum from Italy that the Greek-Albanian border be opened to Italian forces. Greece at the time was neutral, and its rejection of Italy's demand caused it to enter World War II on the side of the Allies. The day is marked by military parades throughout Greece. (*Óchi*, by the way, means no.) October 28.

December

- **St. Nicholas's Day.** A holiday honoring a 4th-century bishop of Myra, in Asia Minor (modern Turkey), who is regarded as the patron saint of children and sailors. The day marks the beginning of Christmas celebrations, with children singing carols accompanied by drums and triangles, December 6.
- **Christmas.** The second most important religious feast of the year (after Easter), celebrated with family gatherings, dancing (especially in the villages), and the serving of special homemade cookies (*kouloúria* and *kourabiédes*). (Gift-giving occurs on St. Basil's Day, January 1.) December 25–26.

3 Health & Insurance

Health

You'll encounter few health problems traveling in Greece. The tap water is safe to drink, the milk is pasteurized, and health services are good. Occasionally the change in diet may cause some minor diarrhea, so you may want to take some antidiarrhea medicine along.

Carry all your vital medicine in your carry-on luggage and bring enough prescribed medicines to last you during your stay. Bring along copies of your prescriptions that are written in the generic—not brand-name—form. If you need a doctor, your hotel can recommend one or you can contact the American embassy or consulate. You can also obtain a list of English-speaking doctors before you leave, from the **International Association for Medical Assistance to Travelers (IAMAT)** in the United States at 417 Center Street, Lewiston, NY 14092 (☎ **716/754-4883**); in Canada at 40 Regal Road, Guelph, ON N1K 1B5 (☎ **519/836-0102**).

If you suffer from a chronic illness, talk to your doctor before taking the trip. For such conditions as epilepsy, diabetes, or a heart condition, wear a Medic Alert identification tag, which will immediately alert any doctor to your condition and provide the number of Medic Alert's 24-hour hotline so that a foreign doctor can obtain medical records for you. For a lifetime membership the cost is $35. Contact the **Medic Alert Foundation,** P.O. Box 1009, Turlock, CA 95381-1009 (☎ toll free **800/432-5378**).

Insurance

Before purchasing any additional insurance, check your homeowner's, automobile, and medical insurance policies as well as the insurance provided by credit-card companies and auto and travel clubs. You may have adequate off-premises theft coverage, or your credit-card company may even provide cancellation coverage if your plane ticket is paid for with a credit card.

Remember, Medicare only covers U.S. citizens traveling in Mexico and Canada.

Also note that to submit any claim you must always have thorough documentation, including all receipts, police reports, medical records, and so forth.

If you are prepaying for your vacation or are taking a charter or any other flight that has cancellation penalties, look into cancellation insurance.

The following companies will provide further information:

Travel Guard International, 1145 Clark Street, Stevens Point, WI 54481 (☎ toll free **800/826-1300**), which offers a comprehesive 7-day policy that covers basically everything, including emergency assistance, accidental death, trip cancellation and interruption, medical coverage abroad, and lost luggage. It costs $44. There are restrictions, however, that you should understand before you accept the coverage.

Travel Insured International, 52-S Oakland Ave., East Hartford, CT 06108 (☎ toll free **800/243-3174**), offers illness and accident coverage, costing from $10 for 6 to 10 days. For lost or damaged luggage, $500 worth of coverage costs $20 for 6 to 10 days. You can also get trip-cancellation insurance for $5.50.

Mutual of Omaha (Tele-Trip), Mutual of Omaha Plaza, Omaha, NE 68175 (☎ toll free **800/228-9792**), charges $3 a day (with a 10-day minimum) for foreign medical coverage up to $50,000, which features global assistance and maintains a 24-hour "hotline." The company also offers trip-cancellation insurance, lost or stolen luggage coverage, the standard accident coverage, and other policies.

HealthCare Abroad (MEDEX), P.O. Box 480, Middleburg, VA 22117 (☎ **703/687-3166,** or toll free **800/237-6615**), offers a policy, good for 10 to 90 days, costing $3 a day, including accident and sickness coverage up to $100,000. Medical evacuation is also included, along with a $25,000 accidental death or dismemberment compensation. Trip cancellation and lost or stolen luggage can also be written into this policy at a nominal cost.

Access America, 6600 West Broad St., Richmond, VA 23230 (☎ **804/285-3300** or toll free **800/424-3391**), has a 24-hour hotline in case of an emergency, and offers medical coverage for 9 to 15 days costing $49 for $10,000. If you want medical plus trip cancellation, the charge is $89 for 9 to 15 days. A comprehensive package for $111 grants 9- to 15-day blanket coverage, including $50,000 worth of death benefits.

4 What to Pack

In summer, wear your lightest clothes. Wear comfortable, *sturdy,* heavy shoes; they're essential for scrambling over all those marble ruins—and not such a bad idea for some sidewalks in Athens. Specifically, wear sightseeing garb. For hiking up steep hills and steps (of which there are countless thousands in Greece), women will probably be happier in shorts or pants rather than skirts. If you're planning to visit one of the sites where donkeys are the standard means of conveyance, long pants are recommended to avoid a case of donkey chafe on your knees. Women should bring along a sweater or jacket (you can buy one there inexpensively) for evenings, cruises, or the mountains. In casinos, men must wear jacket and tie, women should wear cocktail dresses or pantsuits. For dining, jacket and tie are rarely required, but a jacket or sweater may be useful in some air-conditioned restaurants.

Generally, how you dress is up to you. The Greeks dress casually. Shorts or short skirts are now acceptable, although sometimes they are startling to the peasants in the countryside. You're expected to dress in a respectable manner when you enter a cathedral or church (no shorts, sleeveless shirts, short skirts, for example, are permitted), but there are no hard-and-fast rules.

5 Tips for the Disabled, Seniors, Singles, Families & Students

For the Disabled

There are many agencies that can provide advance trip-planning information, among them **Travel Information Service,** Moss Rehabilitation Hospital, 1200 West Tabor Road, Philadelphia, PA 19141-3099 (☎ **215/456-9900**). It charges $5 per package, which will contain names and addresses of accessible hotels, restaurants, and attractions, often based on firsthand reports of travelers who have been there.

You can obtain a copy of *Air Transportation of Handicapped Persons,* published by the U.S. Department of Transportation. It's free if you write to Free Advisory Circular No. AC12032, Distribution Unit, U.S. Department of Transportation, Publications Division, M-4332, Washington, DC 20590.

You may also want to consider joining a tour for disabled visitors. Names and addresses of such tour operators can be obtained by writing to the **Society for the Advancement of Travel for the Handicapped,** 347 Fifth Avenue, New York, NY 10016 (☎ 212/447-7284). Annual membership dues are $45, or $25 for senior citizens and students. Send a stamped, self-addressed envelope.

Fedcap Rehab, 211 West 14th Street, New York, NY 10011 (☎ 212/727-4200), also operates summer tours for members, who pay a yearly fee of $10.

For the blind, the best information source is the **American Foundation for the Blind,** 15 West 16th Street, New York, NY 10011 (☎ 212/620-2000 toll free 800/232-5463).

For Seniors

Many senior discounts are available, but note that some may require membership in a particular association.

For information before you go, write to **"Travel Tips for Senior Citizens"** (publication no. 8970), distributed for $1 by the Superintendent of Documents, U.S. Government Printing Office, Washington, DC 20402 (☎ 202/783-3238). Another booklet—and this one is distributed free—is called **"101 Tips for the Mature Traveler,"** available from Grand Circle Travel, 347 Congress Street, Suite 3A, Boston, MA 02210 (☎ 617/350-7500, or toll free 800-221-2610).

SAGA International Holidays, 120 Boylston Street, Boston, MA 02116 (☎ toll free 800/343-0273), runs all-inclusive tours for seniors, 60 years old or older. Insurance is included in the net price of their tours. Membership is $5 a year.

In the United States, the best organization to join is the **American Association of Retired Persons (AARP),** 1909 K Street NW, Washington, DC 20049 (☎ 202/872-4700), which offers members discounts on car rentals, hotels, and airfares. AARP travel arrangements, featuring senior citizen discounts, are handled by American Express. Call toll free **800/927-0111** for land arrangements, toll free **800/745-4567** for cruises. Flights to and from various destinations are handled by both numbers.

Information is also available from the **National Council of Senior Citizens,** 1331 F Street NW, Washington, DC 20004 (☎ 202/347-8800), which charges $12 per person to join. Members receive a monthly newsletter, part of which is devoted to travel tips. Discounts on hotel and auto rentals are available.

Elderhostel, 75 Federal Street, Boston, MA 02110 (☎ **617/426-7788**), offers an array of university-based summer educational programs for senior citizens throughout the world. Most courses last around 3 weeks and are remarkable values, considering that airfare, accommodations in student dormitories or modest inns, all meals, and tuition are included. Courses include field trips, involve no homework, are ungraded, and emphasize liberal arts.

Participants must be over 60, but each may take an under-60 companion. Meals consist of solid, no-frills fare typical of educational institutions worldwide. The program provides a safe and congenial environment for older single women, who make up some 67% of the enrollment.

For Single Travelers

Unfortunately for the 85 million single Americans, the travel industry is far more geared toward couples, and singles often wind up paying the penalty. It pays to travel with someone, and one company that resolves this problem is **Travel Companion,** which matches single travelers with like-minded companions. It's headed by Jens Jurgen, who charges between $36 and $66 for a 6-month listing in his well-publicized records. People seeking travel companions fill out forms stating their preferences and needs and receive a mini-listing of potential travel partners. Companions of the same or opposite sex can be requested. For an application and more information, contact Jens Jurgen, Travel Companion, P.O. Box P-833, Amityville, NY 11701 (☎ **516/454-0880**).

Singleworld, 401 Theodore Fremd Avenue, Rye, NY 10580 (☎ **914/967-3334,** or toll free **800/223-6490**), is a travel agency that operates tours for solo travelers. Some, but not all, are for people under 35. Annual dues are $25.

For Families

Advance planning is the key to a successful overseas family vacation. If you have very small children you should discuss your vacation plans with your family doctor and take along such standard supplies as children's aspirin, a thermometer, Band-Aids, and the like.

On airlines, a special menu for children must be requested at least 24 hours in advance, but if baby food is required, bring your own and ask a flight attendant to warm it to the right temperature. Take along a "security blanket" for your child—a pacifier, a favorite toy or book, or, for older children, something to make them feel at home in different surroundings—a baseball cap, a favorite T-shirt, or some good luck charm.

Make advance arrangements for cribs, bottle warmers, and car seats if you're driving anywhere.

Ask the hotel if it stocks baby food, and, if not, take some with you and plan to buy the rest in local supermarkets.

Draw up guidelines on bedtime, eating, keeping tidy, being in the sun, even shopping and spending—they'll make the vacation more enjoyable.

Babysitters can be found for you at most hotels, but you should always insist, if possible, that you secure a babysitter with at least a rudimentary knowledge of English.

Family Travel Times is a newsletter about traveling with children. Subscribers to the newsletter, which costs $55 for 10 issues, can also call in with travel questions, but Monday through Friday only from 10am to noon eastern standard time. Contact **TWYCH,** which stands for Travel With Your Children, 45 West 18th Street, New York, NY 10011 (☎ **212/206-0688**).

For Students

The largest travel service for students is the **Council on International Educational Exchange (CIEE),** 205 East 42nd Street, New York, NY 10017 (☎ **212/661-1414**), providing details about budget travel, study abroad, working permits, and insurance. It also sells a number of helpful publications, including the *Student Travel Catalogue* ($1), and issues International Student Identity Cards (ISIC) for $10 to bona fide students.

For real budget travelers it's worth joining the **International Youth Hostel Federation (IYHF)**. For information, write AYH (American Youth Hostels), P.O. Box 37613, Washington, DC 20013-7613 (☎ **202/783-6161**). Membership costs $25 annually, except that under-17s pay $10.

6　Getting There

By Plane

Olympic Airways, the Greek national carrier, is currently the only airline flying nonstop to Athens from New York's JFK Airport—once a day, 7 days a week. In addition, during the summer months, Olympic flies twice a week from Chicago, with one stop en route. **TWA** flies from JFK to Athens with one stop along the way, and from St. Louis and San Francisco with two or three stops along the way, depending on the day of the week. Some **Delta** transatlantic flights connect at Frankfurt with another Delta flight to Athens.

From Canada, Olympic has direct service from Montréal and Toronto, twice a week from each, with one stop along the way in each case.

From other cities in the United States, the obvious plan would be to fly to New York or one of the above-mentioned cities and connect with the Athens flights, but check with your travel agent and you may find that this is not necessarily the most efficient, most convenient, or fastest routing. For example, your connecting flight to New York might take you to LaGuardia Airport rather than to JFK, leaving you the task of getting from one airport to the other in time for boarding. Your travel agent may discover from the computers that it's smarter to fly from Atlanta, Chicago, Houston, or Los Angeles with a European carrier such as **KLM Royal Dutch Airlines** or **Lufthansa** and make your connection at Amsterdam's Schiphol Airport or Frankfurt Airport. It may sound crazy, but in fact both are one-terminal airports that are more efficient than JFK, and your travel time will probably work out about the same—and perhaps even less. The fares will be identical. And for a small additional charge, you will have the option of stopping off for a few days in, say, Amsterdam, thus adding a whole new dimension to your trip.

As you probably know, the fare situation is so complex you almost have to be a lawyer to read the fine print—the restrictions on dates, days of the week, length of stay, advance purchase, and so on. As of this writing, economy-class fares from New York to Athens ranged from more than $2,000 with no restrictions to $938 advance purchase, with a minimum stay of 7 days. Between those two extremes, you can expect fares, with some restrictions, in the region of $998 to $1,600.

Your travel agent may also be able to arrange to buy a ticket through a consolidator, sometimes known as a "bucket shop"— a company that buys tickets in bulk in advance *at special low fares.* These fares range from $420 (AG World Tours & Travel; ☎ 212/947-2208) to $350 (Homeric Tours; ☎ 212/753-1100), in each case one-way based on a round-trip. Finding the *lowest* fares means a lot of extra work for your travel agents but they're usually happy to oblige if you are also using them to book hotels, cruise ships, and sightseeing tours.

By Train

Traveling by train is a long haul, to be sure, but if you're using a EurailPass (☎ 212/697-2100) and you're planning to see other parts of Europe along the way, you have a bargain—and the longer you travel, the better the bargain is. The EurailPass brings you 15 days of unlimited first-class travel for around $498, or 21 days for $648 (about the cost of the round-trip first-class fare from Paris alone).

Frommer's Smart Traveler: Airfares

1. Shop all the airlines that fly to your destination.
2. Always ask for the lowest fare, not just a discount fare.
3. Keep calling the airline—availability of cheap seats changes daily. Airline managers would rather sell a seat than have it fly empty. As the departure date nears, additional low-cost seats become available.
4. Ask about frequent-flyer programs to gain bonus miles when you book a flight.
5. Check "bucket shops" for last-minute discount fares that are even cheaper than their advertised slashed fares.
6. Ask about air/land packages. Land arrangements are often cheaper when booked with an air ticket.
7. Fly free or at a heavy discount as a courier.

Athens & Environs

Dafní Monastery **3**	Piraeus (Pireás) **4**
Elefsís (Eleusis) **2**	Soúnio **11**
Glyfáda **8**	Várkiza **10**
Kaisarianí Monastery **5**	Vouliagméni **9**
Marathon **1**	Vravróna **7**
Mt. Imittós (Hymettus) **6**	

The passes are valid also on ferryboat services between Brindisi, Italy, and Pátra, Greece, but from June through September you may have to pay a surcharge for those segments. Several trains go to Greece, either directly from or with connections from major cities such as Amsterdam, Paris, Frankfurt, and Vienna. If you plan to go by train all the way, you can estimate traveling time from, say, Munich, which is about 36 hours. (However, since these trains go through what was once Yugoslavia, you will use another route until things quiet down there.)

By Car

See "By Ship" below.

By Ship

Once in Europe, you can get to Greece by boat. The usual route is to take the train (or your car) from Rome to Brindisi, where you catch a ferryboat to the island of Corfu or the port city of Pátra, in the western Peloponnese. At Pátra there are special bus services to take you the 4-hour trip to Athens. However, you may not want to head directly to Athens, since many of the sights you have come to Greece to visit are along the way or nearby—Olympia, Corinth, Náfplio, Mycenae, and Epidaurus. You can rent a car in Pátra or take local buses stage by stage to Athens. For more information on connections between Italy and Greece, call Adriatica (☎ 453-3032 in Athens) or Ventouris lines (☎ 324-0276 in Athens).

Package Tours

A great variety of organized tours is offered, from sightseeing in Athens and environs to complete tours of the Greek mainland or air tours and cruises to the many islands. A few of the leading tour operators are: **American Express,** Odós Ermoú 2 (2 Hermes Street; ☎ 324-4976); **CHAT Tours,** Odós Stadíou 4 (4 Stadium Street; ☎ 322-3137, fax 323-5270); **Key Tours,** Leofóros Kallíróis 4 (4 Kallírói Avenue, ☎ 423-3166, fax 923-2008); and **Viking Tours,** Odós Artemídos 1 (1 Artemis Street, Glyfáda; ☎ 898-0729; in the U.S., call toll free **800/841-3030**).

Several U.S. companies offer comprehensive tours of Greece, with dozens of departures from various points in the States. Some examples from the 1994 catalogs (all prices are per person, double occupancy, and do *not* include transatlantic airfares): Grand Tour of Greece (CHAT Tours): 9 days, $752. The itinerary includes Athens (2 days), Corinth, Náfplio, Olympia, Delphi, Metéora, Kalambáka, Thessaloníki Corinth, Pella, and Thermopylae. The tour price includes some meals, some city tours; accommodations are in top-quality Category A hotels.

3

Getting to Know Athens

Everyone's image of Athens is a white, rocky hill with a ruined but glorious temple on top, or maybe an *évzone* in a skirt with pompons on his shoes. But your first impression of Athens will be nothing like that.

Your introduction to Athens will be a marble parthenon of the 20th century—a gleaming, elegant airport terminal that puts you in the atmosphere of a big, modern, successful city.

On your ride in from the airport, you pass through disheveled suburbs of two-story white houses, past women dressed in black; and despite the alien but unmistakable injunction to drink Coca-Cola, you're left with no doubt that you're now in a Mediterranean country.

When you get to your hotel in the heart of the city, you're in a sophisticated European city of avenues, jewelry shops, spacious squares, and terrace cafés. Step a few streets from this chic city, and you're treading in the marbled steps of Aristotle, Pericles, and Sophocles.

In other words, there's no point in trying to put Athens into any kind of category. It's unique. It's a city where you brush shoulders with ancient Greece, Rome, Sparta, Macedonia, Byzantium, the East, the West, Venice, Germany, France, Italy, and America. They've all left their imprint, and you're treated to an intriguing, unbelievably historic, but not particularly beautiful city.

1 Orientation

Arriving

BY PLANE

There are two airport terminals in Athens. If you're flying a foreign airline, you'll arrive and depart from **Ellinikón East Terminal,** which is for international flights by overseas airlines. If you fly anywhere via Olympic Airways, internationally or to the islands or some other city in Greece, you'll leave from the **Ellinikón West Terminal** (sometimes referred to as the Olympic Terminal). Make sure you tell your taxi driver which one you want. There is a shuttle service between the East Terminal and West Terminal every 20 minutes from 6am to midnight.

For information, call East Airport at **969-9466** or **969-9111**; West Airport at **936-9111**; Olympic Airways only, at **936-3363.**

There's airport bus service to and from 4 Amalía Avenue, near the corner of Sýntagma Square, every 30 minutes from 6am to 11pm. Express blue bus 91 leaves for the East Terminal every 30 minutes; the ride takes 30–45 minutes, and the fare is 200 Drs (80¢) each way; there is no charge for luggage. If you're not on a tight budget, the taxi fare is about 1,400 Drs ($6), including luggage, direct from the airport to your hotel (if you're staying around Sýntagma Square). Olympic Airways buses leave from the same corner and from the Olympic downtown terminal at Leofóros Syngroú 96 (96 Syngroú

Avenue) and go directly to the West Terminal at Ellinikón. The ride takes 30 minutes, leaves every half hour from 4am to 10pm, and is free to Olympic ticket holders.

Note: Some of the deluxe hotels operate shuttle-bus service to and from the airport—check out times when you make your reservations.

BY TRAIN

Trains coming from northern Greece or Northern Europe pull into the Laríssis railway station (Stathmós Laríssis) at Karaïskáki Square (☎ 524-0601; trains to and from the Peloponnese use the Peloponnisos station nearby (☎ 513-1601). There are also Greek State Railway (OSE) ticket offices at Odós Siná 6 (6 Siná Street), ☎ 362-4402, and at Odós Filellínon 17 (17 Philhellenes Street), ☎ 323-6747. Trolleys (yellow buses) nos. 1 and 5 will take you to Sýntagma Square, in the center of Athens.

BY CAR

If you arrive from Italy by ship with a car, you'll head into Athens via the national highway from Pátra, which flows into Omónia Square. Two of the most convenient hotels with parking are the Park and the Novotel Mirayia (see Chapter 4, "Athens Accommodations").

Tourist Information

Dial **171** for information (hotels, shops, sports, nightclubs), given in five languages, 24 hours a day.

The EOT information office (see "Information, Entry Requirements, and Money" in Chapter 2) is at Odós Karagheórghi tís Servías 2 (☎ 322-2545).

TRAVEL AGENTS

Here are two reliable organizations: **American Holidays,** Odós Patriárchou Ioakím 58, Kolonáki (☎ 723-3863); and **Wagons-Lits/ Travel,** Odós Stadíou 5 (☎ 324-2281). **Camel Tours,** at Odós Voulís 7 (☎ 323-4617), specializes in rail travel. At **Esperus Travel Agency,** four floors up at Odós Karagheórghi tís Servías 12 (☎ 322-8468), multilingual owner/manager Diamond Carountzos has been paving the way for well-to-do Americans for almost 40 years, but he is not above booking a cabin on the Piraeus-Iráklio (Crete) ferry for more humble travelers.

GUIDES

If you want to hire a personal guide, the rates are from 25,000 Drs to 29,000 Drs ($100 to $116). Call the association of tour guides at 322-9705.

City Layout

Let's begin where Athens began—with the **Acropolis.** From the summit of the hill you get the second-best view of the city. Around the base of the Acropolis is the tourist-famous section of **Pláka,** built on the ancient city (you'll be reading more about it later), with some of the most notable archeological finds—the Agora and the temple of Theseus. To the northeast is the **hill of Lykavittós** (Lycabettus),

Athens Orientation

Acropolis **11**
First Aid Station **7**
Greek Tourist
   Organization **15**
Greek Tourist
   Organization
   Information Desk **14**
Kolonáki Square **4**
Lykavittós (Lycabettus)
   Hill **5**
Monastiráki **13**
National Archeological
   Museum **8**
National Garden **3**
Omónia Square **8**
Parthenon **12**
Pláka **10**
Sýntagma Square **1**
Theseum Station **9**
Záppion **2**

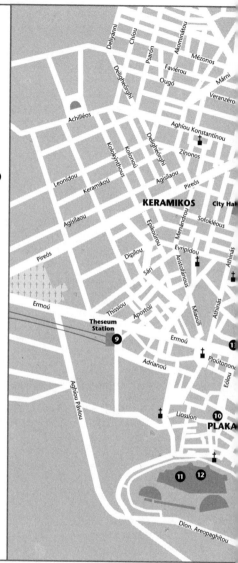

and beyond that are the spreading suburbs and the ring of
mountains separating Athens from the rest of Attica. Between
Lykavittós and the Acropolis is the heart of the city, distinguished
from this height (about 450 feet) mainly by the green patch of the
National Garden and the hint of broad avenues radiating from
Sýntagma (Constitution) **Square.** To the other side, the west and

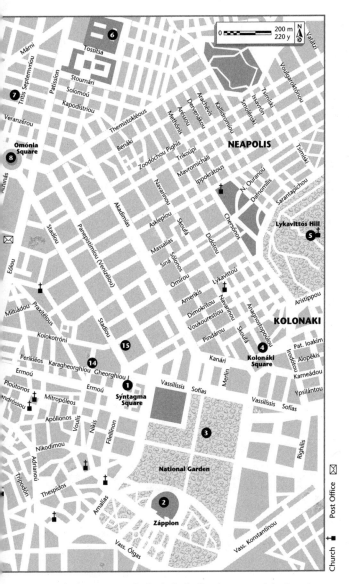

Post Office ⊠

Church ✝■

south, the avenues and suburbs lead off to the coast and the Saronic Gulf, with Piraeus hidden behind a couple of hills.

At street level, the focal point of Athens is Sýntagma Square, a large quadrangle sloping in the direction of the Acropolis. At the upper end is the neoclassical shuttered facade of the Parliament Building, which used to be the old royal palace (the newer palace, next to the National Garden, is now the official residence of the president of the republic). The other three sides are surrounded by hotels and office buildings (including several airline offices and travel agencies). The great attraction of Sýntagma, however, is its cafés, on two sides and in the middle (see p. 104).

There are three streets running from the bottom end of the square, all laden with shops and hotels: **Karagheórghi tís Servías, Ermoú,** and **Mitropóleos.** Mitropóleos leads you to the cathedral, the Agora, the temple of Theseus, and the temple of the Winds; and if you make a left turn when you get to the cathedral, you go up into Pláka and from there up to the Acropolis.

Back to Sýntagma. The broad avenue running off from the top-left corner of the square is variously known as **Venizélou** and **Panepistimíou** (University); it takes you past the magnificent neoclassical facade of the university to the helter-skelter bustle of Omónia Square. **Omónia Square** is to Sýntagma what Times Square is to, say, Rockefeller Center (in New York City). From Omónia Square you can follow the avenue known as **October 28** (28 Oktovríou) or **Patissíon** to the National Archeological Museum.

I've just touched on the major landmarks of Athens in this chapter and will get back to them in detail later on, in Chapter 6.

NEIGHBORHOODS IN BRIEF

Athens, from the Golden Age to the modern age, has always been a very public city. Athenians like to spend time together outdoors: in cafés, tavernas, and plazas or just strolling. Here are a few of the neighborhoods of special interest to visitors who want to mingle with city's denizens. More detailed information is included in the chapters on hotels, restaurants, and nightlife.

Sýntagma Square The city's commercial hub, the square is defined by Amalia Avenue (Leofóros Amalías), Karagheórghi tís Servías Street, Óthonos Street, and Filellínon Street. It's a particularly Greek blend of billboards, banks, and fast foods. The

---

A Note on Street Names

The Greek word for "Street" is *Odós*. The word for "Avenue" is *Leofóros*, abbreviated Leof.

Street names appear in the genitive case. Thus, for example, *Odós Níkis* and *Leofóros Vassilíssis Sofías* should be read as "Street of Nike" (goddess of Victory) and "Avenue of Queen Sophia." The words for "Queen" (*Vassílissa*, gen. *Vassilíssis*) and "King" (*Vassiléfs*, gen. *Vassiléos*) appear in the city's major thoroughfares abbreviated in both cases as "Vass."

For the sake of simplicity, I have, where possible, given the names of squares in the nominative case. Thus, instead of *Platía Syntágmatos* (Square of the Constitution), the main square in Athens, I say "Sýntagma Square." If you were to ask for directions to "Sýntagma," you would be readily understood.

square was recently renovated, and the 3,000 café seats you once had your pick of have been drastically reduced to make space. But what you have now is a beautiful marble plaza with splashing fountains, palm trees, wrought-iron lampposts, carefully manicured landscaping, and Greek statuary, all under the imperial gaze of the ocher Parliament Building. And you can still get a cup of coffee.

Pláka This is the higgledy-piggledy neighborhood that lies between Sýntagma Square and the Acropolis. Here's where you'll find plenty of nightlife, tavernas, bouzouki clubs, and tourists. But you'll also find lovely little walkways, incredible Parthenon views, and all manner of houses, gardens, and fine 19th-century architectural detail. After some years of neglect, Pláka is having a renaissance and has some of the hottest real estate in town.

Kolonáki Lying on the other side of Sýntagma, in a northwest direction, right at the base of Mt. Lykavittós, it's a tony area of chic boutiques and just as chic cafés and watering holes.

Omónia Square The other major commercial center, it lacks the appeal of Sýntagma, but stop for a souvláki here and you'll get the flavor of Athens as a city at work.

Exarchía This area is just up Odós Themistokléous, heading away from Omónia Square. Here's where you'll find the hip and the happening hanging out over coffee and cigarettes, or strolling along the pedestrian-only square.

Fokíonos Négri This is a broad, plazalike street north along 28 Oktovríou, in the Patissíon neighborhood, just beyond the National Archeological Museum. A pleasant little center, it is lined with cafés and restaurants, which at night (and afternoons, for that matter) are filled with animated Athenians.

2   Getting Around

By Public Transportation

If you're staying in downtown Athens, you can walk to almost all major museums, sights, and attractions. However, public transportation is available, inexpensive, and reliable.

BY SUBWAY

The subway goes in a straight line—from Omónia Square to Piraeus and from Omónia Square to the suburb of Kifissiá (the fare is 75 Drs, 30¢, in each direction). Subway cars run every 10 minutes, from 5am to midnight. You probably won't have too many occasions to use it, unless you're staying around Omónia Square and you want to get to Piraeus to catch a ferryboat or cruise ship, in which case it's the fastest and cheapest way to get there.

BY TROLLEY & BUS

The trolleybus and bus routes crisscross the city, and you can get to all the main tourist haunts for no more than 75 Drs (30¢), although you must buy a ticket before boarding. Look for the kiosks that have special ticket-seller signs.

Some of the main routes from Sýntagma Square are the nos. 3, 5, 9, and 12 trolleybuses, which will take you to Omónia Square and the National Archeological Museum; the no. 230 blue bus goes to the Acropolis, the Pnyx, and Philopáppos Hill; the no. 1 trolleybus goes to Omónia Square and the Laríssis railroad station; the no. 161 bus goes to Fálero; and the no. 40 green bus goes from Odós Fillenínon to Piraeus.

If you're in any doubt about which route to take and where to get off, ask your hotel receptionist to write out the number and the stop in Greek and simply show this to the conductor or one of the passengers (unless you're traveling at the peak hours, when everyone's too busy trying to stay upright to have much time to help a stranger).

By Taxi

Taxis are not as cheap as they were in former days, but they're still fairly cheap compared with taxi rates in many U.S. cities. The ride from the airport to Sýntagma Square is approximately 1,400 Drs ($6); the ride from Athens to the next town, Piraeus, costs about 1,000 Drs ($4); and to the nightclubs along the shore it's about 1,700 Drs ($7). If you're sharing with another couple, taking a taxi in Athens is like taking a bus back home. You don't have to tip the drivers, although they've gotten into the habit of expecting to keep the small change at least; and a few of them seem to have trouble counting out your change in the hope that you may just tell them to forget it. The drivers are, on the whole, honest—but erratic. Shut your eyes and don't look. They also have a tendency to have conversations with other cab drivers as they ride along, since many of them can't converse with their foreign passengers. If you're setting off for a night on the town, it's wise to have the doorman or receptionist at your hotel write down the address in Greek for the benefit of your driver. And, of course, like cab drivers everywhere, they disappear at rush hours.

The law allows drivers to pick up additional passengers going in the same direction; conversely, you can now try to flag down a taxi that's already taken (but be prepared to shout out your destination as soon as the cab slows down near you). This is a very practical idea intended to save gasoline and space; but the problem is defining "same direction," and you may find yourself making a few unscheduled detours that add minutes (though *not* drachmas) to your trip.

Although taxi fares are still inexpensive, they have gone up yet again. The meter now starts at 200 Drs ($1) but ticks over at the rate of 54 Drs (22¢) a kilometer; between midnight and 5am rates double. For boarding at an airport, station, or harbor, there's a charge of 100 Drs (40¢); the per-kilometer charge becomes 105 Drs (42¢) beyond the city boundaries. Each piece of luggage is an additional 40 Drs (16¢); waiting time is 720 Drs ($3) per hour. Most drivers, as noted, are honest, but always check to make sure that the meter is on Tariff 1 as you set off.

That's the cost of a cab *if* you can find one! Theoretically, there are taxi stations on or near every major square, but that doesn't necessarily mean there are any taxis at the stations. There is a telephone service for radio-controlled cabs (see below) that adds a 300 Drs ($2) surcharge to your fare. The recent law allowing would-be passengers to flag down taxis that already have passengers in them was supposed to spread the taxis around, but in reality it makes a taxi more difficult to find. There's no easy answer, other than appearing on the doorstep of a deluxe hotel and tipping the doorman handsomely or calling a private "executive taxi" service (☎ 325-5522)—but be prepared to pay $25 and up from downtown to the airport or Piraeus. One further note: Taxi drivers have become absolute pirates when meeting the island ferries; rides back to Athens have been quoted anywhere from 3,000 to 5,000 Drs ($12 to $20). Share a cab; or better yet, take the subway or the no. 40 bus back to Sýntagma Square.

By Car

You could, of course, rent a car, but even a small European car won't free you from the frustrations of one-way streets, blue zones, and parking places. While you're sightseeing in the city, forget about a car; if you're planning to do some trips out into the country or along the coast, then a car makes more sense.

RENTALS

Greece may well be the most expensive country in Europe for both car rentals and gas. It always seems to cost more to rent than you think it will, so the following tips may help.

There are several reliable companies renting cars, and you'll have a fairly wide choice of cars—German, French, Italian, and Japanese, from Ford Fiestas and Volkswagens to luxury Mercedes with air conditioning and automatic transmission. You'll recognize a few old

Average Car-Rental Rates*			
	Peak Season		**Low Season**
	Per Day	**Per Kilometer**	**Unlimited Mileage, Per Week**
Subaru M80 (*Category A*)	4,700 Drs ($19)	67 Drs (26¢)	95,200 Drs ($380)
Nissan Cherry (*Category B*)	5,500 Drs ($22)	75 Drs (30¢)	107,800 Drs\ ($431)
Peugeot 309 (*Category C*)	7,000 Drs ($28)	84 Drs (33¢)	129,500 Drs ($518)
Opel Astra (*Category D*)	10,000 Drs ($40)	110 Drs (44¢)	174,500 Drs ($698)

* Rates are subject to an 18% tax.

faithfuls among the list of companies, such as Avis and Hertz, both of which have desks at the arrivals hall in the airport, but there are also several local European or Greek organizations. Rates vary considerably and can be complicated. Check out possible extra charges for air conditioning, too. Your best bet is to pick out a selection of the rate sheets that seem to be stacked in most hotel lobbies, make a few calculations, and then choose the price that comes closest to your budget. My experience is that most of the local companies are reliable, although some companies, like Hertz, offer special rates if you make your reservations at home, before you leave.

The following five car-rental companies are all reliable and easy to locate: **Avis,** Leofóros Amalías 48 (☎ **322-4951**) and several other locations; **Hertz,** Leofóros Syngroú 12 (☎ **922-0102**) and several other locations; **Batek Europcar-Interrent,** Leofóros Syngroú 4 (☎ **921-5788,** fax 921-5795) and several other locations; **Hellascars,** Odós Stadíou 7 (☎ **923-5353**); and **Kosmos,** Leofóros Syngroú 9 (☎ **923-4697**, fax 324-7898).

If you are unfamiliar with European cars and wonder which one to select, several rental brochures include photographs and descriptions of the cars; but in my experience, the Subaru M70 is a reliable workhorse for the type of driving that you'll be doing in Greece. It accommodates four people comfortably (provided that they don't have too much luggage), and it is light on gas, which can cost as much as 600 Drs ($2.40) a gallon.

Some additional tips: Read through the insurance information included in each brochure; considering the general standard of driving in Greece, it is recommended that you take full insurance coverage. If you pay with cash, you may be able to get a discount of 6% or 10%. When you return the car, stop into a gas station near the rental depot and fill up the tank; otherwise you will pay (a) a higher rate for the gas and (b) the 18% tax on the cost of gas, since the tax applies to every item on the rental bill—including insurance and gas.

Note: If you're renting your car in Athens, double-check to make sure that no odd/even-day-driving antipollution restrictions apply to you.

In the table below, I give some average rates among reputable car-rental companies (local and international). The rates are for peak season (defined by most companies as the period from July 1 through about October 15) and for low season. Note, however, that the rates, like all prices quoted herein, are likely to increase during the lifetime of this edition.

PARKING

When parking in Greek cities, make doubly sure that you're not infringing regulations; if you park illegally, the police may remove your license plates (rental cars are not exempted), in which case you have to trot off to the police station (in Athens, on Odós Aghíou Konstantínou, near Omónia Square) to fight your way through layers of bureaucracy to retrieve your plates and pay a 20,000 Drs ($80) fine (remember to take along your parking ticket). If you happen to arrive at your car as the plates are being removed, do not try, under *any* circumstances, to talk your way out of the dilemma with offers of money or you'll be in real trouble. If you park somewhere really dumb and block other traffic, your car will be towed away.

DRIVING RULES

The **International Driver's License** is officially recommended but not usually required when renting a car. However, it's useful in emergencies, since it may be easier for the local constabulary to understand. For information, contact the **Touring and Automobile Club of Greece** (ELPA), Tower of Athens, Odós Messogíon 2–4 (☎ **779-1615**). For ELPA road assistance, dial 104.

The wearing of seat belts is now compulsory throughout Greece, for both the driver and the front-seat passenger(s). The police conduct frequent spot checks, and the fine for nonuse is 7,000 Drs ($28), payable at the local public treasury office.

The speed limit in Greece is 100kmph (62 mph); you would be well advised to stay well within that limit.

Signs are in Greek, with phonetic English. Regarding the transliteration of Greek place names and street names, see page vi and Appendix A, "Basic Greek Vocabulary."

Outside of Athens, the majority of accidents are head-on collisions caused by careless or foolhardy overtaking on bends or on two- and three-lane highways. When it's time for you to pass, always alert the driver in front by signaling, honking your horn, or flashing your lights. *Never* rely on the driver to look in his rear-view mirror to see what other cars are doing. On narrow roadways, you may drive temporarily on the hard shoulder to allow other cars to pass. Be doubly alert for mammoth coaches and trucks.

Traffic on main roads has priority over traffic on side roads, except that there is also the basic principle of "priority on the right." Most of the time this is not a problem, since most main highways are clearly defined—but never take it for granted. *Always observe traffic on your right with extra caution.*

Never let your tank get too low, since gas stations can be few and far between out in the country, and most of them close around 7pm. If you do get into a tight spot out in the country, head for the nearest village café, which frequently keeps a can or two in reserve for forgetful locals.

All these dire warnings apart, Greece offers some of the most pleasant and interesting driving in Europe, especially off the beaten track. But take along a reliable map. Your car-rental company will probably offer you a basic map, but it may not be completely up-to-date. The most reliable map is considered to be the one published locally by Efstathiádis (available at kiosks and bookstores).

By Boat

Regularly scheduled ferryboats connect Athens with the network of Greek islands. There are also Ceres' hydrofoils *Iliosdolphins* and *Flying Dolphins* (twice the price, but half the traveling time). For more detailed information on island service, see Chapter 10, "Easy Excursions from Athens."

Most boats leave from Piraeus (if you're headed for the Cycladic islands, you'll save time and money by shipping out from Rafina); weekly schedules are available from the Greek Tourist Organization (EOT) in Sýntagma Square. However, while ferries may be scheduled regularly, they do not always depart regularly. It pays to double-check schedules by calling the Port Authority or your shipping line first:

Piraeus

Port Authority	422-600
Flying Dolphins	428-0001
Ceres' Iliosdolphins	322-5139

Rafina

Port Authority	0294-23300
Flying Dolphins	0294-22888

From May through September, there are plenty of embarkation dates to choose from. The rest of the year, service is less frequent; you'll need to plan carefully to make sure you're able to make the connections you want.

Fast Facts: Athens

Abbreviations   There are several common Greek abbreviations that the traveler will frequently encounter. Among them are ELPA, the initials of the Touring and Automobile Club of Greece; EOT (*Ellinikós Organismós Tourismoú*), or Greek Tourist Organization, the abbreviation *within Greece* for the Greek National Tourist Organization, as it's known outside Greece, KTEL, the acronym for the private bus system; OSE (*Organismós Sidirodrómon Elládos*), the Railway Organization of Greece, which also runs a public bus line; and OTE (*Organismós Tilepikinonión Elládos*), the Telecommunications Organization of Greece, which operates telephone centers throughout the country.

Airport   See "Orientation" in this chapter.

American Express   The Athens office is located at Odós Ermoú 2, just off Sýntagma Square (☎ **324-4975**; Banking Division, ☎ **323-4781**). Here you can change money, buy traveler's checks, make travel arrangements, book sightseeing and escorted tours, receive mail, and meet people. Open Monday to Friday from 8am to 2pm.

Area Code   The area code for Athens is **30-1**.

Babysitters   Ask your hotel concierge.

Bookstores   See Chapter 8, "Shopping A to Z."

Business Hours   Athenians have a 5-day workweek. Business offices are open Monday to Friday from 9am to 5pm. Most government offices are open 9am to 1pm. Banks are open Monday to Thursday from 8am to 2pm, Friday from 8am to 1:30pm. Shops are open Monday and Wednesday from 9am to 1:30pm; Tuesday, Thursday, and Friday from 10am to 7pm; Saturday from 9am to 3:30pm.

Business Organizations   Three prominent business organizations in the Greek capital are: Athens Cosmopolitan-Lions Club (☎ **360-1311**); the Rotary Club, Odós Kriezótou 3 (☎ **362-3150**); and the American Hellenic Chamber of Commerce, Odós Valaorítou 17 (☎ **361-8385**).

Car Rentals   See "Getting Around" in this chapter.

Climate   See "When to Go" in Chapter 2.

Currency   See "Information, Entry Requirements, and Money" in Chapter 2.

Currency Exchange   The National Bank of Greece on Sýntagma Square (☎ **322-2738**) is open for currency exchange 8:30am–2:30pm; 4–6:30pm weekdays, Saturday 9am–3pm; and Sunday 9am–1pm. There are Athens branches of a number of American and Canadian banks: American Express, Bankers Trust, Chase Manhattan, Bank of Nova Scotia, National Westminster, Bank of America, Manufacturers Hanover Trust, Citibank, Grindlay's, and Barclays.

   Best bets are the 8am to 8pm or 9pm service of the National Bank of Greece, Odós Karagheórghi tis Servías 2, right on Sýntagma Square (the tourist office is in the same building), and the General Hellenic Bank, also on Sýntagma. Most hotels will also offer this service to registered guests, but the rate will be less favorable. *And remember:* On leaving from Athens airport, change your drachmas back into dollars *before* going into the departure lounge.

Dentists   For dentists who have been trained in the United States or are fluent in English, contact the tourist police (☎ **171**), the U.S. Embassy (☎ **721-2951**), or the State Hospital of Athens (☎ **777-8901**).

Doctors   For doctors who have been trained in the United States or are fluent in English, contact the tourist police (☎ **171**), the U.S. Embassy (☎ **721-2951**), or the State Hospital of Athens (☎ **777-8901**). In an emergency, dial the Athens emergency medical and ambulance service at 166 (English spoken). Taxis are often faster than ambulances, and they are permitted to function as emergency vehicles by flashing their lights and honking their horns.

Documents Required   See "Information, Entry Requirements, and Money" in Chapter 2.

Driving Rules   See "Getting Around" in this chapter.

Drugstores and Toiletries American brands of medicines and toiletries are available in most pharmacy-type stores in Athens and other major tourist centers, but at a price. Bring your own supplies in the interests of economy. European brands are usually less expensive—but reliable. For names of all-night pharmacies (called *farmakía*), dial 107.

Electricity Talk to your concierge before using any U.S. appliances. You will probably need anywhere from one to three adapters, which should be available from reception in the better hotels. However, in Athens and most of the mainland, the current is 220 volts AC. Top hotels also have a 115-volt outlet for shavers.

Elevators Greek elevators are reliable, but they don't operate on the same principles as do those in the United States. Except in modern places, doors don't open automatically; you have to watch for the elevator arriving at your floor, then quickly pull the door open before someone else presses a button on another floor and the elevator shoots off. Others signal their arrival with a "ping." Also, in many cases the button doesn't register the floor you want to go to until after the door is closed tight; so you may have to press your number a second time after the door has closed. Some elevator floors seem to fall out from under you when you step onto them; don't be alarmed—they're simply registering the weight.

Embassies and Consulates The embassy of the *United States* is situated at Leofóros Vassilíssis Sofías 91 (☎ **721-2951**). The hours of its Citizens Services section are 8:30am to 5pm Monday through Friday. Other embassies are: *Canada,* Odós Ghennadíou 4 (☎ **725-4011**); *United Kingdom,* Odós Ploutárchou 1 (☎ **723-6211**); *Republic of Ireland,* Leofóros Vassiléos Konstantínou 7 (☎ **723-2771**); *Australia,* Odós Dim. Soútsou 37 (☎ **644-7303**); and *New Zealand,* Xenías 24 (☎ **771-0112; 777-0686**).

Some embassies also maintain consulates in other Greek cities. The United States has a consulate in Thessaloníki; the United Kingdom has consular offices in Thessaloníki and Pátra, as well as on the islands of Corfu, Crete (Iráklio), Sámos, and Rhodes.

Emergencies In any emergency, dial **171** for the tourist police. In specific emergencies, dial **100** for police service; **104** for help with your car; **107** for all-night drugstores; **166** for an ambulance and **150** for first aid; and **199** for the fire department.

Executive Services For the business traveler who needs a temporary office base in Athens, an organization called Executive Services will provide telephone, telex, secretarial, and translation services; fully furnished, air-conditioned offices, equipped with phones and telex lines, can be rented by the day, week, or month. For details, contact them at the Athens Tower "B," suite 506 GR-11527 Athens (☎ **778-3698;** telex 214227 EXSE GR; fax 779-5509). Executive Services now has a satellite office in the Athens Hilton.

Eyeglasses   See Chapter 8, "Shopping A to Z."

Film   See "Photographic Needs," below.

Hairdressers and Barbers   They're all over the place, but you'll probably feel most comfortable in one of the hotel beauty parlors that cater to an international clientele. Try Costi and Taki at the Hilton or Dino & Gino behind the Hilton at Odós Vrassída 11 (☎ **724-8292**); wash/cut/blow-dry is 7,500 Drs ($30) for women, 4,000 Drs ($16) for men.

Holidays   See "When to Go" in Chapter 2.

Hospitals   In an emergency, dial **171** or **166** for information on how to get to the nearest hospital. There are many hospitals in the Greater Athens area. One that can be fully recommended is the Hygeia (pronounced Yghía) Diagnostic and Therapeutical Center, Odós Erythroú Stavroú 4 at Odós Kifissiás, near the Olympic Stadium (☎ **682-7940**). It is a private hospital and will therefore require that you show proof of payment before you can be admitted (it accepts credit cards).

Information   See "Information, Entry Requirements, and Money" in Chapter 2.

Language   Greek is one of the oldest languages in the world and belongs, as does English, to the Indo-European family of languages. Ancient Greek had three main dialects: Ionian (spoken in Asia Minor and on many of the Aegean islands), Attic (spoken mostly in Athens), and Doric (spoken in Sparta and other cities in the Peloponnese). In the time of Alexander the Great, Attic became the dominant dialect, and from it, later, derived an idiom known as *koiné,* which served for many centuries as a "common" language in the eastern Mediterranean region and what is now the Middle East. (The New Testament, for example, was written in *koiné.*) From it developed modern Greek, which retains much of the vocabulary of ancient Greek but differs from it in grammar and pronunciation. Modern Greek has absorbed many foreign words— Turkish, Italian, Slavic, and now English—and has itself contributed to many other languages; some 15% of English words (largely scientific) are of Greek origin.

Although Greek has a different alphabet, it is not difficult to pronounce (see Appendix A, "Basic Greek Vocabulary"). You may want to learn a little Greek before your trip. There are several excellent phrase books, such as Berlitz's *Greek for Travellers,* which comes with an audiocassette. Don't be shy, once you get to Greece, about using the expressions you have learned; your effort alone, however faltering, will draw an appreciative response.

Laundry and Dry Cleaning   In the Omónia Square area there's the self-service Kokkinis at Odós Didótou 46, near Odós Zoodóchou Pighís and 3 blocks back from Odós Akadimías (☎ **361-0661**). It's open Monday through Saturday from 8am to 9pm. In Kolonáki, there's the Self-Service Laundry at Odós Ploutárchou 7, on the corner of Odós Kleoménous.

Liquor You can buy liquor by the bottle or take your own bottle to the grocery store and get a refill—the cost depends on the amount. Famous brands of scotch whisky cost about 3,200 Drs ($13); vodka costs about 2,500 Drs ($10).

Lost Property To report lost or stolen property, call the tourist police at 171 or the bus/taxi lost and found at **642-1616**.

Luggage Storage and Lockers Pacific, Ltd., a travel agency with offices at Odós Níkis 24 and at the East Terminal at the airport, will store excess luggage while you tour the hinterlands or islands. Call **323-6851** for more details.

Mail An airmail postcard to the United States costs 120 Drs (48¢); an airmail letter costs 120 Drs (48¢) per 20 grams (.7 oz.) weight. Don't even consider surface mail: It could take up to 2 months.

Money See "Information, Entry Requirements, and Money" in Chapter 2.

Newspapers and Magazines English-language newspapers and magazines can be bought throughout Athens. Check with your kiosk around 6pm for that day's edition of the *International Herald Tribune;* British papers arrive around 8pm. The daily *Athens News* and *The Athenian,* a monthly magazine, are worthwhile for restaurant, concert, and theater listings.

Photographic Needs Cameras, accessories, and film are readily available in Greece, but they are much more expensive. A 36-exposure roll of Kodacolor Gold (100 ASA), for example, costs about 1,500 Drs ($6).

Police For emergencies only, dial **100** on the telephone. The tourist police will handle your travel-connected problems. Their address is Odós Stadíou 4, 4th floor. Dial **171** for "Tourist Police Information" in five languages, 24 hours a day.

Post Office The Central Post Office is on Kotziá Square at Odós Eólou 100 (opposite Omónia Square). There are branches at Odós Stadíou 4 (only for parcel post and located in the Spyromílios Arcade), in the lower level of the subway station at Omónia Square, and on Sýntagma Square at the corner of Odós Mitropóleos (open from 7:30am to 8:30pm). There is also a Central Philatelic Service on the first floor above the Central Post Office at Odós Eólou 100; it's open in the morning, in order better to serve the requirements of stamp collectors.

Note: Packages should be left unwrapped until they've been inspected at the post office.

Prices As I've noted elsewhere in this guide, prices are liable to change, probably to increase from 15% to 20%. So be sure to check the rates of hotels, tours, and meals with your travel agent.

Radio and Television Athens has several radio stations, some of which broadcast 24 hours a day, offering a wide selection of music—from classical to Greek, "European" (Western pop), and

American (which is very popular on the airwaves)—as well as news and a variety of entertainment and information programs. All of them broadcast in Greek. But you can catch the U.S. Armed Forces Radio, which provides 24 hours of programming each day, including music, hourly newscasts, and excellent sports reports.

The city, as the center of Greek TV broadcasting, has access to the national television networks and to foreign cable networks, among them British and American. Satellite broadcasts of the Cable News Network (CNN) are available in most hotels; the deluxe hotels now carry in-house movies. Greek television usually features lots of British and American programs and old movies, with Greek subtitles; in the smaller hotels, you'll pay extra to have a TV.

Religious Services   The main non-Greek Orthodox places of worship are St. Dennis Roman Catholic Church, corner of Odós Panepistimíou and Odós Omírou; St. Paul's Anglican Church, Odós Filellínon; St. Andrew's American Church (interdenominational), Odós Siná 66; and the Synagogue, Odós Melidóni 6.

Restrooms   Most public toilets have symbols on the doors that distinguish clearly between the sexes. In case they don't, however, and instead have only the appropriate words in Greek, remember: the Greek word for men, ΑΝΔΡΩΝ ("Andrón"), has six letters, and the word for women, ΓΥΝΑΙΚΩΝ ("Gynaikón"), has eight.

Safety   Whenever you're traveling in an unfamiliar city or country, stay alert. Be aware of your immediate surroundings. Wear a moneybelt and keep a close eye on your possessions. Be particularly careful with cameras, purses, and wallets, all favorite targets of thieves and pickpockets. Athens does not have a high violent-crime rate; however, a few of the side streets off Omónia Square and the area near the food and fish markets are dicey at night.

Stationery   Pallis, on Odós Ermoú opposite the Electra Hotel, probably has the best selection; but as in all stationery stores in Athens, procedures are antiquated and service is slow. You can also have photocopying done here.

Street Names and Addresses   In "Embassies and Consulates" above, you'll notice that the address of the U.S. Embassy is *Leofóros Vassilíssis Sofías 91* (91 Avenue of Queen Sophia) and the address of the U.K. Embassy is *Odós Ploutárchou 1* (1 Street of Plutarch). Note the order in which addresses are given in Greece: first the word "Street" (Odós) or "Avenue" (Leofóros), then the name, and finally the number. The name of a street or avenue appears in the genitive case, which explains why, say, a street named after the ancient Athenian historian Xenophon is written "Odós Xenofón*tos*" (Street *of* Xenophon). Similarly, you'll find Gladstone Street (named after the 19th-century British statesman) written "Odós Gládston*os.*" As if that weren't confusing enough, there's also the question of transliteration—the rendering of Greek sounds in English. Note, for example, that the *ph* in "Xenophon" appears as *f* in the street sign you'll see in Athens. Recognize "Odós Iféstou"? It's named after the Greek god of fire, Hephaestus. "Odós Filellínon" is Philhellenes' Street. The variation in the English spelling of Greek names is a vexing problem for any traveler—and travel writer. See also the discussion of transliterating Greek in Appendix A, "Basic Greek Vocabulary."

Taxis   See "Getting Around" in this chapter.

Telegrams   They are expensive! But if you must send one, the office at Odós Patissíon 85 is open 24 hours a day. Another office, at Odós Stadíou 15, has hours from 8am to midnight. Daily rates to the United States are around 1,226 Drs ($5) plus 77 Drs (30¢) per word, plus 18% tax. There is a 100% surcharge for urgent messages.

Telephones   Public telephones are attached to the sides of kiosks, for local calls only; the cost is 10 Drs (4¢), and you pay the kiosk owner. Phone booths with blue trim are for Athens calls only, and those with orange trim are for calls outside of Athens; in either case, before dialing, you must insert the appropriate coin.

Telephone Service to the United States   *Via the operator:* Station calls (first 3 minutes) cost 903 Drs ($4); person-to-person calls (first 3 minutes) cost 1,204 Drs ($5); each additional minute for person-to-person and station calls is another 301 Drs ($2). The total amount of the call is subject to 18% tax. *Automatic service:* From public telephone offices and coin boxes the cost is 570 Drs ($2) per minute.

You can place telephone calls at offices of the national telephone system, OTE (*Organismós Tilepikinonión Elládos*), or Telecommunications Organization of Greece—Odós Stadíou 15 (open 24 hours a day), Omónia Square (open 24 hours a day)—or dial **161** from any telephone to get the long-distance operator. When you want to communicate directly, you have to dial the international prefix (00), then the U.S. country code (1), and then the area code and local number.

Please note that when dialing, you should dial all digits without pause, and there is no special signal between groups of digits. Dial **169** for recorded instructions for making international calls.

Television   See "Radio and Television," above.

Time   Athens time is 2 hours ahead of Greenwich mean time, 7 hours ahead of Eastern standard time.

Tipping   Porters at the airport and train station receive a fee of 100 Drs (40¢) per bag minimum. Taxi drivers expect you to round off the meter in their favor. Leave chambermaids 100 Drs (40¢) per day for an average stay of 2 or 3 days. Doormen who hail your cab, 200 Drs ($1) to 300 Drs ($2). Tour guides expect 200 Drs ($1) or up, but never coins, although the tourist authorities say they don't have to be tipped at all. Theater ushers traditionally get 100 Drs (40¢) for showing you to your seat. Barbers get from 20% to

30%; public toilet room attendants get 50 Drs (20¢); hatcheck attendants get 50 Drs (20¢); and buspeople in restaurants get the loose change.

Twelve-Step Programs   Alcoholics Anonymous, **962–7122**; Narcotics Anonymous, **361–7089**.

Water   It is safe to drink in hotels and restaurants, but beware of well water. If you get bottled mineral water, make sure the cap is tightly fixed.

Weather   Athens has a moderate, Mediterranean climate, marked by mild winters and long, hot summers; spring starts early. See also the section "Climate" in Chapter 2.

4

Athens Accommodations

WHAT'S THE HOTEL SITUATION IN ATHENS? MOST PEOPLE VISITING Athens for the first time naturally have this question on their minds. After all, Athens is a very, very old city—does it have very old hotels? Do they have private baths? And since summers are hot in Athens, do the hotels have air conditioning?

Well, here's the surprise—most hotels in Athens seem to have been built in the past decade, and those that weren't have been renovated and modernized in the past 20 years. Most of them (except in Classes D and E) have private bathrooms; most of them have air conditioning.

Nevertheless, the outstanding attraction of hotels in Athens is their relatively low rates. Where else in Europe can you get a room with private bath, air conditioning, room service, breakfast, and rooftop pool with Acropolis views smack in the center of a capital city, in peak season, for under $150 a night (under 37,500 Drs)?

If you're seeing Europe on a tight budget, you can probably get a better room, dollar for dollar, in Athens. If you're traveling on a shoestring, you can survive longer in Athens.

Before going on to individual hotels, here are some general notes on the hotel situation in Athens today.

---

1 Choosing a Hotel in Athens

All hotels in Greece are classified by the Greek government. There are six official categories—beginning with L, or deluxe, and then running from Class A to Class E. In this guide, I will confine the reviews to the first four categories (L, A, B, and C) with a quick look at some hotels, guesthouses, and hostels in the lowest price ranges. The factors the government uses in judging hotels are the number of bathrooms and restaurants and the quality of service. According to the official government hotel book, "In the new hotels, all the rooms have private bathrooms and showers. In the majority of old hotels down to category C, most rooms have private bathrooms; these seldom exist in D and E." But in some cases the designations are a holdover from seasons long gone; consequently, some Class C hotels are better than some Class B hotels, and the Class B Athens Gate Hotel, for example, is a better value than the Class A Astir Hotel. In the following pages, you'll read about a few hotels that seem to offer outstanding values.

IMPRESSIONS

From the summit of the Acropolis I watched the sun rise between the two peaks of Mt. Hymettus. . . . Athens, the Acropolis, and the ruins of the Parthenon were bathed in a delicate peach-blossom hue. The sculptures of Phidias, caught in a horizontal beam of golden light, came to life and seemed to be moving, thanks to the changing play of light and shadow on the contours of the marble.
—François-René de Chateaubriand (1768–1848). *Itinerary from Paris to Jerusalem*

Rates

The government establishes and enforces the rates for each category. The minimum price and what it includes must be posted in each room—service, taxes, handling of luggage, central heating, air conditioning, meals, and so on. Usually these signs are in English as well as in Greek. However, this does not mean that you will not encounter misunderstandings here and there, because hotel keepers are allowed to tack on a few extras: "An increase of 10% may be added to room rates if the stay is 2 days or less" or "The room rates of hotels located in summer holiday areas, or spas, may be increased by 20% during the period July 1 to September 15." Throw in a slight language problem, and there could be a minor international incident. You can avoid any misunderstandings if you reserve your room in advance (preferably through a travel agent) and have a written confirmation, *with rates,* in your hand.

Breakfast

Some hotels also quote a rate that includes service charge, tax, *and* breakfast (that is, continental breakfast, which consists simply of coffee with rolls or toast and butter with marmalade or jam). Recently the government instructed hoteliers to add fresh fruit or fruit juice. If breakfast is served in your room, you may have to pay a few extra drachmas. If a hotel offers "English breakfast," it means eggs and bacon with your coffee and rolls. If you're on a very tight budget, you may prefer a rate that does *not* include breakfast, since you can probably walk around the corner to a neighborhood café and have the same thing for half the price.

Half Board & Full Board

The government also controls the prices of meals served in hotels, and one way a hotel keeper will try to boost his income is to insist that guests pay a rate that includes meals—*half board,* with breakfast and lunch or dinner (the equivalent of Modified American Plan and sometimes also known as demipension), or *full board,* with breakfast, lunch, and dinner (the equivalent of American Plan). This may be an advantage if you're staying in a hotel where you can dine on the roof garden; in most hotels, it will probably be a drawback. On

A Note on Hotel Rates

With all these rules and controls, you might think that getting accurate, up-to-date hotel rates would be a simple matter. It isn't. I speak often and at length with the Greek National Tourist Organization and the Hellenic Chamber of Hotels, and I believe I have secured the most up-to-date room rates. When you book your accommodations, however, I suggest you confirm the rates again. For an estimate of 1996 rates, add at least 15% to the prices quoted in this book.

the one hand, the tourist organization advertises tempting waterfront tavernas; on the other, the hotelkeepers force you to dine where *they* want you to dine. Whenever possible, resist half-board and full-board rates and leave yourself the option of dining out.

Seasons

There are basically two seasons for hotels in Athens. The off-season usually runs from November 1 through March 31, but in some cases it may begin on October 1 and in others end on May 31; some hotels add "shoulder" seasons in spring and fall, while a few hotels no longer distinguish between the seasons, so steady is the stream of visitors—whether on business or on vacation—to the city. Get your travel agent to look closely into precise dates, because this may save you several dollars.

Location

Once you've determined what price you want to pay, the situation is fairly simple. Most of the hotels are in one of two clusters in the center of town—either around Sýntagma Square and spreading into the Pláka area or around Omónia Square. A few, such as the Hilton, the Inter-Continental, and the Marriott, are a few blocks farther away but still convenient to the center of town. Most hotels in Athens are within walking distance of almost everything that you want to see.

VIEW FROM THE TOP

The Acropolis is one of the most stunning sights in the world. Every corner you turn in Athens brings you another glimpse of this sacred hill. You'll probably want to sit on your balcony at sunset and watch the Parthenon turn a glowing honey color. You may even want to sit on your balcony in the morning and watch the Parthenon's columns loom through the morning light. There's nothing like it, so try to get a room with a view, even if you have to give up luxury or space or a private bathroom.

Compare before Buying

If you come in the off-season, when the choice of rooms is greater, it's a perfectly acceptable practice to inspect rooms before taking one. If you give yourself half an hour or an hour, you can walk from hotel to hotel, looking at locations and checking out facilities and the view from the balconies or roofs. Even in the hotel you finally decide on, check out the room, because the standards in some of the older hotels vary considerably from one room to another.

Reservations

During the peak season, don't go near Athens without a reservation. You may end up like the Parthenon—without a roof over your head.

IMPRESSIONS

Marvelous things happen to one in Greece—marvelous good things which can happen to one nowhere else on earth.
—Henry Miller, *The Colossus of Maroussi* 1942

In the end you'll very likely find a place to stay, but you may spend half your day finding it. Make a reservation in advance. (More and more Greek hotels now have fax numbers; they are included in this guide, when available.) If you want a room with a view, be sure to specify. In recent years, with more and more visitors flocking to the city, it's wise to make reservations well in advance even during the off-season if you want to be sure of staying in the hotel of your choice. (This is true not only of Athens but also of places out in the countryside, such as Delphi and Náfplio.)

Apartments for Longer Stays

Because hotel rates in Athens are so reasonable, you may be tempted to linger a while in the city. If you do, consider renting an apartment rather than staying in a hotel room. Apartments are usually cheaper and well equipped, and they give you a chance to live a more truly Athenian life. It's a particularly economical idea if you have a family. The **Delice Hotel Apartments** and **Riva Hotel Apartments** both offer one-bedroom and two-bedroom suites with fully equipped kitchenettes and air conditioning, 24-hour reception, and telephone service; the Riva also has bar and restaurant service. The Delice is at Odós Vassiléos Alexándrou 3, and the Riva (☎ **770-6611,** fax 770-8137) is at Odós Michalakopoúlou 114; both are near the Hilton hotel. Double rates are around 20,000 Drs ($80) per night for stays of a month or longer.

Tax, Service Charge & Tipping

As of this writing, the government tacks on an 8% value-added tax (VAT) to all hotel rates; there's also a 4.5% *city* tax on the total bill. In addition, hotels are allowed to add a 15% service charge to the bill. Most hotels, however, quote rates that include both service charge and tax. *All the estimated rates quoted in these pages include the government and city taxes and the 15% service charge.*

The theory behind a service charge was to avoid the confusion resulting from having to tip different members of the hotel staff; a single service charge, added to the bill, would take care of all tipping. But it doesn't: the staff still expects tips. Don't encourage this. Tip only for small *extra* services, such as shining shoes and fetching cabs.

Here are some tips on tipping in hotels: According to the sign in your room, luggage handling is included in the service charge built into the room rate. So you're not obliged to tip any more, but if you feel like it, offer 200 Drs ($1) a bag (the same rate for porters at airports and stations). In a deluxe hotel, you may want to double that. You're also expected to tip the waiter who brings you breakfast in bed, 200 Drs to 300 Drs ($1 to $2), say, depending on the type of hotel. (But remember: there is probably an additional service charge already added to the room service bill.) Doormen who hail your cab also get 200 Drs to 300 Drs.

The Rooms

Greeks like to get out into the open air—and why not, with a climate as balmy as theirs? They'd rather spend a summer evening sitting beneath an olive tree discussing politics or soccer than being cooped up at home watching TV. Since they spend so much time outdoors, they don't bother about spending a bundle furnishing their homes. By American standards, Greek homes are bare; ditto Greek hotels, especially the older ones. The lobbies may be like marble palaces, but upstairs the corridors may be spartan, and the rooms may be furnished with only the essentials. So don't come to Athens expecting all the trimmings you'd normally find in an American hotel (except in places such as the NJV Meridien, the Ledra Marriott, the Inter-Continental, and the reliable Athens Hilton). The rooms will be spotlessly clean and comfortable, but in many cases they won't have wall-to-wall carpeting, armchairs, radios, and writing desks. You may be discouraged at first, but you'll soon discover that it doesn't matter, because you, too, will prefer to spend your evenings beneath an olive tree.

Air Conditioning

The majority of Athens hotels now have air conditioning, at least in the L, A, and B categories. Hotels in other categories probably have air conditioning in *some* of the rooms; you will have to request one of these rooms—and pay an additional charge. Temperatures in Athens in midsummer go up into the 90sF by day and linger in the 70s at night. If you're accustomed to air conditioning back home, you'll probably want it in Athens also, at least in July and August. Moreover, Athens is a rather noisy city, so you may want to switch on the air conditioning and leave windows and shutters closed to keep out the hubbub.

Baths & Showers

There are two types of bathtubs in Athens—the regular kind and the sit-in kind. The sit-in kind is about 3 feet by 3 feet. It's fine for feet that have trudged all the way up the Acropolis and back but inadequate for weary shoulders that have carried camera bags and shoulder purses. If you want a real bath, tell the reception clerk when you're checking in. Many hotels have both types. Most baths of either dimension also have hand-held showers, which have one advantage— when you're in your bath, you can also switch on the shower *underwater* and use it for a whirlpool bath or to massage your weary thighs. If you do get an overhead shower, you may not get a shower curtain. The technique is to let the water splash onto the floor, which has been angled to drain off the surplus. It makes sense—but just remember not to leave your slippers or bathrobe on the floor.

Radio

Many hotels don't have a radio in the room. But if you do get a multichannel model in your room, you may be able to get CNN, the BBC, a Northern European station, or 102.1 FM, which is music and news, 75% of which is in English.

Television

The tube is still not the big thing in everyday Greek life that it is in American life, and although Greece now has satellite channels (including CNN), the amount of programming in English hardly justifies paying an extra charge for the pleasure of watching TV in your room. Only the deluxe hotels in Athens have television in the rooms as a matter of course (most of them carry CNN); other hotels have sets in lounges or special viewing rooms, and others occasionally have sets for rental. But if you're doing what you're supposed to be doing in Greece, you'll have neither the time nor the patience for television.

Swimming Pools

You'll find relatively few hotels with pools in Athens. Of the ones listed in this guide, the Athens Hilton, Inter-Continental Athenaeum, Ledra Marriott, Royal Olympic, St. George Lycabettus, Chandris, President, Stanley, Electra Palace, Dorian Inn, Athens Center, Holiday Inn, Divani Palace Acropolis, and Novotel all have pools. Many hotels have sun decks on the roof. But generally speaking, people come to Athens for sightseeing rather than to get a tan. If you do want to get in some swimming and sun, stay at one of the nearby resorts, such as Glyfáda and Vouliagméni. They're close enough for jaunts into town for sightseeing and dining.

2   Very Expensive

The hotels listed below fall into the L, or deluxe, category. In amenities and service, they rival many of the top hotels in other major European cities.

Athenaeum Inter-Continental, Leofóros Syngroú 89–93. ☎ **902-3666.** Fax 924-3000. 520 rms, 39 suites. A/C MINIBAR TV TEL

Rates: 59,000–80,000 Drs ($236–$320) single; 66,500–87,500 Drs ($266–$350) double; suite from 82,000 Drs ($328). AE, V. **Parking:** Garage for 170 cars.

Completed in 1982, the largest, most expensive, and most extravagant of the city's top-flight deluxe hotels rises 10 floors above the main avenue from the city center to the sea, its white U-shaped, stepped-back facade dominating the not-too-inspired surroundings. Now, with the construction of five floors of bowling lanes across Leofóros Syngroú, only about one-third of the Athenaeum's guest rooms have views of the Acropolis or Lykavittós Hill (you pay more for the Acropolis view, but it's worth it, especially at sunset).

The guest rooms are among the plushest and most tasteful in town: each with separate sitting area (marble floor, flokati rug, desk, sofa, and armchair), carpeted bedroom, and marble bathroom (with wall-mounted hairdryer and bathrobes in suites only). In addition, most of the suites come with a pantry and dining nook; but if you opt for one of the new Golf suites or Olympian suites, you also get a private putting green or a mini–health club, respectively—right there in your room! All units come with direct-dial telephone with message light and bathroom extension, color TV with remote control and video and satellite channels, and radio.

The Athenaeum is self-contained and handsomely accoutred, its multilevel atrium lobby ringed by shopping arcades and the hotel's private collection of works by leading contemporary Greek artists in an array of techniques—kinetic/magnetic, neon assemblage, fiberglass bas-relief, trompe l'oeil, and wood sculptures.

Dining/Entertainment: The Athenaeum's dining facilities include everything from crêpes to chateaubriand to Asian barbecue, served in the Kublai Khan restaurant; a lobby tearoom (the delightful Café Vienna); a classy rôtisserie serving classic cuisine; and the new (and expensive) rooftop Le Première, with international cuisine and Acropolis views.

Services: There's 24-hour room service, and a free shuttle bus running to three locations in downtown Athens.

Facilities: The shopping arcades include jewelry and high-fashion boutiques, art galleries, and a drugstore. In addition, there's a health club, a hairdressing salon, and a business center with telex and fax machines.

Athens Hilton, Leofóros Vassilíssis Sofías 46. ☎ **725-0201.**
Fax 725-3110. Telex 215 808 HILT GR. 453 rms. A/C MINIBAR TV TEL
Rates: 62,744–75,400 Drs ($251–$302) single; 71,346–88,550 Drs ($285–$354) double. AE, DC, MC, V. **Parking:** Indoor.

The Athens Hilton is not so much a hotel as it is a city. On weekends, its lobby is filled with wide-eyed Athenians who can't afford a trip to New York but want to see what America is like. There's plenty for them to see—but it's not America. Not with all that marble. There's probably enough marble in the Athens Hilton to have built a second Parthenon—30,000 square yards of it, of 11 types, from Árta, Tínos, Mt. Pendéli, Ioánnina, and Salamís. You arrive at the hotel beneath a great curving portico with brown-and-white marble (a work of art that later centuries may dig up and prize as highly as we prize fragments from Knossós). You walk through hallways with marble floors and marble pillars, down marble steps to a lounge with dozens of plush armchairs, then down a few more marble steps to another, wider, furnished lounge where you can have afternoon tea and look out on the marble pathways leading to the swimming pool and the poolside café.

All the guest rooms have views of the Acropolis or Mt. Pendéli, and a few have views of both the Acropolis and Lykavittós Hill. Spacious and comfortable, as you've come to expect of Hilton hotels everywhere, the guest rooms feature five-channel radio, satellite TV with in-house movies, wall-to-wall carpeting, and, of course, sliding glass doors opening onto spacious balconies. Two floors are now given over to the Executive Club, with its own hostesses and exclusive lounge; another floor, the ninth, is now all nonsmoking rooms; and the three presidential-style suites have been completely redesigned with Jacuzzis, custom-designed Greek embroideries, and Murano glass—even the doorknobs are works of art.

Dining/Entertainment: One of the favorite spots for the Athenian sightseer is the Byzantine Café, where Greeks sample American coffee, American hamburgers, and American apple pie, and Americans, in turn, sample varied cuisines on special evenings. Downstairs is the distinguished restaurant Tá Nissiá.

On the Hilton roof, 12 floors above the city, you'll find the Galaxy Bar with dancing to a live band. No ordinary nightspot this. When you step off the elevator you'll see why. Ahead of you, through floor-to-ceiling windows, lies one of the most spellbinding views in Europe—the distant star-speckled mass of the Mediterranean sky, the twinkling lights of the city, and, smack in center stage, the floodlit Acropolis and Parthenon. Since it's open only in summer, you can also sit outside on the terrace itself and soak in the view and the soft Athenian air.

Services: The Hilton's maids fix your room twice a day and turn down the sheets while you're up on the roof dancing. The hotel has 24-hour room service, a sharp concierge team, executive services, and a shuttle bus to Sýntagma Square, five minutes away, and to the airports.

Facilities: Just inside the hotel entrance are two courtyards (the traditional Greek atrium) with 200-year-old olive trees in the middle and boutiques and shops around the sides—jewelry shops, an antiques store, a bank, an optician, a beauty salon, a barbershop, a photo shop, a florist, travel agencies, an airline office, and an Avis Rent-a-Car office. Without ever leaving the Hilton, you can buy designer clothes, records, jewelry, flowers, books, souvenirs, hand-crafts, copperware, rugs, bags, and cigars. There's also a large swimming pool, sauna, and massage.

$ Holiday Inn, Odós Michalakopoúlou 50. ☎ **724-8322.** Fax 724-8187. Telex 2188 HINN HOLIDEX. 190 rms. A/C MINIBAR TV TEL

Rates: 26,400 Drs ($106) single; 30,800–35,200 Drs ($123–$140) double. AE, EC, DC, MC, V. **Parking:** Underground garage for 150 cars.

The striking gray facade of the Holiday Inn rises eight stories above Odós Michalakopoúlou, a broad street just beyond the Hilton, a short walk from the U.S. Embassy. Indoors, it makes most other Holiday Inns look like country cousins, with its lobby in dazzling decor, a glass-paneled shopping arcade, and a contemporary bar/lounge. Guest rooms have two double beds and are decorated in cool soothing colors. Only 35 rooms are singles, so solo visitors may be offered a double room at a special rate (one reason, perhaps, why 60% of the hotel's guests are businesspeople).

Dining/Entertainment: Attractive coffee shop, open to 2am; American piano bar in lobby.

Athens Accommodations Very Expensive

Services: Hairdresser. Shops for books, jewelry, clothing, luggage, toiletries, crafts, and souvenirs.

Facilities: Underground parking; outdoor rooftop swimming pool with bar; safe boxes in guest rooms.

⭐ **Hotel Grande Bretagne,** on Sýntagma Square. ☎ **323-0251.** Fax 322-8034. Telex 215346 HBRT GR. 450 rms. A/C MINIBAR TV TEL

Rates: 62,500–75,000 Drs ($250–$300) single; 73,750–86,250 Drs ($295–$345) double. AE, DC, MC, V.

The Grande Bretagne was built in 1862 as a 30-room annex to the royal family's summer palace (now the Parliament Building) across the street and put in the care of Eustace Lampsa, chef to the royal household, who knew all the preferences of the royal visitors who'd be staying there. In 1991 it became part of the prestigious CIGA Hotels, and the original three-story building is now seven stories. Generations of distinguished guests have created a unique atmosphere at the GB (no one refers to it as the Grande Bretagne). Its doors have been whisked open by uniformed attendants for princes, czars, tycoons, and millionaires; for composer Richard Strauss and the Grand Duchess Helen; and for Liz Taylor and Peter Ustinov, as well as Bruce Springsteen and Sting. During World War II, the GB served as Nazi headquarters; at the end of the war, Sir Winston Churchill stayed there for a few nights and narrowly escaped an assassination attempt that involved using the labyrinthine sewers of the hotel. Today the GB is virtually a "reviewing stand" for state occasions at the Parliament Building and the Tomb of the Unknown Soldier in front of Parliament.

The lobby is one of those monumental Athenian halls of marble—marble floors, green marble walls, marble pillars, with Asian carpets and plushly upholstered sofas and fauteuils; beyond it is an equally comfortable and spacious lounge, with a decorative glass ceiling, and beyond that is the dignified, classical dining room.

The GB is one of *the* grand hotels in Europe; and although it may have been overtaken by others in terms of sheer plushness (its decor dates from more elegant days), its furniture is regularly reupholstered and refiligreed—and always polished. The prize rooms are those facing the square (especially those on the sixth floor), all now with double French doors and windows to block out traffic noise; but the huge inner courtyard has been restored in its neoclassical style, complete with window boxes and fragrant flowers, and these rooms will be welcomed by people who like to sleep with their windows open—there are no traffic sounds here.

Dining/Entertainment: Two contemporary touches are the intimate, dimly lit cocktail lounge in one corner and the GB Corner café-restaurant in the other, both with live piano music in the evenings. If you simply want to sample the opulence of the GB's public quarters, drop into the marble Winter Garden off the lobby for a coffee; it costs a few drachmas more than it would cost in one of the cafés in the square, but it comes to you in a china pot with matching cup and saucer, on a silver tray, with a silver milk jug and silver sugar bowl—plus a glass of chilled water, served with great style. Or treat yourself to afternoon tea.

Services: Concierge, 24-hour room service, currency exchange, laundry and valet service.

Facilities: Beauty parlor and barbershop; lobby bookstand; special desk for tours and car rentals.

Ledra Marriott, Leofóros Syngroú 115. ☎ **934-7711.** Fax 395-8603. Telex 22-1833. 259 rms and suites. A/C MINIBAR TV TEL

Rates: 25,000–51,600 Drs ($100–$206) single; 25,000–56,700 Drs ($100–$226) double; up to 260,000 Drs ($1,040) suite. AE, DC, EC, MC, V. **Parking:** Nearby.

The Marriott is a near neighbor of the Athenaeum. It has a balconied facade of white marble separated from the avenue by a service road and driveway.

The Marriott's guest accommodations come in four categories, including sumptuous suites. But even the most "modest" rooms are above average with elegant designer decor (soft tans, ecrus, and browns) that was refurbished in 1990, all-marble bathroom with built-in hairdryer and sunlamp, radio with extension speaker in the bathroom, armchair and sofa, and extravagant closet space with drawers and sliding doors that positively glide. A whole *extra* set of double-glazing *and* double doors have been added to the windows and balconies on the lower floors, which let in the light and the views but keep out the sounds of Syngroú. Only one-third of the Ledra's rooms have views of the Parthenon, but in nice democratic fashion, every guest (and only hotel guests, by the way, no "local memberships" allowed) can lounge on the rooftop deck, plunge into a big pool, or soak in a hydrotherapy pool while admiring the Parthenon. Overall you'll find the Ledra staff young, enthusiastic, and efficient.

Dining/Entertainment: The hit of the Ledra is, surprisingly, the city's first Polynesian/Japanese restaurant, the lavishly waterfalled and batiked Kona Kai, which is one of *the* smart places for Athenians to be seen and entertained. Other restaurants include the stylish Panorama (which from June to October serves 75 different dishes from around the world) on the roof, beside the pool; and the wicker-and-lattice Zéphyros coffee shop, featuring a popular Sunday buffet lunch, including champagne and orange juice on the house, for about 5,400 Drs ($21). There's also a rooftop bar and, on summer evenings, Greek music. Ledra guests may also relax in the Crystal Lounge piano bar, in the lobby, underneath a huge 1,000-crystal chandelier.

Services: 24-hour room service, concierge, free shuttle bus to Sýntagma Square, laundry and valet service, voice mail, cable TV with in-house movies.

Facilities: Rooftop deck, swimming pool, hydrotherapy pool.

NJV Meridien Hotel, on Sýntagma Square. ☎ **325-5301.** Fax 323-5856. 152 rms, 25 suites. A/C MINIBAR TV TEL

Rates: From 52,900–65,800 Drs ($211–$263) single; 56,400–75,000 Drs ($225–$300) double; 89,000–136,000 Drs ($356–$544) suite. AE, DC, EC, MC, V. **Parking:** Nearby.

Open the door to one of the NJV Meridien's suites, say no. 808, and you seem to be walking right into Apollo's sun. An entire wall is sliding glass doors—one in the sitting room and one in the bedroom, both of them opening onto a terrace with almost perfect views of the Acropolis (marred only by one of Sýntagma Square's newer and bigger obnoxious billboards) and, on a good day, of the mountains and the sea.

All of the Meridien's white-and-gold rooms are done in classic Ionic or Doric style, which means that the detailed molding and occasional columns vary. The sitting area has comfy leather chairs and couch, and brass lamps; the bedroom has twin beds (ask if you want a double—there are some king-size, too), ample closet space, electric trouser press, marble vanity and night tables, with all the room controls at your fingertips: lights, air, radio, TV, alarm clock. Carpeting, bedspreads, and drapes reflect the Doric or Ionic pattern and are done up in pleasant ecru, Greek blue, and purple.

After a day of checking out your Acropolis view on site, you can return here to bathe your weary body in total comfort. The white and gold-flecked marble bathrooms are large and well appointed. The suite's Greek blue is picked up, gold detail added by way of fixtures. There's a bidet; hand-held and full shower and tub; and all the amenities: oversize bath towels, terrycloth robes, toiletries, and a phone extension.

The NJV Meridien shares the same block as the GB and boasts a sleek efficiency that the older hotels might envy. Soundproofing has been built in from the beginning. (It does cut down on the outside noise, but in some rooms you can hear the sound of the elevator and occasionally hallway Muzak or the music of young lovers next door.)

Services: Concierge; 24-hour room service; currency exchange; laundry and valet; car rental; safe deposit; babysitting; complimentary newspapers.

Facilities: Business center; small gift shop.

Andromeda Hotel, Odós Vássou 2. ☎ **643-7302.** Fax 646-6361. Telex 218386. 30 rms and suites. A/C MINIBAR TV TEL

Rates: From 48,000 Drs ($192) single; 54,000–61,000 Drs ($216–$244) double; 72,000–85,000 Drs ($288–$340) suite. All major credit cards. No parking.

The only new hotel in Athens in several years will, one hopes, set a trend. Other cities have their small luxury boutique hotels, but the Andromeda, when it opened in 1991, was a first for Athens. Vássou is a relatively quiet street, located more conveniently for business travelers—anyone with appointments at the U.S. Embassy and the Athens Tower office complex—or for music lovers and performers attending the city's new Concert Hall. Some guests may welcome its quieter, less polluted neighborhood.

The Andromeda is a brand-new building, its lower two floors faced with elegant marble, the upper levels with office-building tinted glass. The lobby and reception area is sparely furnished, stylish, but small, and the elevator is barely large enough for one guest, one porter, and one carry-on. The walls in the lobby and throughout the guest rooms are marbleized. The 30 rooms, studios, and suites are about as plush as they come in Athens, in a style that's a cross between "Greek traditional" and "international boudoir"; rear rooms and suites are the prime locations, overlooking the swimming pool and tennis court of the U.S. ambassador's residence. In addition to the usual amenities, each room comes with wall-to-wall carpeting, wingback chairs, a circular dining table, and a not too practicable combination desk and dressing table. The surprise is the bathroom: room enough to swing a towel or two, lots of marble, brilliant lighting, reflective ceiling, stainless-steel washbasin, and oodles of towels.

Services: Room service 7am to 2am; kitchenettes in five suites; facilities for fax and computers; limousine service, on request, to and from the airport.

Facilities: The four-stool bar, nine-table Michelangelo Restaurant (from breakfast to midnight) and the tony White Elephant Restaurant serving Asian cuisine (see "Athens Dining").

3   Expensive

The following hotels are officially in the L category, but in terms of facilities and furnishings they are really only a cut above Class A. Fortunately, their rates are considerably lower than those of the L group above.

Amalia Hotel, Leofóros Amalías 10. ☎ **323-7301.** Fax 323-8792. Telex 215161 AMAL GR. 98 rms. A/C TV TEL

The Amalia's balconied facade is known to thousands of visitors who have never stayed here—it's simply the place where airport buses and hotel shuttles begin and end their downtown trips. It's conveniently located just around the corner from Sýntagma Square and across the avenue from the National Garden (about one-third of the hotel's rooms have balconies overlooking the foliage). And of course, if you're bound for the international airport (Ellinikón East), you couldn't be in a handier spot.

Upper floors facing the avenue have sliding glass doors that open onto a generous-size balcony with fantastic views. Head-on there's the stand of royal palms that mark the entrance to the National Garden; beyond the Parliament Building to the left is Mt. Lykavittós, particularly beautiful at night with its golden crown of lights; and off in the distance are the surrounding hills, where you can see lights twinkling as cars travel up the winding roads. Rooms in the back, from the fourth floor up, have partial views of the Acropolis.

Compared with the views, the Amalia's rooms are uninspiring: neutral beige tones; not too thickly piled carpeting; undistinguished dark wood beds, vanity, and chairs. Marble bathrooms are small, but have hand-held shower, full tub, and a phone extension.

Dining/Entertainment: A streetside and air-conditioned coffee shop in the lobby and a spacious restaurant, serving breakfast, lunch, and dinner: A TV lounge one floor up.

Services: Room service.

Facilities: Lobby has an electronic map of Athens that will show you the route to and location of the city's major sights.

Athens Chandris Hotel, Leofóros Syngroú 385. ☎ **941-4824.** Fax 942-5082. Telex 218-112 ATCH GR. 386 rms and suites. A/C MINIBAR TV TEL

Rates (including buffet breakfast): 29,000–34,000 Drs ($116–$136) double. AE, DC, MC, V. **Parking:** On site.

On Syngroú, the long, straight avenue that links the city with the sea, you'll find one of the landmarks in the new-style Athens: the glistening Athens Chandris Hotel, which opened its automatic doors in 1977. It's close to the sea, equidistant from downtown Athens, downtown Piraeus, and the airport, and facing the Ippódromo, or racetrack (hippodrome). The interior is a glistening art-deco extravaganza of holiday colors, marble, and contrasting textures. The furniture, imported from Italy, is all Milan Modern—the bedside lamps are like giant ice cubes, the chrome trim of the headboards has a built-in radio, and the ultramodern suites must be among the smartest in Athens. On the roof, eight floors up, guests can have lunch, snacks, and a buffet dinner; or just enjoy vast views of the city, the mountains, and the Saronic Gulf; many guests also have a grandstand view of the races from their windows.

Dining/Entertainment: Four Seasons Restaurant and a late-night coffee shop.

Services: Room service; free shuttle bus every 30 minutes to Sýntagma Square.

Facilities: Rooftop swimming pool, snack bar, bar.

Divani Caravel Hotel, Leofóros Vassiléos Alexándrou 2. ☎ **725-3725.** Fax 723-6683. Telex 214401 CH GR. 471 rms and suites. A/C TV TEL

Rates: 28,000–33,000 Drs ($112–$132) single; 35,000–43,000 Drs ($140–$172) double; from 35,200 Drs ($185) suite. About 20% less in the off-season. All major credit cards. **Parking:** Limited.

The big, modern Caravel, a near neighbor of the Hilton, has just joined the Divani chain of hotels. Lobby facilities include a piano bar and a battery of shops (Greek art, souvenirs, jewelry, clothing, electronics, cameras, *two* art galleries—one of them a studio where you can have your portrait painted).

The Caravel's guest rooms, recently renovated, are spacious, functional, and soothing, many with small balconies. Rooms at the rear (a few with distant views of the Acropolis) are most popular because they're quieter. All rooms are equipped with minibars.

Dining/Entertainment: An array of restaurants includes the attractive Lido, for Greek cuisine, and the Ilissos, a roomy coffee shop on the lower level where you can have omelets for 1,200 to 2,400

Drs ($5 to $10) and sandwiches from 960 Drs ($4). There's the Lord Byron Piano Bar, and the Constantinople Bar.

Services: 24-hour room service, closet safes, beauty parlor, car hire, and tour desk in lobby.

Facilities: Rooftop sun deck and viewful health club with sauna and Jacuzzi.

$ Divani Palace Acropolis, Odós Parthenónos 19–25. ☎ **922-2945.** Fax 921-4993. Telex 218306 DIVA GR. 260 rms. A/C MINIBAR TV TEL

Rates: 27,500 Drs ($110) single; 30,800 Drs ($123) double. AE, DC, EC, MC, V.

This place was recently upgraded all the way—to the deluxe category. Outside there's a waterfall of flowering vines cascading off the balconies; inside there's a whole new wing that adds five floors of guest rooms and another full lounge area with marble pillars, huge chandeliers, soft seashell-pink couches, and glass doors that lead to an azure-tiled pool outside. A gift shop shares a foyer with a glass-enclosed expanse of the Wall of Themistocles, dating from 479 B.C. The new rooms are good-sized and have sparkling marble floors, flocked wallpaper, dressing tables, and double beds; all have balconies, some with Acropolis views. Rooms in the front of the older wing have angled views of the Parthenon, but those at the rear on the upper floors have unobstructed views of Philopáppos Hill. This is an ideal location if you're planning to spend much time at the Athens Festival performances in the Herod Atticus Odeum, which is a 5-minute walk away, or if you'd just rather sip an ouzo at twilight at the Divani roof garden restaurant. Divine.

Dining/Entertainment: Off the cool marble lobby there's a pleasant dining room downstairs that offers a three-course lunch or dinner for 4,000 Drs ($20) and a lounge/bar on the left; upstairs there's a roof-garden restaurant that serves drinks and buffet dinner.

Services: 24-hour room service.

Facilities: Swimming pool; gift shop.

Park Hotel, Leofóros Vassilíssis Alexándras 10. ☎ **883-2712.** Fax 823-8420. Telex 214748 PARK GR. 111 rms. A/C MINIBAR TV TEL

Rates (including American breakfast): 18,300 Drs ($73) single; 24,600 Drs ($98) double. AE, DC, MC, V.

The Park Hotel is smaller and more intimate, welcoming guests in a clublike lobby of wood paneling and leather decorated in muted colors. It's across the street from Areos Park, one of the city's most spacious parks, and many of the upper rooms have pleasant views overlooking the treetops. Pampering seems to be the philosophy here: marble bathroom with direct-dial telephone; and bedside controls for the gadgetry—message light, door lock, DO NOT DISTURB sign, color TV (with CNN), radio, and music channels.

Dining/Entertainment: In addition to a 24-hour coffee shop, the Red Horse, the Park's Latina Restaurant offers Greek and international dishes. In summertime the Blue Peacock bar on the roof garden gives you an even better view of the treetops and a refreshing breeze.

Services: 24-hour room service.

Facilities: Parking garage.

$ Royal Olympic Hotel, Odós Diákou 28. ☎ **922-6411.** Telex 215753. 295 rms, 15 suites. A/C TV TEL

Rates: 23,000 Drs ($92) single; 27,000 Drs ($108) double. AE, DC, EC, MC, V.

The Royal Olympic is just 10 blocks from Sýntagma Square. But what a location! If you have a room facing the front, you can throw back the drapes, open the sliding windows, step out onto your balcony, and . . . there, in live wide-screen Cinemascope, is the entire temple of Olympian Zeus spread out before you. And right behind it, almost growing out of the temple's cluster of columns, is Lykavittós Hill, with the greenery of the National Garden filling the gap between. It's a breathtaking sight that is well worth the 10 blocks between you and Sýntagma Square. Into the bargain, this hotel is handsomely furnished—the bedrooms as well as the public rooms.

The Royal Olympic's guest rooms are roomy and modern. There are carpets on the floor, radio, balcony, sliding doors of double-glazed glass, amply fitted closets, chairs, coffee tables, a well-equipped bathroom complete down to a second phone, and big towels. The hotel's corner suites can keep an entire family in comfort (with even an icebox attractively disguised as a wood-grained cabinet). There are also suites with sliding screens to separate sleeping area from working area; these are equipped with a full-size desk, studio couch, refrigerator, and coffee table. The choice rooms are on the sixth floor. They're a shade more "designed," and they have larger balconies—and, of course, the higher you are, the more stunning the view and the more muffled the sound of the traffic. But take a room on any floor as long as it's at the front. They all have a different decor, an enormous bed, carved inner doors, big oval bathtub, and large silk prints of recumbent maidens. However, if you check into a room without a view, you can always head for the lounge overlooking the temple.

Dining/Entertainment: The bar separates the lobby from the square swimming pool at the back of the hotel, and on the left of the lobby there's an elegant dining room decorated with engravings of old Athens. One of the most attractive of the public rooms is the lounge, up a few marble steps to raise it above the level of the traffic so that you can get an undisturbed view of the temple. (Even if you're not staying at the Royal Olympic, remember that this grandstand lounge is a place to drop into for morning coffee or afternoon tea.) The dining room of the Royal Olympic is a spruce, chandelier-bright place, and there's also a specialty restaurant called the Templars' Grill, specializing in steak.

Services: Room service.

Facilities: Swimming pool, sauna, and fitness center.

$ St. George Lycabettus Hotel, Odós Kleoménous 2.
☎ 729-0711. Fax 729-0439. Telex 214253 HEAM. 150 rms and
suites. A/C MINIBAR TV TEL

Rates: 26,160–39,040 Drs ($105–$156) single; 33,000–46,100 Drs
($133–$184) double; 64,400–90,350 Drs ($257–$361) suite. Rates are
20% less during the off-season. AE, DC, EC, MC, V. **Parking:** Limited.

The St. George Lycabettus is located on a residential street on the
side foot of Lykavittós Hill. Automatic glass doors open to cool, spacious elegance; gleaming black marble floors are highlighted with
upholstered chairs and couches in blends of caramel, pumpkin, and
gold and smoky-glass tables with brass accents.

The accommodations are trim and contemporary—light blue
wall-to-wall carpeting, pale blue upholstery, wood paneling, furniture with brass trim, and a luxurious bathroom with tile walls and
marble floors. The plushest rooms are the corner suites, especially
those on the fourth and fifth floors, because these have balconies on
two sides, breathtaking views, two rooms, two bathrooms, and a sense
of spaciousness that you might miss in the basic rooms. The St.
George Lycabettus (don't get it confused with the plain Lycabette
Class B hotel farther down the hill) is popular with visitors (especially business travelers) who want modern facilities and comfort in
a quieter location, with Sýntagma Square still only a 7-minute walk
downhill and a $2 cab ride back up.

Dining/Entertainment: Tony's Bar, off the lobby and down a
few steps, is not very exciting to look at, but the bartender is one of
the friendliest in town and speaks perfect English. (One floor below
that, going down the hill, there's a restaurant/coffee shop with a
summer terrace across the street.) Crowning it all is a rooftop restaurant, Le Grand Balcon, eye-to-eye with the pine groves of Lykavittós.

Services: Room service.

Facilities: The 30-foot-long rooftop pool is surrounded by Astro
Turf—style matting, with comfortable chaises, poolside showers, and
a small bar. Other facilities include a garage, a beauty parlor, and a
barbershop.

4 Moderate

The following are Class A and B hotels. Some of the best buys and
some of the most attractive accommodations are to be found in
Classes A and B, and for most travelers the hotels described below
are most likely to match their tastes and budgets. Rates listed include
continental breakfast and, of course, taxes, service charge, and air
conditioning, unless otherwise mentioned.

Near Syntagma & Plaka

Adonis, Odós Kodroú 3. **☎ 324-9737.** Fax 323-1602. 26 rms. TEL
Rates: 7,500 Drs ($30) single; 11,000 Drs ($44) double. Reduced rates
for stays longer than 2 days. AE, MC, V.

This cheerful hotel, which received the 1993 "Cleanest-Hotel-in-Athens" award, has a modern, unadorned facade and brightly striped awnings shading balconies on the upper floors. What the Adonis has to boast about is a roof terrace for breakfast or evening snacks against a stunning backdrop of the looming Acropolis.

Astor Hotel, Odós Karagheórghi tís Servías 16. ☎ **325-5555.**
Fax 325-5115. 131 rms. TEL
Rates: 12,000 Drs ($48) single; 16,000 Drs ($64) double; 20,000 Drs ($80) triple. AE, DC, V.

The Astor is right in the center of one of the busiest areas of town, with taxis and people constantly passing up and down Karagheórghi tís Servías on their way from Pláka to Sýntagma Square. Once inside, however, you won't be too conscious of noise. The hotel sits back from the street, with its entrance under an arcade that blocks out the traffic noises as well as the harsh sun.

The Astor has 11 air-conditioned floors, with the top floor given over to the Roof Garden. One of Athens's few year-round roof gardens, it sprawls over the terrace in summer, but in winter it's enclosed in glass that doesn't confine the view. And what an incredible view! Look up from your table and there's the Acropolis looking as though it's across the street. In the opposite direction, you can see Lykavittós Hill, and over on the left is Mt. Pendéli. You can have lunch or dinner up there for about 3,500 Drs ($14) per person.

Most of the Astor's rooms above the sixth floor have views (except for the singles, which are all at the rear), and most of them also have a balcony. Bathrooms have a small tub and hand-held showers. The furniture is nothing to write home about, and the place needs sprucing up, but you may be too busy looking at the view from your balcony to care much. Down in the basement there's a well-stocked

---

Frommer's Smart Traveler: Hotels

Value-Conscious Travelers Should Take Advantage of the Following:

1. Off-season rates. They vary from hotel to hotel (some hotels, among them the Hilton, have a year-round rate); but generally, if you travel after October and before April, you can save on hotels.

2. Avoid MAP (Modified American Plan) rates—in this day and age there's no justification for a city hotel (as opposed to a resort) insisting that guests have dinner in the hotel.

Questions to Ask if You're on a Budget:

1. Do rates include breakfast?

2. Do rates include all taxes and service charges?

3. Do rates include air conditioning?

souvenir shop and a beauty parlor, and just off the lobby is a small bar.

Athens Gate Hotel, Leofóros Syngroú 10. ☎ 923-8302.

Fax 923-7493. Telex 214 202 DTB. 100 rms. A/C TEL

Rates: 14,850 Drs ($60) single; 18,150 Drs ($73) double. AE, DC, EC, MC, V.

This is one of Athens's top budget values—especially since half the rooms have television. It's a 5-minute walk from Sýntagma Square and directly across the avenue from the temple of Olympian Zeus. There's a gleaming black-leather, chrome, and marble bar and lounge on the ground floor, but don't linger—head straight for the elevator and press the top button. The roof is eight stories up—a walk-around marble sun deck with a view. All the sights are there: Olympian Zeus and the attendant Hadrian's Gate; the National Garden and the famous Záppion exhibition hall with its Corinthian portico, the Parliament Building, and the former Royal Palace (now the official residence of the president of the republic); Lykavittós Hill farther off; the Olympic Stadium; the towering Acropolis on the other side; and away in the distance the Saronic Gulf.

Most of the rooms come with balconies, and depending on location, you'll probably enjoy some part of this vista without leaving your room. Get your reservation in early, ask for a room on the seventh floor at the rear, and you'll get a large, plant-filled terra-cotta terrace rather than a balcony, with room for breakfasting or sunning while you look up at the looming Acropolis. The rooms themselves are livelier than the usual in Athens—with drapes, carpeted floors, functional mahogany furniture (desk/dresser and armchair), radio, and bedside lamps. Other facilities include room service until midnight; a cheery 100-seat restaurant on the mezzanine floor; and a roof-garden restaurant with bar, barbecue, and breathtaking views of the Parthenon, temple of Zeus, Lykavittós Hill, and Hadrian's Gate. Now a Best Western hotel.

$ Hotel Electra, Odós Ermoú 5. ☎ 322-2323. Fax 322-0310. 120 rms. A/C MINIBAR TV TEL

Rates: 21,700 Drs ($87) single; 27,400 Drs ($110) double. AE, DC, EC, MC, V.

This modern hotel looks more like an office building—especially at street level, where the narrow glass entrance is surrounded by shops and cafés. Once you step into the lobby, however, you're unmistakably in a first-class, businesslike, cosmopolitan hotel. The 120-room Electra reopened in 1994 after a top-to-bottom renovation and is now one of the best values in town, complete with satellite TV, minibars, direct-dial telephones, hair dryers, sound-proofed windows, and central air conditioning with individual controls. Some rooms also have terraces.

Esperia Palace, Odós Stadíou 22. ☎ 323-8001. Fax 323-8100.

Telex 215067 ESPE GR. 185 rms. A/C MINIBAR TV TEL

Rates: 16,800 Drs ($67) single; 22,700 Drs ($91) double. AE, DC, MC, V.

Stadíou Street is one of the big thoroughfares that link Sýntagma Square with Omónia Square, and 22 is closer to Sýntagma than to Omónia. It's a convenient location, but it can get noisy at rush hours, so ask for a room high up (there are nine floors) on the side or at the rear. The Esperia is yet another of those Athenian palaces with acres of marbled space—a two-story lobby, with marble floors and columns, and marble hallways on each floor—and the inevitable highly polished floors. The rooms are sparely done up, but the furniture's a shade more substantial and comfortable than usual in Greece. All the rooms have balconies; the ones on the sides have views of Lykavittós (from the sixth floor up) or the Acropolis (fourth floor up). There's also an attractive wood-paneled restaurant and café on the main floor and a big comfortable lounge at the top of the spiral staircase. Room service is available.

Hotel Acropolis House, Odós Kodroú 6–8. ☎ **322-2344.**
Fax 324-4143. 19 rms (9 with shower). TEL
Rates: 7,344 Drs ($29) single with shower; 8,813 Drs ($35) double with shower.

The Hotel Acropolis House claims to offer its guests "comfortable rooms and realistic prices at the gateway of the old city." True, but there are better bargains in the area. The hotel is located on the corner of Odós Voulis (Parliament Street), just 4 minutes on foot from Sýntagma Square (maybe 10 with a backpack or suitcase). This family-run Class B pension fills a handsome century-old villa with many of the original architectural devices preserved (decorative ceilings and friezes, intricate plasterwork and moldings, that sort of thing) and a "newer" 60-year-old wing. The breakfast room just to the left of the lobby is a high-ceilinged, old-style salon, and the owners, the Choudalakis family, are warm and welcoming. The guest rooms, nine of which are air-conditioned, come in various shapes and sizes, some with balcony and a few with Acropolis views. The decor is spartan at best and jarring at worst, with wallpaper patterns, spreads, and linoleum all at war in some rooms; most rooms could use a fresh coat of paint.

Hotel Arethusa, corner of Odós Mitropóleos and Odós Níkis.
☎ **322-9431.** Fax 322-9439. Telex 21-6882. 87 rms. A/C TEL
Rates: 11,200 Drs ($45) single; 15,800 Drs ($63) double. AE, MC, V.

While the outside of the hotel is gift-wrapped in what looks like aluminum foil, the interior decor is a lively blend of marble, polished hardwoods, and fabrics in once-sprightly colors. All rooms in this attractive hostelry are decked out with mostly contemporary furniture, wall-to-wall carpets, radio, and clean, tiled bath and shower. Up top there's an indoor/outdoor roof garden (with a superb view and dinner for around 2,400 Drs or $10), and you can have an after-dinner drink in the modern bar (with TV), one hushed floor above busy Mitropóleos Street. The Arethusa is unusually handsome as Class B hotels go, and the rates are still reasonable.

Olympic Palace Hotel, Odós Filellínon 16. ☎ **323-7611.**
Fax 923-3317. 90 rms. A/C TV TEL

Rates: 14,500 Drs ($58) single; 19,500 Drs ($78) double. AE, DC, V.

Turn right into Filellínon Street from Mitropoléos Street, at the corner of Sýntagma Square, and three blocks later you come to a small square with an old Byzantine church and tower and three palm trees. The Olympic Palace is the modern building just across the street, with the neat square verandas on three sides. The lobby is the usual palace of glass and marble, leading into a larger lounge with almost enough armchairs to seat every guest in the hotel. There's also a small bar with comfy upholstered chairs; one floor up is a big bright dining room with lots of windows and flowers.

All the Olympic Palace's rooms were renovated in 1990, and they have music channels, modern furniture, and bathrooms with marble floor and floral wallpaper. Most rooms have (albeit small) balconies. There are corner suites that sleep three. Despite its location close to Sýntagma Square and Pláka, the Olympic Palace is a relatively quiet hotel; and despite the tempting photograph on its brochure, none of the rooms has a proper view of the Acropolis, although some pleasantly overlook the church square.

Omiros Hotel, Odós Apóllonos 15. ☎ **323-5486.** Fax 322-8059.
37 rms. TEL

Rates: 9,732 Drs ($37) single; 14,364 Drs ($57) double.

Apóllonos Street is hotel row. It runs for half a dozen blocks from Pláka to Sýntagma Square, and it's full of good budget hotels. The Omiros Hotel is one of the newer and smaller ones. Rooms come with pink- or green-tiled bathrooms and radios. The lobby has handsome wood paneling with ancient Greek ceramic decorations on the walls and a coffee corner at the back. There's also a small but pleasant breakfast room. The rooms are equally compact, some with head-to-head beds along one wall and a small couch along the other. The rooms facing the street have a balcony overlooking the narrow, typically Athenian street, with balustrades, arcades, shutters, and pots of flowers. Some of the back rooms (ask for no. 504 or 505) have huge terraces. Most of the rooms have scatter rugs on linoleum floors; the furnishings are standard: twin beds, desk, and wardrobe. There's taped pop music everywhere at the Omiros—in the lobby, in the elevator, in the rooms, and on the roof.

Beyond Sýntagma Square

⭐ **Athenian Inn,** Odós Cháritos 22, in Kolonáki. ☎ **723-8097.**
Fax 721-5614. Telex 224092 INN GR. 25 rms, 3 suites. A/C TEL

Rates: 12,800 Drs ($51) single; 19,110 Drs ($76) double; 22,190 Drs ($89) suite. AE, DC, V. **Parking:** Nearby.

Kolonáki is one of the most fashionable neighborhoods in Athens, much sought after by bankers and novelists, but the Athenian Inn lets you stay here in a quiet residential street, surrounded by high-rent apartments, for reasonable prices. Entered by a flower-decked entrance just 2 blocks from Kolonáki Square, the Athenian Inn is owned by a Greek couple who've decorated it tastefully in "Greek village" style (dark beams, white stucco walls, and tile floor). The lounge/breakfast room/bar features an open fire, rustic furniture, and watercolors by local artists; the guest rooms have wall-to-wall carpeting, quaint rustic-style wooden beds, and radios; all but five of them have a balcony, some with a view of Lykavittós Hill.

⭐ **Best Western Ilissia Hotel,** Odós Michalakopoúlou 25. ☎ **724-4051.** Fax 724-1847. Telex 4924 GR. 90 rms. A/C TV TEL **Rates:** 9,000–11,600 Drs ($36–$46) single; 17,400–21,000 Drs ($70–$84) double. AE, MC, V.

The Class B Ilissia tucks its trim and tidy rooms (only 18 of them singles) into a corner site just around the corner from the Hilton. The friendly owners don't insist on half board (they don't have a restaurant, but they do serve light snacks until midnight). The hotel caters primarily to business travelers, many of them connected with the nearby U.S. Embassy. All rooms have a bath or shower, a TV, and a refrigerator (unstocked); some have balconies.

Hotel Lycabette, Odós Valaorítou 6. ☎ **363-3514.** Telex 22-1147. 39 rms. A/C TEL **Rates:** 10,900 Drs ($44) single; 16,200 Drs ($65) double. AE, DC, MC, V.

This Class B hotel is a 5-minute walk from Sýntagma Square, on one of the quieter shopping streets that are now part of a pedestrians-only mall. All the rooms on its seven floors have telephones, radios, and balconies. The best of the bunch are on the upper floors (where the balconies are bigger). The Lycabette is a friendly little place—not a steal, but a good value considering the location and the coziness. It has now sprouted a smart little coffee bar and terrace, Café Fiorian, offering pies and burgers and a fresh salad bar, from 800 to 1,400 Drs ($3 to $6).

President Hotel, Leofóros Kifissiás 43. ☎ **692-4600.** Fax 692-4968. Telex 218585. 513 rms. A/C MINIBAR TV TEL **Rates:** 10,685 ($43) single; 14,260 Drs ($57) double. AE, DC, MC, V. **Parking:** Indoors.

This high rise is one of Athens's biggest Class A establishments, although its stylishly modern lobby (acres of marble in earthy colors with concealed lighting and pop music) might lead you to believe that you'd stepped into a deluxe hotel; bars, lounges, and dining facilities are equally spacious. The guest rooms, on the other hand, are dainty, pretty to look at, and fitted with balconies. The 22d floor is given over to a swimming pool, sun terrace, and discotheque, but the President's basement may be the best feature if you plan to do a lot of driving—it has space for 500 cars. The fact that you don't have to take a half-board rate even in summer may compensate for its slightly inconvenient location. The President is located on one of the main avenues leading north from Athens (convenient for touring by car), but it is about a 15-minute taxi ride from Sýntagma Square.

Makriyánni

This part of town is a predominantly residential area bounded by the Acropolis (the side opposite Pláka); the temple of Olympian Zeus; and Leofóros Syngroú, which is rapidly becoming one of the main business and commercial centers of the city.

⭐ **Hotel Herodion,** Odós Rovértou Gálli 4. ☎ **923-6832.** Fax 923-5851. Telex 21 9423 HERO. 90 rms. A/C TV TEL

Rates: 15,950–23,000 ($63–$92) single; 21,250–29,500 Drs ($85–$118) double. AE, MC, V.

The Herodion is located on a quiet side street but so close to the Herod Atticus Odeum, at the foot of the Acropolis, that it's especially popular with performers and culture buffs during the Athens Festival. Since it's also just a 5-minute walk from Pláka and a 5-minute bus ride from Sýntagma Square, the Herodion is a good address at any time of the year. The hotel has been completely renovated. Its spacious marble lobby leads to a lounge and patio garden, where you can have drinks and snacks beneath the trees; the dining room is taverna style, with ceramics and native rugs on white stucco walls. The Herodion's guest rooms are tastefully decorated, many of them have a balcony, and in any case there's a solarium/roof terrace with a stunning view of the Acropolis.

   Note: The Herodion manages the nearby Philippos Hotel, Odós Mitséon 3. Renovated in 1993, the 50-room Philippos offers rates about a third lower than those at the Herodion.

Hotel Christina, Odós Petmezá 15 at Odós Kalliróis. ☎ **921-5353.** Fax 921-5569. Telex 219304. 89 rms. A/C TEL

Rates: 11,800 Drs ($47) single; 15,050 Drs ($60) double. AE, DC, EC, MC, V.

The cabin-size guest rooms are convenient to the Olympic downtown terminal. The Christina is on a very busy main road, so rooms may be noisy. If other area rooms are booked, this may be an option because you can still cross Syngroú Avenue and stroll through Makriyánni or up to the Acropolis.

Near Omónia Square

Athens Center Hotel, Odós Sofokléous at Odós Klisthénous. ☎ **524-8511.** Fax 524-8517. Telex 221761. 136 rms. A/C TEL

Rates: 2,100–3,100 Drs ($84–$124) single; 11,500–16,000 Drs ($46–$64) double. MC, V. **Parking:** Garage for 25 cars, at 1,500 Drs ($6).

If you enjoy browsing around markets, the Athens Center puts you within walking distance of the central meat, fish, vegetable, and fruit markets, and close enough to the flea markets at Monastiráki. The hotel bustles with small tour or sports groups, and there's an amiable atmosphere around the lobby TV lounge/bar. The rooftop terrace also has a bar and a swimming pool to add to the fun. Colorwise, the rooms are drab but good sized and have small, tiled baths or showers and carpeting; a few have balconies (ask for an eighth-floor room, with a huge terrace and formerly stunning views which are now partially blocked by a new office building). Other amenities include a convivial snack bar and restaurant.

Dorian Inn Hotel, Odós Pireós 15–17. ☎ **523-9782.** Fax 522-6196. Telex 214779 DORI. 117 rms, 29 junior suites. A/C TEL

Rates: 13,000 Drs ($52) single; 19,500 Drs ($78) double. AE, DC, MC, V.

All the comfortable rooms and junior suites here have wall-to-wall carpeting and three-channel music; half of them have balconies. There's room service from 7am to 10pm, a restaurant; a bar/lounge with TV; and another bar on the roof, 12 floors above the city, with an excellent view of the Acropolis and Lykavittós Hill. But the Dorian's main attraction for many people will be the rooftop pool.

Hotel Ionis, Odós Chalkokondýli 41. ☎ **523-2311.** Fax 524-7360. Telex 218425. 102 rms. A/C TEL

Rates: 8,000 Drs ($32) single; 14,000 Drs ($56) double. No credit cards.

At first glance, the Ionis looks like yet another modern office building on a street of undistinguished office buildings, but once you step through the smoked-glass doors, you enter an oasis of style. Gleaming gray marble, polished wood, and brightly colored ceramics create a welcoming lobby; a marble stairway winds up to a mezzanine restaurant, spacious lounge with TV, and a bar with ceramic friezes depicting willowy nymphs. Corridors are carpeted; cheerful curtains and bedspreads are color coordinated; and each room has a two-channel radio. Rooms on the street side have balconies (on the upper floors, terraces rather than balconies). Although Chalkokondýli is not the "smartest" street in town, it has some advantages: It's quiet in the evening when all the office workers have gone home; it's only a 5-minute walk from Omónia Square and 15 to 20 minutes away from the National Archeological Museum; and rooms cost less than they would on more fashionable thoroughfares.

Hotel Stanley, Odós Odysséos 1 at Karaïskáki Square. ☎ **524-1611.** Fax 524-41611. Telex 216550 STAN. 400 rms. A/C TEL

Rates: 12,558 Drs ($50) single; 16,964 Drs ($68) double. AE, V. **Parking:** On premises.

This is another moderately priced Class B hotel with a pool on the roof. It's a slight distance from the center of town, but its roof is one of the coolest, breeziest places in Athens at high noon, with a great view as a bonus. The Stanley dominates the big square at the end of Leofóros Aghíou Konstantínou, between Omónia Square and the Laríssis railroad station.

Every room in this modern hotel has a bath or shower and a balcony. The rooms are big and have been outfitted with dark wood beds, vanities, and so forth. The rooftop pool and garden are open from May through October. An attractive first-floor restaurant with Scandinavian decor and mottled marble floor is open year-round (with three-course meals for 2,250 Drs or $9) and there's an inexpensive cafeteria as well as a bar and TV lounge.

Despite its size, the Stanley is usually full, so if you don't have a reservation, call ahead first. It's a good value.

Hotel Titania, Odós Panepistimíou 52. ☎ **330-0111.**
Fax 330-0700. Telex 214673 1FEL. 400 rms, A/C TV (on request) TEL
Rates: 14,800 Drs ($59) single; 19,800 Drs ($79) double. AE, DC, EC,
MC, V. **Parking:** Available for 400 cars.

A stylish, tinted-glass facade rising eight floors above a street-level
shopping arcade (look for the hotel sign *inside* the arcade) identifies
the Titania. Up on the roof, the terrace and bar (sometimes with
music) have impressive views of Lykavittós Hill and the Acropolis.
The Titania's rooms and suites fill six floors; all the rooms have fitted wall cabinets, writing desks, three-channel music, and tiled bathrooms with tubs and hand-held showers. The color schemes vary from
floor to floor; rooms at the back of the hotel are sunny and quiet and
have balconies. Public facilities include a colorful coffee shop (there's
also room service from 7am to 11pm), spacious restaurant, and
lounge/writing room on the mezzanine. It's a good value in a convenient location, with parking for 400 cars. The traffic hurtling along
Panepistimíou Street is not too intrusive with the windows closed,
but if you want complete quiet, ask for a room at the rear.

King Minos Hotel, Odós Pireós 1. ☎ **523-1111.** Fax 523-1361.
Telex 215-339 HERO GR. 200 rms. A/C TEL
Rates: 14,950 Drs ($60) single; 20,750 Drs ($83) double. AE, MC, V.

Although this Class A hotel is only a few steps from Omónia Square,
its glass-and-grillwork facade is more reminiscent of the Caribbean.
The hotel has a spacious lobby, with a marble frieze of King Minos's
Palace in Knossós dominating one wall. Up on the mezzanine floor
are acres of comfortable lounges, two desks with typewriters, an
American bar, fountains, birds in a gilded cage, and a restaurant.
There are seven floors of rooms, and the King Minos was fully renovated in 1987, including repainting and installing double windows
to block street noise. The room furnishings are fresh and modern,
with roomy closets, chairs and desks, radios, and marble balconies;
studios have twin beds, arranged at right angles around a brace of
chairs and a coffee table; bathrooms have full-size bathtubs, marble
floors and walls, and piles of towels. If you feel cramped, you can
always sit out on the balcony and watch the action in Omónia Square
or go up to the roof to sunbathe.

Novotel Athens, Odós Vodá 4–8. ☎ **825-0422.** Fax 883-7816.
195 rms. A/C MINIBAR TV TEL
Rates: Year-round 20,000 Drs ($80) single; 23,500 Drs ($94) double;
36,000 Drs ($144) suite. AE, DC, MC, V. **Parking:** Indoors.

With its smart lines, spacious ambience, and stylish interiors, the
Novotel is a better buy than many of the city's so-called deluxe hotels. The Novotel is located about a 7-minute walk from the National
Archeological Museum in one direction, a few paces less from the
railroad station in the other. The French hotel chain's first venture
in Athens is a handsome eight-story structure of white stone, its first
two floors set behind two-story windows, the top two floors stepped
back behind balconies and verandas, and the remainder trimmed with

window boxes trailing geraniums. The shiny marble lobby leads to an inviting café/restaurant, Le Grill, designed as a sort of conservatory with arched-glass ceilings and floor-to-ceiling walls overlooking a decorative courtyard with still more geraniums. But it's the Roof Garden that's the real stunner here: a big tiled swimming pool surrounded by split-level sunning terraces, blue-and-white striped awnings for shade, with terraced gardens at one end and behind them a panoramic view of the Acropolis and Lykavittós.

With the exception of five suites on the seventh floor, the Novotel's rooms are identical except for location: With double-glazed windows and additional soundproofing throughout, traffic noise is unlikely to be a factor on the street side; and with the window boxes and decorative courtyard at the rear, rooms at the back are more appealing than usual. All rooms come with a modern bathroom, alarm clock, double beds, and sofa—all done in light, soothing colors. Additional public features include underground parking for 150 cars, room service, and business facilities.

5   Inexpensive

The following are Class C and D hotels. Here's good news for budget travelers: The official hotel guide to Athens includes more names in categories C and D than in all the others put together. In all, there are well over 100 hotels in Athens offering rooms between $25 (6,250 Drs) and $65 (16,250 Drs) a night for doubles in peak season. This guide can't possibly review all of them, but in the following pages you'll find a selection of some of the best budget hotels in the city.

Near Sýntagma & Pláka

Hermes Hotel, Odós Apóllonos 19. ☎ **323-5514.** Telex 224202. 45 rms (all with bath or shower). A/C MINIBAR TEL
Rates: 6,250 Drs ($25) single; 10,300 Drs ($41) double. AE, V.

This small hostelry has a modest lobby with a relief map of Greece; its severe facade is softened somewhat by hints of shrubbery draping over the balconies. Rooms are actually double-size, and all have balconies. The ones at the rear look out on a school playground. There's also quiet bar/lounge to the rear of the lobby.

$ Hotel Hera, Odós Falírou 9. ☎ **923-5618.** Fax 924-7344. Telex 223941 STIM. 49 rms (all with shower). TEL
Rates: 11,000 Drs ($44) single; 15,000 Drs ($60) double. No credit cards. **Parking:** On premises.

Here's a real little find, opened in 1983. The Hera faces a small square in a residential section between the Acropolis and Leofóros Syngroú, a 5-minute walk from Pláka. The stylish facade, like a miniature Ledra Marriott, fronts a spick-and-span split-level lobby that opens onto a lounge with TV and a coffee shop with marble-topped tables, which in turn leads to a quiet, sunny patio café. The guest rooms, on five floors, are compact to be sure but sensibly designed (plenty of storage space for suitcases or backpacks), each with radio, twin beds covered with brightly colored spreads, and skimpy drapes covering sliding windows that shut out most neighborhood noise. The bathrooms are spotless. For Acropolis views you have to head for the rooftop terrace. The Hera is a good value.

$ Hotel Nefeli, Odós Iperídou 16A. ☎ **322-8044.** 18 rms (all with bath). TEL

Rates: 8,500 Drs ($34) single; 10,500 Drs ($42) double. No credit cards.

For people who want to be in the heart of things, you can't be much closer to the heart of old Athens than the intersection of Odós Iperídou and Odós Satíros in Pláka. The 16-year-old Nefeli squeezes spick-and-span rooms into a three-story wedge, each of its chambers equipped with trim furniture and windows that open onto cheery geranium planters. It's nothing fancy, but it's comfortable and functional. The spacious, cool lobby is dominated by an orange plastic phone bubble, and there's a pleasant breakfast room/lounge right on the corner. It's obviously not the quietest spot in the city, and when Pláka wakes up so will you; but you'll get modern rooms in a central location. First choice in this category.

Imperial Hotel, Odós Mitropóleos 46. ☎ **322-7617.** 21 rms (19 with bath).

Rates: 5,500 Drs ($22) single; 7,200 Drs ($30) double. **Parking:** Free tourist parking across the street.

The five-floor Imperial Hotel has a slightly Germanic facade—square cut with small windows. It doesn't have a lobby at the entrance, but when you go up one flight you'll find a pleasant sitting room; the manager, G. Klissouris, who speaks English, is anxious to please and enjoys meeting all the guests who stay in his hotel. The simple, clean, and large guest rooms have balconies and central heating, but no air conditioning. They also have wildly clashing wallpaper: stripes, patterns, diagonals, and that may all be in one room! Singles have double beds and tend to be roomier than most singles in this price range. Most of the balconies look toward the cathedral and Acropolis.

Phaedra Hotel, Odós Cherefóntos 16. ☎ **323-8461.** 21 rms (none with bath).

Rates: 5,300 Drs ($21) single 6,500 Drs ($26) double.

The location of the Phaedra Hotel belies the ominous overtones of its legendary namesake—on a quiet little square facing the palm-filled courtyard of St. Catherine's Church, surrounded by neighborhood tavernas and narrow streets, one block from Odós Filellínon, near the monument to Lysicrates. The rooms are relatively big, decor is dormlike, with some crazy-quilt linoleum slapped down. There are washbasins in each room and three toilets to every floor. Some rooms have tiny balconies—but some very big views!

Near Omónia Square

Hotel Exarchion, Odós Themistokléous 55, In Exarchía Square. ☎ **360-8684.** Fax 360-3296. 64 rms (all with bath or shower).

Rates: 5,900 Drs ($24) single; 8,800 Drs ($35) double. No credit cards.

Exarchía Square is a charming triangular plaza lined with trees and cafés, with its apex at the Hotel Exarchion. This Class C hotel has a rooftop bar, six floors up, with a splendid view across the city. Most of the rooms have balconies. If your first stop in Athens is the National Archeological Museum and you want to be in an area that's Athenian rather than touristy, then this is a good address to head for.

Hotel La Mirage, Odós Kotopoúli 3. ☎ **523-4755.** Fax 523-3992. Telex 222598 SASA. 208 rms. A/C MINIBAR TEL
Rates: 11,200 Drs ($45) single; 16,400 Drs ($66) double.

One of the best buys in the Omónia district is Category C Hotel La Mirage, adjacent to the Omónia Hotel and right in the square, despite its official address. It rises seven stories above the square, its double-glazed windows blocking out the sounds, and each room with tiled bathroom (some with bathtub), radio, reading lamps, and desk. The second floor is given over to spacious lounges (with satellite TV), a bar, and restaurants, all with picture windows overlooking the square and the fountain—and worth keeping in mind for a moderately priced lunch or dinner (lunch, at 1,900 Drs or $8, is slightly more expensive than it is in Pláka tavernas). Popular with tour groups, who can overwhelm the check-in desk.

Hotel Museum, Odós Bouboulínas 16 at Odós Tossítsa.
☎ **360-5611.** Fax 360-0507. 59 rms (all with shower). TEL
Rates: 5,400 Drs ($22) single; 8,000 Drs ($32) double. AE, MC, V.

The Hotel Museum is a friendly, pleasant, and spotless Class C hostelry located right behind the National Archeological Museum. Of its rooms, 52 are doubles with balcony, all at the front, and the remaining seven are singles, all at the rear; all rooms have taped music. The mezzanine floors are given over to a cafeteria and a bar/lounge. The rates make the Museum popular with visiting professors and students.

Hotel Nestor, Leofóros Aghíou Konstantínou 58. ☎ **523-5576.**
Fax 524-3207. 50 rms (all with bath or shower). TEL
Rates (including continental breakfast): 5,000 Drs ($20) single; 8,000 Drs ($32) double.

The Hotel Nestor has a rather olive-drab exterior, but the rooms themselves are bigger than usually found in this category—bright, with handsome furniture and pastel-colored walls and balconies. There's also a café and a dining room. It's a friendly hotel in a sometimes marginal area.

Hotel Pythagorian, Leofóros Aghíou Konstantínou 28.
☎ **524-2811.** Fax 524-5581. Telex 2238634. 56 rms (all with bath).
A/C
Rates: 5,200 Drs ($21) single; 8,000 Drs ($32) double. DC.

This is another of those good-buy Class C hotels with a very friendly staff, in the region of Omónia Square. The lobby/lounge/dining room has been renovated. The rooms, spread over seven floors and topped with a roof garden, all have a typical lino-floor/

plain-modern-furniture decor. Rooms at the front have balconies, and bathrooms have bidets.

Omónia Hotel, on Omónia Square. ☎ **523-7211.** Fax 522-5779. 275 rms (all with shower). TEL

Rates: 6,114 Drs ($24) single; 8,427 Drs ($34) double. V.

The Omónia has 10 floors and rooms with iron balconies and picture windows that give the building an airy appearance. The lobby, one floor up, above the entrance to the subway, is surrounded by a nondescript bar/café facing the square, with a restaurant at the rear. There's always plenty of activity around this friendly, spotless hotel. The rooms, which have very modest, slightly worn but comfortable furniture, are particularly spacious, especially the singles. Higher-floor rooms with balconies have Omónia Square and partial Acropolis views, but many rooms just face an inner courtyard, so check first.

6 Budget

In a city such as Athens, where 6,250 Drs ($25) will set you up in a single room in a very nice hotel in the off-season, you hardly need to bother with the local rock-bottom prices. However, thousands of young (and some not so young) people arrive in Greece each year with minimal dollars in their pockets and backpacks on their shoulders; Athenians seem to go out of their way to cater to them, although the government has clamped down on many of the pensions and hotels offering dormitory-type accommodations.

There are two types of hostels: youth and student. In Athens, call or apply to the Greek Youth Hostels Association, Odós Dragatsaníou 4 (☎ **323-4107,** fax 323-7590).

YWCA, Odós Amerikís 11. ☎ **362-4291.**

Rates: 3,000 Drs ($12) single without bath, 4,500 Drs ($18) single with bath, 6,250 Drs ($25) double with bath.

The YWCA, or XEN in Greek, hardly deserves the title "rock-bottom," because it's in a big, modern building that at first glance seems more like a first-class hotel; it's also in a convenient location, just a couple of blocks from Sýntagma Square and the American Express office. XEN has kitchen and laundry facilities on every floor. Each impeccably clean room has beds, tables, chairs, and marble floors; there's no air conditioning, but the sunless rooms at the rear are cool even at midday in the middle of summer.

5

Athens Dining

SINCE ANCIENT TIMES, GREEK DINING HAS BEEN MARKED BY SIMPLICITY. THE fare is varied and delectable, but prepared and served without ostentation; for the meal is less the object in itself than a pretext for family and friends to gather at the end of the day and enjoy each other's company (*paréa*), as well as the animated discussion that invariably accompanies a Greek meal and makes it a social experience to be savored.

In Greece a meal is meant to last beyond the time it takes to gobble down the contents of one's plate. Dine at one of the city's many neighborhood restaurants and you'll see families linger for hours over their meal, unhurried by overzealous waiters eager to seat the next customer.

TYPES OF EATING PLACES Athens, as a cosmopolitan city, offers a wide selection of international cuisines, from French and Italian to Mexican and Japanese. For a taste of Greek cuisine—and of the leisurely pace that still distinguishes life here, despite the increasing demands of the European Union—try that peculiarly Greek institution called the **taverna**.

The simplest tavernas (and for many people, these are the most enjoyable) are plain rooms in nondescript buildings or in patios and gardens under arbors and olive trees; furnishings usually consist of plain-Jane wooden tables and chairs, the tables covered with white paper on which your waiter sets glasses of water. The kitchen is usually open to view, and the selection of food is either still in the pots or spread out in glass-enclosed showcases—diners simply walk over to the pots or the display, size up the various dishes, and then indicate to the waiter what they want. It's simple—especially for foreigners who don't speak Greek. Most menus follow the same basic pattern—that is, moussaká, *dolmadákia* (stuffed grape leaves), *arní soúvlas* (grilled lamb), *barboúnia skáras* (grilled red mullet), and some regional variations of these basic dishes.

In some tavernas, on the other hand, you have no choice, and it matters not whether you speak Greek or Swahili, because waiters simply arrive at your table with platters of food, beginning perhaps with the selection of *mezédes* (appetizers).

There probably was a time when a taverna was something quite distinct from a restaurant—and even more distinct from a nightclub. But that's no longer the case. A taverna can be a pub, a restaurant, a café, a nightclub, or a combination of all of them. Restaurant-type

IMPRESSIONS

We are lovers of the beautiful yet simple in our tastes, and we cultivate the mind without loss of manliness.
—Pericles, in Thucydides, *The Peloponnesian War*, c. 430 B.C.

The climate and country [of Greece] were such as to gratify every appetite for pleasurable sensation, without enervating or relaxing the frame or allowing the mind to sink into an Asiatic torpor.
—J. C. and A. Hare, *Guesses at Truth*, 1847

tavernas will be listed in this chapter. Since many of them, however, provide music and are really for an evening on the town, you'll read about some of them in Chapter 9, "Athens Nights."

The other unusual feature about Athenian eating places is the **roof garden.** Apparently the roofs of Greek houses used to be flat in order to collect rainwater, which was then drained off and fed into a tank under the soil; when proper plumbing and water systems came along, people didn't need their roofs as dams, but they then discovered that they were refreshingly cool places to spend an evening. So they started turning them into gardens, or at least terraces. The idea spread to restaurants. Now many of the new hotels in Athens include a roof garden, and you should certainly plan to spend at least one evening up there. There are also basic, authentic roof gardens on tavernas in Pláka.

Athens at midday in midsummer is often too hot for sitting down to a meal, and this has probably given rise to the city's varied types of **snack bars**—the Western-style snack bar, the tea and pastry shop, the fig-and-nut store, the pastry vendor, and the souvláki shop. Keep these snack bars in mind if you're on a budget or if you're having problems adjusting to the curious meal hours in Athens.

The Greeks, like any other people, have sweet tooths. But shamelessly so. *Baklavá* is a gooey goody made of layers of paper-thin pastry called phyllo (Greek for "leaf"), filled with nuts and covered with honey. *Kataífi* is equally gooey but filled with sweetened nuts and shredded wheat and in its most glorious state is served with a mound of Chantilly cream. *Galaktoboúreko* is much simpler—a hollow pastry filled to overflowing with custard cream. Greek chocolate, like Greek olives, is bitter, and you can sample it in the form of layer cakes, tube cakes, or flaky mounds. Many pastry shops, or *zacharoplastía,* in Athens also sell coffee, so you can sit down and enjoy yourself right there and then—simply pointing to what you fancy.

Fig-and-nut shops sell figs, dates, prunes, walnuts, pistachios, almonds, honey, raisins, syrup, and so on. You buy by the drachma, and these goodies hit the spot if you're on a budget or if it's a long time until your nine o'clock dinner date.

Pastry vendors, the local equivalent of pretzel vendors, sell two, sometimes three, items. First, there are rolls and hero-style breads, plus a large, thin bagel, known as *kouloúri,* with sesame seeds on top; it costs only a few drachmas—the perfect inexpensive snack. The pastries include plain *bourékia,* made of doughnut dough with sugar sprinkled on top. You can buy them either in a "long-john" shape or in a rounded shape with a redundant smidgen of jelly in the middle. *Bougátsa* is a pastry pie with cream inside and sprinkled with powdered sugar. When filled with apples rather than cheese, it's known as *milópita.* Some pastry vendors also have ham sandwiches or *piróski* (bread with sausage inside).

As in most other Mediterranean countries, people in Greece pop into a coffeehouse, or *kafenío,* at the slightest opportunity. In winter, they'll have a quick espresso as a pick-me-up; in summer, they'll have something cooler. The *kafenío* is an institution, almost an epidemic. The waiters are no less immaculately attired and competent than their counterparts in restaurants. Even the simplest order is attended to with style. Ask for a lemonade, and they'll bring you a tall glass with freshly pressed lemon juice, a carafe of water, and sugar on a silver tray—all for something like 650 Drs ($3). And having paid your dues, you're free to sit in this informal "club" all afternoon, watching the world go by, flirting, dozing, and writing postcards. In Athens, as in other parts of Europe, it's perfectly proper to sit at an empty chair even when there are other people at the table.

DINING TIPS The following few nuggets of information will make eating your way around Athens easier:

Dining Hours Meals are probably later than what you are accustomed to (see "Food & Drink" in Chapter 1).

Prices This is probably the most tempting part of the subject, despite inflation. You can go to the finest restaurant in Athens, pick out the most expensive dish, and still end up spending less than you would on an average meal back home. If you want to shoot the works, Athens is the place to shoot. If you have to survive on pennies a day, you needn't get skinny in Athens. In this guide, there are plenty of restaurants where you can eat, and eat *well,* for under 2,500 Drs ($10) per person.

Restaurant prices, like hotel prices, are controlled by the government, specifically by an organization referred to on the menus as the "marketing police." Each type of restaurant is fitted into a category and must supply meals within those limits. Individual items will vary on the à la carte menus of different restaurants, but all restaurants within a given category, except deluxe, must supply fixed meals at a fixed price.

Tipping Despite the service charge, most people round out the figure on the bill and leave the change as a bonus tip. You don't have to, but some Greek restaurants, even the humblest, are swarming with busboys and assistant waiters who rely heavily on tips. If your busboy, or *mikrós* ("little one"), is particularly attentive about getting rid of empty plates and so forth, tip him separately by placing a few 20-drachma coins *on the table,* not in the saucer.

1 Restaurant Dining

Tavernas

In addition to the places listed below, two typical neighborhood tavernas are located in the residential district of Kolonáki. **Rodia,** at Odós Aristípou 44 (☎ **722-9883**), fills a whitewashed courtyard in summer, a pink-walled chamber in winter; the prix-fixe dinner costs 4,000 Drs ($16), a bottle of beer less than $2 (open Monday through Saturday, 7:30pm to 3am). **Philippos,** at Odós Xenokrátous 19 (☎ **721-6390**), is a popular gathering spot, in summer or winter, for local artists, writers, and actors attracted by the friendly staff, barrel wine, and good values—around 5,000 Drs ($20) for two, with wine. In summer, Philippos overflows onto a tiny terrace tucked into the steep sidewalk or across the street on a narrow sidewalk beneath a clump of bitter orange trees, with the action beginning at noon and running continuously until 12:30am weekdays, until 4:30pm only on Saturdays.

EXPENSIVE

⭐ **Taverna Myrtia,** Odós Trivonianoú 32–34. ☎ **924-7181** or **924-7175.**

Cuisine: GREEK TAVERNA. **Reservations:** Required.
Prices: Fixed-price meal 11,500 Drs ($46). AE, DC, MC, V.
Open: Dinner Mon–Sat. **Closed:** Aug.

The Taverna Myrtia, behind the Panathenaic Stadium, is the most famous of the fixed-menu tavernas. It's fairly typical of its kind, with rush-matting walls, beamed ceiling, a collection of island pottery and copper lamps, and a few paintings. Myrtia also regales you with a strolling trio. It's the most expensive of the tavernas listed here, but your meal consists of innumerable courses (probably more food than you can manage) plus wine. It lends itself to convivial evenings: The tables are covered with jolly red cloths, and waiters squeeze and maneuver through the crammed tables with platefuls of shrimp, mussels, and meatballs, followed by moussaka, and then tas kebab, followed by lamb stew, roast pork, and fruits. Myrtia also has garden seating during the warm months.

Xynou, Odós Anghélou Ghéronta 4. ☎ **322-1065.**

Cuisine: GREEK TAVERNA. **Reservations:** Recommended.
Prices: Appetizers 750–1,560 Drs ($3–$6); main courses 1,500–2,100 Drs ($6–$8); average meal (including house wine) under 5,500 Drs ($22). No credit cards.
Open: Dinner Mon–Sat 8pm–2am. **Closed:** Winter.

Many Athenians will tell you that this is one of the best traditional tavernas. Located on a back street in Pláka, it's basically a cluster of leafy courtyards with soft lights, murals of life in ancient Athens, and a trio of balladeers singing gentle songs. Xynou is where well-to-do Athenians dine (you'll see more jackets here than in most tavernas); prices are moderately expensive.

MODERATE

Taverna Costoyannis, Odós Zaimí 37. ☎ **821-2496.**

Cuisine: GREEK TAVERNA. **Reservations:** Recommended. **Taxi:** 950 Drs ($4) from Sýntagma Square.
Prices: Appetizers 450 Drs ($2); main courses 1,700 Drs ($7), average meal. No credit cards.
Open: Dinner Mon–Sat 7:30–2am.

Situated one block behind the National Archeological Museum and popular with students and well-to-do Athenians as well as with visitors, this big, rambling, busy taverna serves consistently good meals. Unlike other restaurants that remove only the roof in summer, Costoyannis discards its walls, too, so you can dine virtually in a garden surrounded by whitewashed walls and luxuriant creepers. Costoyannis has a stunning selection of appetizers, with a special recommendation for shrimp with bacon, tzatzíki, eggplant Imam, and swordfish souvláki. Visit Costoyannis with a few friends, order half a dozen dishes, and dip in. Call for a kilo (about 1 quart) of the house wine, called "brusco," or *kokkinélli,* and you'll still be amazed when your bill comes. If you can squeeze in yet another dish, then try the grills, both meat and fish; they're excellent. Costoyannis fills up from 9pm on, so go early or reserve unless you don't mind waiting for a table.

Aerides, Odós Márkou Avrilíou 3.

Cuisine: GREEK TAVERNA.
Prices: Appetizers 800–1,200 Drs ($3–$5); main courses 1,100–2,000 Drs ($4–$8); 3-course meals 2,000–3,400 Drs ($8–$14). No credit cards.
Open: Breakfast, lunch, dinner, 8am–12 noon.

At the Aerides, located on the edge of Pláka, you'll be seated at tables placed right out on the pavement opposite the Tower of the Winds; from here you have a glimpse of the Erechtheum up on the Acropolis and of the hills away in the distance. For winter dining there's also a raffia- and greenery-covered patio and a couple of rooms upstairs in an old Pláka house. A good selection of wines complements the taverna-style menu.

★ Socrates' Prison, Odós Mitséon 20. ☎ 922-3434.

Cuisine: GREEK TAVERNA.
Prices: Appetizers 200–400 Drs ($1–$2); main courses 800–1,700 Drs ($3–$7). No credit cards.
Open: Dinner Mon–Sat 8pm–1am.

Head for Makriyánni, the neighborhood on the far side of the Acropolis, walk downhill from Odós Dionysíou Areopaghítou, and enter this split-level taverna with stenciled archways, high, wooden ceilings, and big wine casks mounted overhead. You won't find a menu in English (your waiter will explain what's cooking), but you will find things like a grilled shrimp dish that's indescribably rich and without doubt the best at the price in Pláka. The Socrates has seasonal garden seating and is popular with Greeks and tourists alike, so be prepared for crowds.

Taverna Strofi, Odós Rovértou Gálli 25. ☎ 921-4130.

Cuisine: GREEK TAVERNA.
Prices: Appetizers 700–1,200 Drs ($3–$5); main courses 1,700–2,700 Drs ($7–$11). AE, MC, V.
Open: Mon–Sat. 7pm–2am.

Strofi is just a few blocks away from Socrates' Prison, where Rovértou Gálli Street meets Propyléon Street. The decor is old-fashioned— dark wood moldings, wrought-iron chandeliers—and whimsical, with ballet slippers, photos, and dance programs from the performers at the Herodion Theater covering one wall. The fare is traditional taverna: mixed grills, kebabs, dolmádes; but if you think all Greek country salads and table bread are alike, you're in for a pleasant surprise at the Strofi.

BUDGET

⭐ **The Cellar of Plaka,** Odós Kydathinéon 10. ☎ **322-4304.**
  Cuisine: GREEK TAVERNA.
  Prices: Appetizers 250–750 Drs ($1–$3); main courses 700–1,200 Drs ($3–$5). No credit cards.
  Open: Daily 8pm–2am. **Closed:** Summer.

Pláka is filled with colorful tavernas, and this is one of the more colorful—literally. The walls of the Cellar are completely covered with murals of Pláka life: the strollers, merrymakers, and imbibers all painted at their archest. The kitchen is up front and open, so you can check out the octopus, pork chops, garlic salad, and fried eggplant before pointing to your order. Wine is served out of the barrel. So tuck into a meal and raise a few glasses, then go upstairs and outside to watch the Cellar murals come to life.

Taverna "Damigos" Bakaliarakia, Odós Kydathinéon 1.
  ☎ **322-5084.**
  Cuisine: GREEK TAVERNA.
  Prices: Appetizers 250–750 Drs ($1–$3); main courses 600–800 Drs ($2–$3). No credit cards.
  Open: Daily 7am–12am. **Closed:** July–Sept.

This taverna is at a crossroad farther down Pláka's main street. Established in 1865, "Damigos" claims to be the oldest taverna in Athens. True or not, it certainly retains a venerable atmosphere. The back dining room is filled with Greeks, all of whom seem to be eating fried codfish, a local specialty; the kitchen is open for looking and smelling, and when you've finished off the garlic salad, the Greek salad, the eggplant, and the lamb chops, the waiter will write out your bill right on the tablecloth.

The 5 Brothers, Odós Eólou 3. ☎ **325-0088.**
  Cuisine: GREEK TAVERNA.
  Prices: Appetizers 600 Drs ($2); main courses 1,800 Drs ($7). No credit cards.
  Open: Daily 8am–1am.

This taverna, right across from the Tower of the Winds, has cloth-covered tables with big white sun umbrellas set out on the sloping sidewalk. Meals here (mainly lamb and veal dishes) are adequate, but the Acropolis views are magnificent.

Platanos, Odós Dioghénous 4. ☎ **322-0666.**
  Cuisine: GREEK TAVERNA. **Reservations:** Recommended.
  Prices: Appetizers 400–1,000 Drs ($2–$4); main courses 1,000–1,400 Drs ($4–$6). No credit cards.
  Open: Lunch Mon–Sat noon–4:30pm; dinner Mon–Sat 8pm–midnight.

Head down Dioghénous Street away from the Tower of the Winds and in 30 seconds you'll find yourself in a quiet, shady little square with tables and chairs under the trees, where Platanos and a little café face each other. Platanos is another Pláka taverna that's been around for decades, and you'll find plenty of Greeks here sitting down to a roast lamb or swordfish dinner, relaxing over a half kilo (about 1 pint) of wine from the barrel.

See Chapter 9, "Athens Nights," for names of additional nightclub/tavernas in Pláka.

Other Typically Greek Restaurants

EXPENSIVE

⭐ **Kouti,** Odós Adrianoú 23. ☎ **324-4794.**

Cuisine: GREEK/INTERNATIONAL. **Reservations:** Recommended.
Prices: Appetizers 1,500–1,900 Drs ($6–$8); main courses 2,100–2,500 Drs ($8–$10). DC, V.
Open: Lunch daily noon–6pm; dinner daily 8pm–1am.

One of the newest—and hottest—eating spots in the city, Kouti is tucked into a century-old town house, handsomely restored with timber ceiling beams and galleries and a wooden bar with traditional Greek chair stools. A few tables (for fours and sixes only) on the gallery have views of the Acropolis. The wood-and-marble tables are set with artfully designed paper mats featuring the Kouti logo; since *koutí* means "box," the fresh bread arrives on the table inside a vintage container. The food is delicious, from the spiced yogurt dip for the bread to desserts of Levantine gooeyness.

The menu is in Greek and the waitress may be shy about translating, but eventually you'll end up with an interesting meal—say, avocado stuffed with crab as an appetizer and lamb Moroccan-style or veal with honey for the main course.

Adrianoú is one of the streets that weave through the lower elevations of Pláka: At this point it has passed the Monastiráki metro (subway) station, not a spot that inspires instant confidence after the stores have shuttered up for the night. I walked to test the waters and didn't feel too uncomfortable (it certainly doesn't deter the Athenians who flock to the place). Take a taxi, if you have any qualms. In summer, the restaurant spills out onto both sides of the street, but it's worth the inconvenience of the cars to enjoy the stunning view of the Acropolis, the Stoa of Attalos, and the floodlit observatory on a distant hilltop.

Vladimiros, Odós Aristodímou 12. ☎ **721-7407.**

Cuisine: GREEK. **Reservations:** Recommended.
Prices: Appetizers 850–2,500 Drs ($3–$10); main courses 1,800–3,650 Drs ($7–$15). AE, DC, MC.
Open: Dinner daily 8pm–2am.

This is a delightful restaurant on the way up to the Lykavittós Hill funicular. It's an ideal spot for American visitors—a neighborhood restaurant catering to a local clientele who may want a change from their native moussaká, so without acting like a tourist you can enjoy beef, pork, lamb, and veal dishes cooked over charcoal and garnished in continental style. Vladimiros is equally popular in summer for its garden beneath the pine trees of Lykavittós and in winter for its piano bar and cozy rooms filled with paintings.

MODERATE

Fatsio's, Odós Efroníou 5. ☎ **717-421.**

> **Cuisine:** GREEK. **Reservations:** Recommended.
> **Prices:** Main courses under 1,500 Drs ($6).
> **Open:** Lunch daily noon–5pm.

A bright little restaurant in an apartment building, Fatsio's is a few blocks from the Hilton and the Caravel hotels. The walls and ceilings are hand-painted in the style of Thessaly, with cornucopias and flowers in sunny blues, yellows, and reds. The menu includes baked veal with eggplant, baked swordfish, veal with tomato sauce.

Gerofinikas, Odós Pindárou 10. ☎ **363-6710** or **362-2719.**

> **Cuisine:** GREEK. **Reservations:** Required.
> **Prices:** Appetizers 1,000–1,500 Drs ($4–$6): main courses 1,900–3,200 Drs ($8–$13). AE, DC, MC, V.
> **Open:** Daily 12:30–11:30pm.

Located between Sýntagma Square and Kolonáki, Gerofinikas (pronounced *Gherofínikas*) is considered by many to be the finest of the Greek/Levantine restaurants, and a recent lunch there (from 2 to 4 pm!) coincided with visits from a TV celebrity and the Greek foreign minister. You enter it through a long, narrow passageway that leads into a wood-paneled room with the air of a mountain lodge. Displays of Asian desserts and great bowls of fresh fruit greet you at the door, and off to the left there's a big open kitchen with the day's dishes set out for your inspection—lamb fricassée, eggplant Bayildí, grilled veal as well as moschári (veal) with vegetables cooked in a paper bag. The succulent desserts include the syrupy ekmek kataífi, topped with Chantilly cream in summer and with thick cream in winter. Gerofinikas is one of the best buys in town.

French & Continental Restaurants

★ **L'Abreuvoir,** Odós Xenokrátous 51. ☎ **722-9061.**

> **Cuisine:** FRENCH. **Reservations:** Recommended.
> **Prices:** Appetizers 2,000–2,500 Drs ($8–$10); main courses 3,500–4,500 Drs ($14–$18). AE, DC, MC, V.
> **Open:** Lunch daily noon–4:30pm; dinner daily 8:30pm–1am.

Up in Kolonáki, the elevated, tree-shaded terrace at the corner of Xenokrátous and Aristodímou Streets is something of a gourmet's corner, home to two fine continental restaurants long popular with well-to-do Athenians. And with well-to-do visitors, too: At L'Abreuvoir in recent months diners might have found themselves sharing the 12-table terrace with Elizabeth Taylor and friends or with Luciano Pavarotti and friends. The restaurant proper occupies the lower floor of a low-rise 1960s apartment building—an elegant room with fashionably contemporary colors and furnishings and with original works of art. The real attraction, however, is dining on the terrace beneath the mulberry trees and the stars.

Out there, you still get the same fine china with the L'Abreuvoir cartouche and the same smart waiters with their napkins over their wrists; and you're still served fresh butter, rather than fiddly little packets, with your crisp toast fingers.

Although L'Abreuvoir bills itself as a French restaurant, the main courses are mostly variations on steak—try the escalope du chef, with red wine sauce, for a hearty meal. The escalope du chef may be *too* hearty a dish for lunch, but the staff will be just as pleasant if you order something lighter—and less expensive—such as a salad or omelet. Be sure to begin the meal with the spinach tart (*tarte à l'épinard*), which is delicious.

Prunier, Odós Ypsilántou 63. ☎ 722-7379.

Cuisine: FRENCH. **Reservations:** Recommended.
Prices: Dinner 6,850–8,300 Drs ($27–$33) AE, DC, MC, V.
Open: Dinner daily 8pm–1am. **Closed:** July–Aug.

Prunier, one of the most highly regarded French restaurants in town, has an interesting menu and attentive service. The award-winning, pretty little three-room bistro is 2 blocks from the Hilton.

Bajazzo, Odós Tyrtéou 15. ☎ 729-1420.

Cuisine: CONTINENTAL/GREEK. **Reservations:** Recommended.
Prices: Dinner 15,000–18,000 Drs ($60–$70). AE, DC, MC, V.
Open: Dinner Mon–Sat 8pm–3am.

One of the most stylish restaurants in the city, Bajazzo celebrates its tenth year of culinary acclaim by moving from its elegant town house in Kolonáki to a restored mansion in the up-and-coming neighborhood of Metz, near the Olympic pool. Decor in the new quarters retains the animated puppet clowns that give the restaurant its name. German chef and owner Klaus Feuerbach offers a serendipitous selection of dishes (one recent meal consisted of grilled aubergine, seabass in ouzo, and herb ice cream with marinated cherries). There's no printed carte; the evening's specialties are presented course by course—a "live menu," as they call it. Whatever's on the oversized platters, an evening at Bajazzo is an evening on the town just by itself.

Mona Lisa, Odós Loukianoú 36. ☎ 724-7283.

Cuisine: ITALIAN. **Reservations:** Recommended.
Prices: Appetizers 800–1,200 Drs ($3–$5), main courses 1,600–2,600 Drs ($6–$11). DC, V.
Open: 1pm–1am.

This used to be Jimmy's Cooking, a slightly off-the-beaten-track location in Kolonáki, with a half dozen candlelit tables set up on a sidewalk terrace notched into the hillside. The menu ranges from salade treviazana (with beans and onions, for 1,700 Drs ($7) to spaghetti siciliana (1,600 Drs or $6) and scaloppine al vino blanco (2,600 Drs or $10), all meticulously prepared and presented by simpatico waiters.

Boschetto, Álsos Evanghelismoú (at the intersection of Leofóros Vassilíssis Sofías and Leofóros Vassiléos Konstantínou). ☎ 721-0893.

Cuisine: ITALIAN. **Reservations:** Required.
Prices: Appetizers 1,200–3,000 Drs ($6–$16); main courses 2,800–3,500 Drs ($15–$18). AE, DC, V.
Open: Dinner Mon–Sat 8:30pm–12:30am. **Closed:** Aug.

The Boschetto ("Little Forest") is one of the prettiest restaurants in Athens, set down among the trees in a small grove (*álsos*) across the avenue from the Hilton. A circular terrace for alfresco dining is ringed on one side by a low-profile structure rather like a semicircular stucco-and-glass hacienda. The air-conditioned interior has an outer salon with tables along the curving glass and an additional conservatory-style room surrounded by the garden at the rear. The setting has charm, but the service and reception, alas, are charmless—you almost get the impression that the staff had been specially schooled in the offhandedness of New York's latest "hot" eateries.

The *cucina,* as the name implies, is Italian, with an authentic Italian chef to prepare the *tortino de patate con radicchio e gorgonzola* and the *medaglioni coda di rospo.* The menu is complemented by a fine wine list that blends modest Italian labels with some boutique (but not overexpensive) Greek vintages. Neither the Italian cuisine nor the Greek wines are enhanced by background music that runs to masterpieces like "Crash, bang, Alakazam, wonderful you came by."

Al Convento, Odós Anapíron Polémou 4–6. ☎ **723-9163.**

Cuisine: ITALIAN.
Prices: 450–720 Drs ($2–$3).
Open: Dinner Mon–Sat 8pm–1am.

If the prices at Da Walter (see below) are too stiff, then try this restaurant located just around the corner—a relaxed neighborhood bistro serving, as you would expect, pizzas and other light Italian fare.

$ Da Walter, Odós Evzónon 7. ☎ **724-8726.**

Cuisine: ITALIAN. **Reservations:** Recommended. **Taxi:** About 600 Drs ($2) from Sýntagma Square.
Prices: Appetizers 470–760 Drs ($2–$3); main courses 1,900–2,400 Drs ($8–$10), average dinner 4,000 Drs ($16). AE, DC, MC, V.
Open: Dinner daily 8pm–1am.

Located in a modern apartment building at the corner of Anapíron Polémou in Kolonáki, Da Walter is attractive and friendly; the fresh flowers and lemon-colored napery tell you that the dapper staff is proud of the place. You can order petti di pollo alla marsala or filetto Voronoff (veal in a cognac and mustard sauce) for your main course; but if you're on a budget, try to avoid pricey appetizers, such as prosciutto crudo and salame da Milano. In summer, there's a small patio screened from the street by bushes.

★ Eden, Odós Fléssa 3. ☎ **324-8858.**

Cuisine: GREEK VEGETARIAN. **Reservations:** Not accepted.
Prices: Appetizers 500 Drs ($2); main courses 1,500 Drs ($6). No credit cards.
Open: noon–11pm.

This is one of the more interesting—and healthy—restaurants in Pláka. The menu is strictly vegetarian, but who needs meat when you can feast on *bouréki*, a delicious zucchini, potato, and feta cheese combination, or eggplant stuffed with cheese and topped with toasted nuts and onions? There's even moussaká with soya, and with your meal you can enjoy a bottle of retsina or the house red wine or a nonalcoholic beer.

Far East, Odós Stadíou 7. ☎ **323-4996.**
Cuisine: KOREAN/JAPANESE/CHINESE.
Prices: Main courses 2,750–12,500 Drs ($11–$50). AE, DC, MC, V.
Open: Daily 12:30pm–1am.

This small, elegant dining room has carved high-back chairs, white tablecloths, and Asian china. The huge menu features house specialties, such as crispy whole duck, Mongolian seafood, and tender beef in oyster sauce. Sushi is also available but must be ordered in advance. There is also an extensive wine list.

Kona Kai, in the Ledra Marriott, Leofóros Syngroú 115. ☎ **934-7711.**
Cuisine: POLYNESIAN/JAPANESE. **Reservations:** Required.
Prices: Average meal 9,000–12,000 Drs ($36–$48). AE, DC, MC, V.
Open: Dinner Mon–Sat 7:30pm–1am.

The lower-level location of the Kona Kai, one of the most popular restaurants in Athens, is deftly disguised with waterfalls, pools, hanging batiks, and a striking backdrop photograph of a South Sea isle matched in extravagance only by the exotic cocktails. (Try the "Kona Grog," served in a skull mug; it's deadly.) In addition to Polynesian fare, there are several Japanese teppanyaki tables.

Michiko, Odós Kydathinéon 27. ☎ **322-0980.**
Cuisine: JAPANESE. **Reservations:** Recommended.
Prices: Main courses 4,500–6,800 Drs ($18–$27).
Open: Mon–Sat 12:30pm–2:30pm; 6:30pm–midnight.

Tucked away in a narrow street (near Farmáki Square) in Pláka, Michiko sits in a Japanese courtyard, complete with fish pond, fountains, butterfly bridge, and kimono-clad waitresses. The 20-odd tables are distributed along flagstone paths on two raised terraces beneath frilly red awnings, and the whole place is sheltered by a venerable tree and decorated with colored lanterns. Sukiyaki and sushi may not be what you've come to Pláka to savor—they're not exactly bargains here—but they're there if you feel like a change of pace from moussaká and eggplant some evening.

Steak Houses

Steak Room, Odós Eginítou 6. ☎ **721-7445.**
Cuisine: STEAK. **Reservations:** Recommended.
Prices: Appetizers 1,100–2,000 Drs ($4–$8); main courses 2,300–3,500 Drs ($9–$14). AE, DC, MC, V.
Open: Dinner Mon–Sat 7pm–1am. **Closed:** August.

The Steak Room, located between the Hilton and the U.S. Embassy, is one of those restaurants that you might want to try if you weary of moussaká and veal. The lunch menu also includes such non-Greek dishes as wienerschnitzel and hamburgers. The air-conditioned Steak Room claims to have been the first steak house in Athens, and if so, it started quite a trend. They're now all over the place.

2   Casual Budget Dining

Despite the steady rise of prices in Athens in the past few years, there are still many inexpensive entries thanks to the devaluation of the drachma. Some of those restaurants and tavernas mentioned in the previous section have a few items on their menus that could, with judicious selection, bring you a meal for under 1,900 Drs ($10); conversely, some restaurants in this section list a few expensive dishes that *could* put your meal over the 1,900 Drs figure. On the whole, however, you should have no problem keeping within your budget at any of the restaurants, cafés, and snack bars listed below. There's no need to detail the menus in each of these places: They all follow a basic pattern—moussaká; dolmadákia; *keftédes* (meatballs); and various lamb, veal, and pork dishes in assorted Greek styles. Many of them also have a sprinkling of international dishes, such as omelets, spaghetti, schnitzels, and scallops (but not too much seafood, which is now relatively expensive throughout Greece). In most cases, the waiter will offer you a menu in English. You can expect a cover charge of 30–50 Drs (15¢–25¢), and a small charge for bread and butter.

Around Sýntagma & Pláka

RESTAURANTS

$ Delphi, Odós Níkis 13. ☎ 323-4869.
Cuisine: GREEK. **Reservations:** Not required.
Prices: Main courses 850–2,200 Drs ($3–$9). DC, MC, V.
Open: Daily 11am–11:30pm.

The two-story, air-conditioned, wood-paneled Delphi, just off Sýntagma Square, has a wide-ranging menu, including grilled chicken with rice, shrimp with rice, rice with minced meat, veal with okra, moussaká, and a choice of unusual salads featuring squash, dandelion, beetroot, and cabbage. Don't come looking for a leisurely, relaxed meal—those waiters *move.*

Diros, Odós Xenofóntos 10. ☎ 323-2392.
Cuisine: GREEK.
Prices: Appetizers 215–610 Drs ($1–$2); main courses 450–2,100 Drs ($2–$8); side dishes 230 Drs ($1); average meal (including wine) 2,300 Drs ($9).
Open: Daily noon–11:30pm.

The tables of the new, air-conditioned Diros spill out onto the sidewalk beneath the stoa. A refrigerated glass case displays some of the attractions within—roast veal, moussaká, omelets, grilled grouper, and grilled shrimp. A half bottle of retsína is 800 Drs ($3). You can easily put together a meal with wine at a budget price.

Drugstore, Odós Koraí 4. ☎ **322-6464.**

Cuisine: ECLECTIC.

Prices: Appetizers, main courses, and desserts 600–2,000 Drs ($2–$8).

Open: Daily 8am–2am.

Located in a shopping arcade off Odós Klafthmónos and Odós Stadíou, this eatery doesn't have quite the personality of its Parisian namesake. But if you're in no hurry, you can linger over items on an eclectic menu, from cheese pie to hamburgers, to a tasty variety that includes cuttlefish and fried cheese in the ouzerí section.

$ **Kentrikon,** Odós Kolokotróni 3, in the arcade. ☎ **323-2482.**

Cuisine: GREEK.

Prices: Appetizers 270–490 Drs ($1–$2); main courses 650–840 Drs ($2–$3).

Open: noon–5pm.

A restaurant in the down-to-earth Greek style, Kentrikon serves moussaká, dolmadákia, omelets, and spaghetti. It overflows into the arcade just off Kolokotróni Square, next to the National Historical Museum, and is popular with local media people.

SNACK BARS

The **Karagheórghi American Coffee Shop,** on the corner of Karagheórghi tís Servías and Níkis Streets, offers nostalgia (for Americans) for just over a couple of dollars—charbroiled hamburgers and omelets or two eggs any style. Open daily from 7am to midnight. Another all-day eatery is the **Elysée** snackbar, located in the arcade on the corner of Mitropóleos and Fillenínon Streets; its main attraction is an array of tables beneath a blue awning outside the post office across the street. Dawdle over a cup of espresso (550 Drs or $2), cheese pie (700 Drs or $3), or a salad (750 Drs to 1,350 Drs or $3 to $5). Two doors down from the arcade (on Mitropóleos, although the official address is Sýntagma 3), the new **Neon Restaurant** greets diners not with neon but with an equally glittery mass of chrome and mirrors—and rows of display cases with sandwiches, pastries, omelets (580 Drs or $2.50) and four-cheese rigatoni (for around 980 Drs or $4). Open daily from breakfast through midnight snacks. There are also branches of Neon in Kolonáki at Odós Tsakáloff 6, near Omónia Square at Odós Dórou 1, and over near the National Archeological Museum at Odós Patissíon 43.

Higher up Lykavittós Hill, the snackbar and coffee shop of the St. George Lycabettus Hotel, now known as **Mediterraneo,** goes alfresco much of the year in a comparatively quiet, tree-shaded terrace of whitewashed stone with white wrought-iron chairs and comfy green padding; the "everything" menu now has a Mediterranean flavor to match the name—Italian pastas and pizzas, Spanish salads and paellas, Greek moussaká, and chickenburgers (rather than hamburgers), with most dishes ranging from 1,500 Drs to 2,600 Drs ($6 to $10). There's a cover charge of 350 Drs.

Around Omónia Square

Over in the Omónia Square area, prices tend to be a few drachmas cheaper than those found around Sýntagma Square.

Athinaikon, Odós Themistokléous 2.

Cuisine: GREEK.
Prices: Appetizers 250–500 Drs ($1–$2); main courses 1,000 Drs ($4).
Open: Mon–Sat 8am–midnight.

The Greek sign of this 60-year-old *ouzerí*-restaurant says "Athenian"—and Athens is where many of the customers inside seem to come from. The service may be gruff, but the lunch fare is good: fried sweet peppers; fried shrimp in the shell; *tzatzíki* (a flavorful yogurt-cucumber-garlic dip, here spelled "djadjiki"); and a tasty garlic relish.

Ellinikon, Odós Satovriándou 3.

Cuisine: GREEK.
Prices: Main courses 460–1,020 Drs ($2–$4).
Open: Mon–Sat 8am–midnight.

Just off the square, Ellinikon is one of the busiest eating spots (at least at lunchtime) in this neighborhood; it can seat 100 diners. You can order such items as moussaká, pastítsio, spaghetti, and meat pie.

Ideal, Odós Venizélou 46. ☎ 361-4604.

Cuisine: GREEK.
Prices: Appetizers 750–1,500 Drs ($3–6); main courses 920–1,780 Drs ($4–$7). AE, DC, EC, MC, V.
Open: Mon–Sat noon–2am.

Still near Omónia Square but a block or two toward Sýntagma Square, the Ideal serves omelets and various meat dishes, plus a "grillerie" for *kokorétsi* (charbroiled lamb entrails), swordfish, and "drunkard's tit bit's." The restaurant has become more upscale recently, renovating to a belle-époque design and piping in classical music. Prices have gone up accordingly.

Kapabaki, Odós Themistokléous 3. ☎ 363-7660.

Cuisine: GREEK.
Prices: Appetizers 325–825 Drs ($1–$3); main courses 1,300–3,400 Drs ($5–$14).
Open: Mon–Sat 8am–midnight.

On a narrow, quiet street (where Odós Panepistimíou meets Omónia Square), this delightful eatery has a pretty wood trim, Cycladic-blue two-level interior and, in summer, a few wicker chairs and white-marble tables outside.

Nea Olympia, Odós Benáki 3.

Cuisine: GREEK.
Prices: Appetizers 300–600 Drs ($1–$2); main courses 1,250–1,600 Drs ($5–$6).
Open: Mon–Sat 8am–midnight.

Between Panepistimíou and Stadíou Streets, you'll find one of the most attractive and spacious restaurants in this area—the wood-paneled Nea Olympia. Its extensive menu includes dolmadákia, omelets, and beef dishes.

Taygetos, Odós Satovriándou 4. ☎ 523-5352.

Cuisine: GREEK.
Prices: Appetizers 500 Drs ($2); main courses 800–1,320 Drs ($3–$5). AE, DC, V.
Open: Daily 9am–1am.

Step into this cheerful corner grillroom with its yellow walls and smart wooden trim, and you'll probably smell the delicious chicken and lamb dishes before you even see the open kitchen. Taygetos has been serving these tasty dishes since 1925.

3 Dining Outside Athens

In summer most Athenians don't come into the center of town for dinner: They drive out to their favorite hideaways on the outskirts of town—in the countryside or by the sea. You might want to follow suit, in which case here are some tips on where to go.

Kifissiá

Kifissiá is a suburb some 10 miles from the city center; in recent years it has become a home away from home for many Americans who have come to live and work in Greece. It's not the sort of place you'd come to if you're in Athens for only a few days, but you may want to spend an hour or two here to cool off in summer or stop off for a meal on your way to Delphi or other points in the hinterlands. You can get to Kifissiá for 75 Drs (30¢) on the subway from Omónia Square or by taxi for about 3,000 Drs ($12); once there, take a 20-minute ride around the town center in a horse-drawn carriage before or after your meal or pay a brief visit to the **Goulandris Natural History Museum** and view its displays of flowers and zoology.

Some of the most popular restaurants in Kifissiá are **Edelweiss, Blue Pine Farm, La Belle Hélène, Alt Berlin,** and the small but stylish **Lotophagus.** At the restaurant of the **Grand Chalet Hotel,** you can sit in the garden as you sip or dine and look across at the marble quarries on Mount Pendélin. These are all pleasant spots for a meal, but they are "international" rather than Greek in flavor; for more typically Greek settings, go to **Varsos** or **Taverna Moustakas.**

Mikrolímano

The other popular dining spot on Athens's outskirts is in the opposite direction, by the sea, 1,500 Drs ($6) away by taxi. Until a few years ago, it was known as Turkolímano (Turk Harbor), but signposts now direct you to Mikrolímano (Little Harbor). It's a marina filled with sailboats from the seven seas and crowned on the far hill by the ultra-chic Hellenic Yacht Club. The entire waterfront is ringed with seafood restaurants, each with its terrace set up beneath brightly colored awnings across the street by the edge of the quay. Some of these restaurants have no-nonsense, unadorned interiors, while others (the newer ones) are interior-decorated; on the whole, they're all expensive. A few of them have their own fishing boats or their own sources of supply, and theoretically they should sell less-expensive fish, but it doesn't always work out that way—as you'll discover on a stroll along the waterfront checking out prices. **Note:** All fish prices are quoted automatically "per kilo" but are invariably sold *whole;* therefore the price you pay is the price per kilo (2.2 lb.) times the weight of the fish.

When you visit Mikrolímano, here's the procedure: Check out the restaurants and menus to see what the day's catch has been and how much you'll have to pay. Next, find yourself a table across the street by the quayside and order an ouzo or a bottle of Demestica wine. Then go back to the restaurant, ask the waiter to open the icebox with the fish, and make your selection—*barboúnia* (red mullet), *garídes* (shrimp), *glóssa* (sole), and so on. Have your waiter weigh the fish right there and then and tell you how much your choice will cost. Finally, tell him how you would like to have it cooked—*stí skára* (on the grill) or *tiganitó* (fried). Before returning to your waterfront table, select as an appetizer one of the Mikrolímano specialties—baked shrimp with tomatoes and feta cheese or *pikilía* (literally, "variety"), a selection of seafood hors d'oeuvres (one portion is usually enough to appease two appetites until the main course is ready). Then you can settle back and spend the rest of the afternoon or evening sipping your wine and listening to the water lapping the hulls of the

---

Frommer's Cool for Kids: Restaurants

Neighborhood Tavernas   Dining in Athens is a family affair. Kids are therefore welcome in most restaurants and particularly neighborhood tavernas, even after 9pm. Since most of the places have alfresco seating, the youngsters won't be bored; there's always the house kitten coming around for a helping.

Wendy's and McDonald's   If the youngsters' yearning for fast food proves too strong to placate with a souvláki from the street vendor, take them to Wendy's, Odós Stadíou 4, to McDonald's, Sýntagma Square at Odós Ermoú, or to Pizza Hut at Fokíonos Négri in Kypséli. Prices at Wendy's run 300–1,250 Drs ($2–$5), and 850 Drs ($3) at McDonald's.

Dionysos-Zonar's   The Athenian *zacharosplastío* (pâtisserie) par excellence, Zonar's at Odós Panepistimíou 9 is the place to take kids for fancy ice-cream sundaes or any other delectable dessert. There's also a Zonar's atop Lykavittós Hill (to reach it take the funicular at the head of Odós Ploutárchou above Kolonáki Square); here, for the price of a salad or sandwich (1,500–2,100 Drs or $6–$8), you can also enjoy a spectacular view of Athens.

schooners and yawls. You could almost be in Hydra or Mýkonos or one of the other romantic Greek islands—yet you're only a short cab ride from your hotel.

Every Athenian has his or her favorite restaurant in Mikrolímano, although there is really only a marginal difference in prices, usually in the region of 3,100–4,200 Drs ($12–$17) a kilo (2.2 lb.)—which should work out to 6,000–8,000 Drs ($24–$32) a head per meal, without wine. (Prices used to be much lower, but fish are getting scarce, and no one wants to go fishing anymore, even in Greece.) In summer you may have little choice between one restaurant or another—you simply grab whatever table is available; if you do have your choice, you should check out **Semiramis, Zefiros, Ta Prasina Trehantiria, Kokkini Varka,** the newish, three-story **Aglamer,** or perhaps most famous of them all, **Canaris.**

Zéa Marina

If you go one bay beyond Mikrolímano, you come to a larger harbor known as Zéa Marina, which is the part of Piraeus given over to pleasure boats rather than to cruise ships; and if you're joining one of the Greek shipping tycoons for a cruise, chances are this is where you'll come to board his floating palace. Zéa Marina is a pleasant spot to keep in mind on a stifling Athens day when you want to get a breath of fresh air. Take the subway or bus to Piraeus and join the folks on a stroll around the promenade, stopping off now and again to admire a particularly handsome yacht or taking a break in one of the cafés near the marina, such as **Landfall,** at Odós Makriyánni 3 (☎ 452-5074).

4 Specialty Dining

Cafés

In some cases, the cafés in the budget price range are also snack bars; they may also have restaurants serving full meals. I've listed them here because their main attraction is their role as cafés—places where you can idle away hours over a cup of coffee or a glass of lemon juice or soda, or where you can dawdle over a light lunch.

Until 1991, Sýntagma Square was the city's major café neighborhood, with hundreds of relaxing chairs deployed around its sidewalks and around the fountain in the center of the square, shaded by cypress, laburnum, and a few palm trees. Then the gardens were restyled and the number of tables reduced to a handful. Currently, the center of the square is a shambles while the tunnelers are building a stretch of the new subway system. What Sýntagma will be like when the clutter is cleared is anyone's guess; but I doubt if the square will ever return to the elegance it once had, one of the most pleasurable urban oases in Europe, since some of Sýntagma's most relaxing cafés have been replaced by a McDonald's and a Kenny Rogers Restaurant, the latter blaring relentless, grating, totally inappropriate music.

Skip Sýntagma, then. If you are in the neighborhood and gasping for your shot of java, walk one block to Odós Voukourestíou, between Stadíou and Panepistimíou Streets, where the tiny **Brazilian Coffee Store** serves 600 of the best cups of coffee every day—which you can also enjoy at stand-up counters inside and out on the street. Coffee and pastries only. Inside the arcade next door, you'll find **Galeria de Brasília** a small, split-level mecca with chairs and tables and a menu of snacks.

Walk farther up Odós Voukourestíou, a pedestrians-only mall, and around the corner to Odós Valaorítou, and you come to a sort of coffee heaven. **Biffi** couldn't be more convenient for shoppers. Bright as a new pin with a spacious, high-ceilinged interior decorated in cream-and-asparagus art deco, it has tables and counters inside and a few tables outside in the mall. An espresso here will set you back 400 Drs ($2), but the overstuffed, baguette-style sandwiches and pastries are good value at 460 to 850 Drs ($2 to $3).

On Odós Valaorítou, long-time favorite **Jimmy's Café** has been joined by **Café Florian** in the Hotel Lycabette, **MG Café,** and **Janetto's** (around the corner, opposite the Amis des Livres bookstore). They're all in the same price range, serving good coffee, sandwiches, and salads (Florian has a self-service salad bar for about $3 to $6). How do you decide? It often depends on the position of the sun and the availability of a shaded table.

One block up, at Odós Akadímou 14, **Précieux Gastronomie** has been spreading its delectable wings. The lower floor of the townhouse still looks like a chocolaterie/pâtisserie, with its showcases glittering and gleaming with candies and sweetmeats; but the adjoining café has been augmented with a cool, spacious restaurant one floor up. Gateaux or spinach pies are 500 to 860 Drs ($2 to $3); the salads and sandwiches upstairs add a touch of refinement to the usual snack-bar scene. Précieux Gastronomie is also a take-out café and gourmet shop, with Fauchon teas, coffees, and honeys as well as pies and sandwiches for picnics in the park.

If Sýntagma Square is where the tourists go, Kolonáki Square is where the Athenians sip their coffee, share gossip, talk politics, and compare notes on the surrounding boutiques. Kolonáki Square is something of an oasis, with a garden in the center and terrace cafés lining the west and south sides. At rush hour, though, it can be like a parking lot, so you may want to head for the opposite side of the square, in the direction of Leofóros Vassilíssis Sofías, to **Plateia Kolonáki** 18a and the **Café Bibliotheki.**

In the opposite direction from Sýntagma, the square in front of the cathedral, Platía Mitropóleos, has been cleared of traffic, relaid with cobblestones, and generally spruced up; now it also has one of the most congenial cafés in the city, **Café Metropolis,** on the corner of Odos Pandróssou. Its terrace is the perfect spot for watching the comings and goings at the cathedral (weddings, inevitably, are the most colorful events) while sipping a fancy ice cream concoction for 850 Drs ($3) and up or a café frappé for 500 Drs ($2). It's also a neat place to have breakfast, for around $5.

Between the Hilton and the Caravel, you'll come upon a small square called Platía Santiago de Chile but known among the locals simply as Caravel Square. Here, in the evening, gather tourists and neighborhood yuppies, filling the cluster of cafés that extend to the edge of the square's garden and mingling their animated chatter, in Greek and a variety of foreign tongues, with the blend of aromas emanating from the cafés. It's a good place to end up in, after a day of sightseeing, if you and your party are not sure what kind of cuisine you want. For here you'll find, within a few yards of each other, such choices as **Oroscopo** (pizzas and pastas), **Krikelas** (Balkan specialties), **Etoile** (primarily a café and bar), and the popular **Le Palmier.** The last, on the corner of Odós Antínoros and Odós Iofóntos, sports an inviting white-on-white interior, which opens onto a small terrace with wood-topped tables and wicker chairs. Prices at Le Palmier are inexpensive; salads go for 720 to 850 Drs ($3 to $4), crêpes with minced meat and cheese for 890 Drs ($4), and burgers for 2,000 Drs ($8).

Fokíonos Négri, our next café haunt, is over in Odós Patissíon, the residential neighborhood just beyond the National Archeological Museum and slightly off the beaten tourist track. But if you're spending more than a couple of days in Athens and you want to get beneath the surface of Athenian life, hop into a taxi or take the no. 3 trolleybus and ask the conductor to let you off at the stop nearest Fokíonos Négri. Now blessedly traffic-free except at intersections, this street is sometimes called (but never by Athenians) the Via Veneto of Athens, and you'll soon see why: It's a broad, plazalike street with hedgerows, fountains, and café tables and umbrellas in the center, and a café, it seems, on each corner. The remainder of the street is taken up by boutiques, flower shops, food shops, and other services pampering to the needs of Athenian society. Here, again, you can choose almost any café; but if you want to sample some of the local favorites, head for **Select, Floca,** or **Oriental.** For meals, there are two popular, moderately priced tavernas, **I** (pronounced *Ee*) **Thraka** and **Violetta,** and a good Italian restaurant, **Cesare,** among other choices. But, as elsewhere in town, many of the traditional Athenian spots threaten to give way to the likes of Wendy's and Pizza Hut and their local versions, **Soulatsos** and **Cruising.**

If you want to experience a perfect evening in Fokíonos Négri, begin with a leisurely aperitif at Select or Oriental; from your sidewalk perch, in between sips, observe the native and foreign strollers who fill the mall as the sun sets over Attica. Then take a stroll yourself around the street to scan the menus. At the café of your choice, pick a table under an acacia or mulberry tree and, casting aside Western prandial habits, get ready to enjoy a meal in the Athenian style—unhurried and unostentatious, marked by plenty of conversation and helped along by a bottle of Boutari. Then, as the hour approaches nine or ten, amble over to Floca for coffee and some delectable pastry. The whole evening, for two, may cost you $20 to $30. Add to that $5 for the taxi ride back to Sýntagma Square.

SELF-INDULGENCE ON ODÓS PANEPISTIMÍOU

One of the most famous *zacharoplastía* (pâtisseries) in Athens is, in fact, on none of the city's major squares, but on Odós Panepistimíou, a block from Sýntagma Square. **Dionysos-Zonar's** is the huge café on the corner with a row of red tables and chairs beneath a bright-red awning. The interior of Zonar's is an Expo for sweet tooths—with display cases piled high with candies, chocolates, pastries, baklavás, galaktoboúreko, and bougátsa, as well as the classical pastries you'd find in Vienna or Munich. Even the decor carries through the theme—chocolate-brown walls, cream-colored ceilings, icy chandeliers, and marble-topped tables. At the rear, a few steps lead up to the restaurant and a few more lead down to the cozy American bar. You can have snacks here—sandwiches are 500 Drs to 1,250 Drs ($2 to $5)—but most people come to savor the pastries at 500 Drs to 750 Drs ($2 to $3) and sip the espresso, cappuccino, Viennese coffee, Nescafé, French coffee, or Greek coffee. Zonar's is a haven for self-indulgence. Don't miss it.

Much to the dismay and regret of Athenians (and who knows how many thousands of visitors), the 100-year-old *zacharoplastío* next door to Zonar's, the delightful **Floca,** closed its doors for the last time in 1988—to be transformed into, eventually, a bank. But the joys of Floca live on despite progress and big bucks in various branches around the city—the nearest Floca being on the pedestrians-only square known as Koraí, a few blocks along Panepistimíou, opposite the university.

The Ouzerí

Here's a leisurely, carefree, and relatively inexpensive way to sample some local color—visit an *ouzerí.* The ouzerí is a sort of neighborhood bar/pub/café where Athenians stop in at any time of the day for a quick pick-me-up of ouzo, wine, or coffee, accompanied by bite-size delicacies such as sagnáki (toasted cheese) and dolmadákia. The decor is usually basic and functional, the clientele mostly male, and the conversation covers mostly soccer or politics. Now the ouzerí is making a comeback, partly because of the new working hours and partly because of a general tendency to eat lighter food—and the clientele is more mixed and the decor more inviting.

One of the city's old-style ouzerís is just 3 blocks from Sýntagma Square, in the arcade at Odós Panepistimíou 10, where the high-ceilinged **Apotsos** lines its well-worn walls with posters and mirrors advertising the pleasures of biscuits, whisky, and mustard. Another traditional spot is **Athinaikon,** at Odós Santaróza 8, near Omónia Square, a gathering place for lawyers and judges from the nearby law courts.

Among the newer ouzerís, two, located in the Kolonáki district, are particularly attractive and convenient for shoppers as well as for visitors to the Benaki, Byzantine, and Cycladic Art museums nearby. **Yali Kafines,** at Odós Ploutárchou 18, features a contemporary interior in dark wood and polished brass; in summer a few tables are set up at an incline on the sidewalk beneath the acacia trees. The menu includes English translations (sometimes obscure: "baby white pat" turns out to be a cousin of the sardine), with 50 types of mezedes from 600 Drs to 1,400 Drs ($2 to $6) and a variety of salads from 750 Drs to 1,100 Drs ($3 to $4). Open daily from 12:30 to 5pm and from 8pm to 2am. **Kafenion,** one block over at 26 Odós Loukaníou, comes with the more traditional, wood-paneled interior and pubby ambience. It has a similar menu and prices. Open daily from 12:30pm to 12:30am. Both are welcome stops for walkers heading up the hill to the Lykavittós funicular.

Hotel Dining

⭐ **GB Corner,** in the Hotel Grande Bretagne, Odós Panepistimíou. ☎ **323-0251,** ext. 858.

Cuisine: GREEK INTERNATIONAL. **Reservations:** Recommended. **Prices:** Average meal 5,000–12,000 Drs ($20–$48). AE, DC, MC, V. **Open:** Daily 6am–2am.

The GB Corner is in the prestigious Hotel Grande Bretagne, with one entrance in the glittering, elegant lobby and the other on the street. It has an Edwardian, masculine air, all dark wood and cut glass, brightened by clusters of globe lamps. Its moderately priced menu includes hamburger chasseur and Oriental spring rolls, as well as a variety of regional Greek dishes. It's a pleasant place to visit any time of the day or night for a drink or a cup of coffee, or for a full meal, which could be cheap or expensive, depending on whether you want to order fancy caviar and chateaubriand. A pianist plays throughout the evening.

Ta Nissia, in the Athens Hilton, Leofóros Vassilíssis Sofías 46. ☎ **722-0201.**

Cuisine: INTERNATIONAL. **Reservations:** Recommended. **Prices:** Appetizer buffet 3,150 Drs ($13), main courses 3,900–5,650 Drs ($16–$23). AE, DC, MC, V. **Open:** Dinner daily 7:30pm–12:30am.

Ta Nissia (the islands) is a bright, pastel-and-planter version of the traditional Greek taverna, with an appetizing blend of international and Greek cuisine—including a Greek "Mezedakia Experience" for appetizers, a Greek version of bouillabaisse known as kakaviá, and gourounáki soúvlas or crusty suckling pig à la broche. There's an outstanding wine list to match your choice of entrée.

Dining with a View

💲 **Astor Hotel Roof Garden,** Odós Karagheórghi tís Servías 16. ☎ **325-5555.**

Cuisine: GREEK. **Reservations:** Recommended, especially in peak summer.
Prices: Appetizers 650–1,250 Drs ($3–$5); main courses 1,500–2,400 Drs ($6–$10); fixed-price dinner 3,400 Drs ($12). AE, DC, V.
Open: Dinner daily 7–10:30pm.

You can get a close-up view of the Acropolis from one of the city's few year-round aeries. (In winter, it's enclosed in glass that doesn't block the view.) This is another place for lingering, although it closes when most Athens restaurants are just warming up, and you may be surrounded by large tables of tour groups. Once you get up there, order a bottle of Santa Helena or Cimarosa, and slowly scan the menu; you'll be reluctant to rush through your meal and get back down to earth, literally and otherwise. Enjoy roast lamb, shish kebab, or the fixed-price dinner with moussaká or soup as a first course, roast lamb or chicken with rice, dessert, and/or feta cheese. If it's still too early to drag yourself away, order some Greek coffee. Then follow it up with a Metaxa. Two people can still leave with change from 7,000 Drs ($28)—having enjoyed a better view (as well as a better value) than diners in the pricier places.

Dionysos-Zonar's, Rovértou Gálli 43. ☎ 922-1998.

Cuisine: GREEK/CONTINENTAL. **Reservations:** Recommended.
Prices: Restaurant appetizers 1,150–1,800 Drs ($4–$7); restaurant main courses 1,100–3,200 Drs ($4–$13); fixed-price dinner 5,400 Drs ($22); courtyard tourist menu 4,300 Drs ($17).
Open: Daily noon–11pm.

The Dionysos, on the far side of the Acropolis, near the Herod Atticus Odeum and Philopáppos Hill, has one of the best views of the Acropolis in the entire city. In decor, it has a sort of dated chic and is difficult to fit into one category, since the Dionysos is really several restaurants in one: It serves Greek food and continental food (*shish kebab à l'orientale,* escalôpe Holstein, and spaghetti carbonara) in its glass-walled restaurant and terraced garden and snacks in its vine-covered courtyard café, which is almost right opposite the main entrance to the Acropolis. In the courtyard, there are tourist menus and simple dishes, such as omelets, spaghetti, and sandwiches. With these prices and this setting, Dionysos is a very popular place.

Dionysos-Zonar's, atop Lykavittós Hill. ☎ 722-6374.

Cuisine: GREEK/CONTINENTAL. **Reservations:** Required.
Prices: Appetizers 600–1,200 Drs ($2–$5); main courses 750 Drs ($3); full dinners 4,000–5,300 Drs ($16–$21); lunches 2,400 Drs ($10). AE, DC, MC, V.
Open: Daily noon–11pm.

This is the no. 1 spot for dramatic dining (and the highest in the city). The decor is utilitarian, but the menu is eclectic—salads, Greek food, and continental dishes, such as escalôpe Holstein and spaghetti bolognese. Add in the view and you have quite a bargain.

Picnic Fare & Where to Eat It

What with all that sunshine and all those scented lemon trees, you may want to find a corner of some centuries-old agora and have a picnic. To stock up, visit a grocery store or the Prisunic Marinopoulos supermarket. Start with some cheese. The main types are *graviéra* (Greek-Swiss), *feta* (Greek goat cheese), *kefalotíri* (a yellow, salted cheese), *kasséri* (a hard, yellow cheese), and Roquefort (which in these parts is any kind of blue cheese). The olives are stored in large wooden barrels and aged for months (order them by the drachma). Yogurt is ladled from large vats and spread onto wax paper. You'll never taste fresher yogurt than in Greece (try it served with honey for breakfast).

With so much dining taking place out of doors, and with restaurant and café meals so moderately priced, there is less incentive in Athens to have a picnic. However, if the heat of a summer day puts you in the mood for a quiet snack in the shade, grab some food from street vendors or neighborhood stores and head for one of the parks: Areos, a few blocks north of the National Archeological Museum; the National Garden across the street from Sýntagma Square; or Syngroú Grove behind the Hilton. Or find a bench or stone wall among the pines on the slopes of Lykavittós Hill. Picnicking on the hillside leading to the Acropolis is fine on days when the sun is not blinding and oppressive—in early spring or late fall. You probably don't have to be reminded about leaving garbage behind; but since trash cans are not ubiquitous, remember to take along some sort of container as temporary storage for your bits and pieces.

6

What to See & Do in Athens

I F YOU HAVE ONLY ONE DAY IN ATHENS, YOUR BEST BET IS TO TAKE A GUIDED sightseeing tour. But even if you're staying a few days and plan to do a lot of sightseeing, it's still advisable to take the tour to get an idea of the lay of the land and find out what really interests you. Then you can go back yourself and take in the spots that you want to cover in depth.

Let's assume, however, that you plan to see the city on your own and have decided to begin with breakfast in **Sýntagma Square.** The square itself is a sightseeing attraction (you've already read about its cafés—*but note* that much of the square is currently roped off because of the expansion work being done on the Athens subway). On the southern side you have one of the highlights of the square as far as Americans are concerned—the office of **American Express,** usually surrounded by swarms of visitors, young and old, rich and poor, booking trips to the islands and waiting for mail or money from home. The mail, by the way, is delivered at 5pm, and this is the time to be there to meet old friends, catch up on gossip, make new friends, and sympathize with those who didn't get that check.

However, the main sight of Sýntagma is the **Parliament Building,** which at one time was the royal palace. This is a large, squarish ocher building with a marble forecourt facing the square. Apparently, this site was chosen personally by young King Otto, the Bavarian who was put on the throne after the war with Turkey; his site-selection technique was to hang pieces of meat in various parts of town and select the location where the maggots were slowest to develop. The main attraction here, apart from the constant arrival and departure of dark limousines, is the **changing of the guard.** This ceremony, complete with *évzones* and their pom-poms, takes place every hour at 20 minutes before the hour and on Sunday at 11am, accompanied by a regimental band. If you get there late, you can always photograph the new *évzone* on duty at the **Tomb of the Unknown Soldier,** in front of the building.

You can spend whole days sitting in the cafés of Sýntagma Square enjoying the daily routine of the city: the crowds cramming into the offices in the morning; the lottery-ticket sellers promising riches; the sponge sellers, more interested in sitting in the shade than in selling a record number of sponges; the jet-setters dashing in and out of the NJV Meridien and Grande Bretagne; the tourists checking into the airline offices; the limousines heading for Parliament; the Americans clustering around American Express; the shoppers disappearing into the arcades of Odós Ermoú and Odós Karagheórghi tís Servías; the crowds streaming out of their offices and cramming into the buses; the young, foreign blondes, and the young Greeks trying to pick them up; the elderly gentlemen who've been congregating there through several reigns and regimes, as timeless as the Acropolis.

But sooner or later you'll want to leave the comfy café chairs and the shade of the awnings and go see the other sights of Athens, mainly the Acropolis. **Note:** In the pages that follow, "winter" means the period from November 1 to March 31, and "summer" means the period from April 1 to October 31—but there's a lot of leeway.

Did You Know?

- Athens is the southernmost capital in Europe and, as such, offers a unique blend of Western and Near Eastern cultures.

- In antiquity, at the height of its power, Athens was called the "school of Hellas" by Pericles because it was the center of Greek culture and influence.

- By the time of the Greek War of Independence (1821), after many centuries of different foreign occupations, Athens had been reduced to little more than a village.

- Today a sprawling metropolis, Athens is the home of some 40% of Greece's approximately 11 million people.

- In 1896, Athens was the host of the first modern Olympic Games, for which the city's gleaming marble Panathenaic Stadium was built on the site of a 4th-century B.C. stadium.

- The height of buildings in Athens is limited by law to ensure that the city's skyline does not obscure the Acropolis.

- In 1991, Athens celebrated the 2,500th anniversary of the birth of democracy.

Suggested Itineraries

If You Have One Day

Head first for the Acropolis. It's *the* site to see, but it also gives you an eagle-eye view of the city. From there, make your way down the hill, through the winding streets of Pláka, stopping off at the Kanellópoulos Museum to view the eclectic collection of one of Athens's most famous families, then going on to see the ancient Agora (*archéa agorá* in Greek), the temple of Theseus, and all the archeological wonders around Monastiráki. From there, walk up Odós Mitropóleos to the cathedral, then proceed to Sýntagma Square and the Parliament Building (for the changing of the guard). If you have time or energy left, walk down Leofóros Amalías to the temple of Olympian Zeus.

If You Have Two Days

Day 1 as above. On Day 2, head right for the National Archeological Museum on Odós Patissíon (also known as Odós 28 Oktovríou), one of the world's preeminent repositories of antiquities. From there, take a leisurely stroll to Lykavittós Hill, where you may decide to have a midday repast above the din and fumes of the bustling city. Then wend your way through the boutique-lined streets of Kolonáki to the new Museum of Cycladic Art, on Odós Neophýtou Douká, to see the ancient marble figurines, some of them dating from as far back as 3300 B.C. and executed in a surprisingly "modern" abstract style;

if you still have time, take in the nearby Benaki Museum, on Leofóros Vassilíssis Sofías, to view its famous treasures of Byzantine and later Greek art.

Having treated yourself to more than five millenniums of Greek art (enough for one day!), you may want to pause at the National Garden, across from Sýntagma Square, and quietly contemplate what you've seen. Find a seat at the large outdoor café by the Záppion exhibition hall (a short walk from the garden's main entrance on Leofóros Amalías), order a refreshing drink, and stay for some lively Greek entertainment, which begins around sunset.

If You Have Three Days

If you have three days in Athens, you have some flexibility in planning an itinerary: You can space out the activities suggested above for Day 1 and Day 2 so that they spill over into Day 3; or you can stick to the somewhat crowded schedule for the first two days and use Day 3 for an excursion either to an ancient site (Cape Soúnio, Delphi) or to a nearby island. Your choice of excursion depends, of course, on your particular interests—history and archeology or sun and fun; if the choice is too difficult to make, consider going to the island of Aegina, only a short boat ride (ferry or hydrofoil) from Piraeus.

In Aegina you'll find a famous 5th-century B.C. temple dedicated to the goddess Aphaea (protectress of women), an archeological museum containing objects from the 3d millennium B.C. to Roman times, and several medieval structures (in the historic town of Paleochóra, once a pirates' den, and in Aegina town), *as well as* a popular resort, Aghía Marína, with sandy beaches and frolicking tourists. If you're tired after two days of hectic museum-going in Athens, you may want to relax by having a leisurely lunch at a portside taverna (try the grilled *sfirída,* a local fish); from your table, shaded perhaps by a thatched awning or a pergola, you can observe the active seaside scene or sink into idle ruminations as you watch the yachts glide by in the distance.

But if you've allowed yourself only three days in Athens, you're probably headed for the islands—where, of course, you'll get all the sand and sun you came to Greece for. So use your third day to visit the ancient oracle at Delphi, a favorite excursion site just three hours away by bus. (The bus leaves from the station at Odós Liossíon 260; to get to the station, take bus no. 24 from Leofóros Amalías, in front of the National Garden.) It was to Delphi that the Greeks would trek to hear the oracle's answer to whatever question worried them: "Will our city be invaded?" "Will my business prosper?" "Is my wife faithful?"

See where the pythian priestess stood as she uttered—in a trance believed to be divinely induced—her "delphic" responses. Every answer required some kind of votive offering to Apollo, and as evidence of the thriving business done at Delphi you can see the treasuries of Athens and some of the other Greek city-states that still stand there, albeit bereft of their contents, amid the ruins of a vast temple to Apollo, an amphitheater, and a stadium. The whole can be put into context by a visit to the archeological museum nearby.

If You Have 5 Days or More

If you have nearly a week in Athens, you have enough time to devote to whatever combination of activities interests you: the Acropolis plus a museum or two in the morning; a refreshing swim at Glyfáda or Vouliagméni in the early afternoon; a stroll through the city's shopping district or residential areas (Kolonáki, Fokíonos Négri) in the late afternoon; a concert or an ancient Greek play in the evening—concluding with a late repast *à l'athénienne* at a lively taverna with bouzouki, dancing, and if the mood sets in, a broken plate or two. These activities may describe your first couple of days in Athens; the other 3 days you may choose to set aside for an excursion to some of Greece's famous historical sights (Mycenae, Marathon) or for a cruise to some of the islands off the eastern coast of the Peloponnese (Hydra, Spárses) or in the Aegean. See Chapter 10, "Easy Excursions from Athens," for further suggestions.

1   The Top Attractions

The Acropolis

Admiring visitors huff and puff up the hill for a closer look at the Acropolis ("High City"), built by the ancient Athenians to house their city's treasure and artworks, as well as their most sacred buildings, such as the Parthenon (temple of the goddess Athena). The Acropolis rests on a rock 515 feet above sea level. The rock has been there, presumably, since the Creation, and the walled fortress on top of it has been there for many millenniums; but the Acropolis you see today dates from the 5th century B.C., when Athens was at the pinnacle of its glory, the leading power in the Greek world, with an empire that provided the money to indulge in such grand public works. The Acropolis is the entire plateau; it contains four ancient buildings and one very discreet modern building, which is the Acropolis Museum.

The first of these ancient structures is the **Propylaea** ("Foregates"), an imposing entrance consisting of a central gateway with two wings (one of which was originally a picture gallery, the Pinacotheca). Just to the right of the Propylaea is a small temple known as **Athena Nike** (or Níke Ápteros, "Unwinged Victory"). It was built to

IMPRESSIONS

Above the low roofs of Athens the Acropolis rises on its pedestal of rock: astonishing, dramatic, divine, with at the same time the look of a phantom.
—Edmund Wilson, *Europe Without Baedeker,* 1947

Since 146 B.C. Greece has been selling foreigners the Age of Pericles, and this is what meets the traveler on arrival.
—Kevin Andrews, *Athens,* 1967

commemorate the victories of the Greeks over the Persians, and its beautiful friezes portray scenes from that war.

The **Erechtheum** was begun in 421 B.C. and completed in 407 B.C. on the site of a temple to Erechtheus, a legendary king of Athens. In some ways, this is the most hallowed spot on the hill, because it is the spot where, according to legend, Athena, the guardian of Athens, created the first olive tree. Legend also has it that the invading Persians destroyed this tree; but when they were driven off, the tree miraculously grew again. It's a curious temple by Athenian standards: It's built on two levels, it's asymmetrical, and its two porches have no relationship to each other. The smaller porch is the famous one supported by six stone maidens known **Caryatids.** During the Ottoman occupation, the military governor housed his 40 wives there.

The crowning glory of the Acropolis, however, is the great temple dedicated to the virgin goddess (*parthénos*) herself, the **Parthenon.** At one time, the temple sheltered a gigantic statue of Athena, finished in ivory and gold, and its anterooms were stacked high with the treasures of the city. The Parthenon was built during the time of Pericles, between 447 and 432 B.C., and it was designed by what may have been the most successful architectural team of all time—Phidias, Ictinus, and Callicrates. They started out with a very uneven foundation, so that one end of the building rests on 35 feet of marble to bring it level with the rest of the structure; the temple lies east to west, with 17 columns on the north and south walls and 8 columns on the other two sides.

But the numbers mean little compared with the grace and grandeur of the temple's lines. The Parthenon has no straight lines, although they appear to be. To counteract the effects of optical illusion, horizontal lines curve in the middle, and the 50 columns bulge in the center and then taper off toward the top. Traces of iron in the marble (from Mt. Pendéli, on the edge of the city) give it a golden glow. In its youth, the Parthenon had statues and friezes and other decorations, but over the years they've been removed by various conquerors or explorers. (The British Museum's famed Elgin Marbles come from the Parthenon.) But long before Lord Elgin scrambled up the hill, the Parthenon had undergone various humiliations—for a thousand years it was a Christian church, then it became a Muslim mosque complete with minaret, and then it became a Turkish arsenal. It was hit by a Venetian shell during a siege in 1687, and that one fateful shell destroyed the interior and the roof of the temple. All the bits and pieces that were left lying around were put back into place during a restoration project that began in the 19th century and didn't end until 1930.

Take a breather now. What you see from up on the Acropolis—the stoa of Attalos, Pláka, the Areopagus, Pnyx Hill—was the extent of the city of Athens in its Golden Age. This was where the action was. Pericles, the orator, aristocrat, general, and statesman, was the grand panjandrum. The tragedies of Aeschylus, Sophocles, and Euripides and the comedies of Aristophanes were premiered at the

Theater of Dionysus. Philosophers and men of learning were gathering there and exchanging their wild ideas: Anaxagoras with his absurd theory that the universe was an organized system; Democritus mumbling that all matter was made up of atoms; Herodotus, the father of history, researching his book on the Persian Wars. It must have been an extraordinary, exciting place.

Now for the rest of the Acropolis. The **Acropolis Museum** is a low structure tucked into the southeastern end of the plateau, hidden from the outside world. It was built in the last century to store the various statues and fragments of stone reliefs found on the surrounding hills: pediments, friezes, the *Moschophoros* ("Man with Calf"), *Athena Meditating,* and a collection of statues of women, known as *Kórae,* famous for their smiles (which certainly make a change from *Mona Lisa* and her mystic smile). The museum helps you visualize how the buildings must have looked centuries ago.

Please check the open hours and admission charges listed below when you get to Athens (☎ **321-0219**), before hiking up that hill, because they may change due to preservation work. The preservation of the Erechtheum is nearly complete; the Caryatids have been moved to the museum for preservation, and now replicas stand in their stead. The actual temple will reportedly soon be open to visitors. On the whole, the preservation work will continue for several years, but there's a good chance that the priceless treasures will survive for a few more centuries.

Admission (including Acropolis site and museum): 1,500 Drs ($6).

Open: Acropolis site, Mon–Fri 8am–5:30pm, Sat–Sun 8:30am–2:30pm. Museum, Mon 11am–5:30pm, Tues–Fri 8am–5:30pm, Sat–Sun 8:30am–2:30pm.

National Archeological Museum, Odós Patissíon 44.
☎ 821-7717.

When you arrive here, don't rush in. Enjoy the setting first. From Patissíon, you walk through a spacious garden with cafés beneath palm trees, up to a long, classical facade above a sweep of marble steps—usually crowded with footloose young travelers in search of a heritage or a companion and crowds of tourists pouring from sightseeing buses. It's not unusual for 8,000 people to visit this museum in one day.

Once in the exhibition rooms proper, you're left with no doubt that here is the world's grandest collection of antiquities. Years after you've visited the museum, its treasures will still be imprinted on your mind. You need several hours, if not several days, to see everything here. Go on your own rather than on a tour, when you'll be whisked through so quickly that you won't remember a thing; on the other hand, if you have time for several visits, you might want to take a tour the first time, make a mental note of exhibits you want to see in a more leisurely manner, then return again on your own.

All the treasures from Mycenae are here in Athens, and the distant site really comes alive before your eyes when you see the fantastic collection of objects discovered at the dig by the famous

Athens Attractions

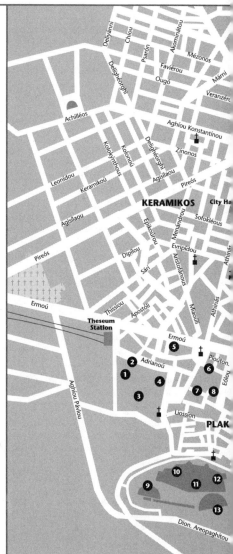

9388

German archeologist Heinrich Schliemann. Note the magnificent beaten-gold mask of a man with beard and moustache taken from the fifth Shaft Grave: Schliemann claimed, when he removed the mask, to "have gazed upon the face of Agamemnon." The Mycenaean Hall contains a staggering variety of finds: intricate gold and silver

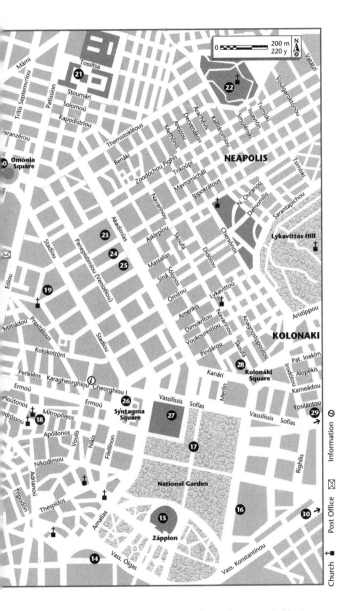

Church ╬■ Post Office ⊠ Information ❷

dagger blades, gold-leaf portrait masks, breastplates, swords, libation cups, and many representations of animals and birds—all dating from around 1550 B.C.

Contrast these objects of exquisite craftsmanship with the comparatively crude statues of the 7th and 6th centuries B.C.—the stiff, upright *Koúros,* or youth, is represented naked with one foot forward and the *Kóre,* or maiden, is draped. Examples of this sculptural style have been found all over mainland Greece and the islands. Another remarkable category of exhibits (not grouped together) consists of bronzes, some of which have lain beneath the sea for the past 2,000 years.

You should also visit the exhibition of the finds from Santoríni—the frescoes alive with colorful representations of swallows, monkeys, dolphins, and elegant figures of youths and maidens. Santoríni, called Thíra, was an island civilization that flourished at the same time as the Minoan, back in the second millennium B.C. The islanders built luxurious homes and decorated them with gorgeous murals and pottery. But one day, as legend has it, "Enceladus in the bowels of the Earth was roused with undescribable fury," and the ensuing earthquake wiped out Thíra.

These paragraphs describe maybe one-millionth of this museum's treasures; unless you have time to pay several visits, confine your tour to a couple of halls, and within each focus on a couple of showcases—such as the displays of gold rings, bracelets, and seals. Otherwise you'll go daffy.

There are three other museums adjoining the National Archeological Museum, mostly of specialized interest—the **Epigraphical Collection** (inscribed monuments from all parts of Greece), the **Numismatic Collection,** and the **Display of Plaster Copies of Antiquities** (both for display and for sale). The hours are similar to those of the National Archeological Museum and the same ticket will get you into all of them.

Admission: 1,500 Drs ($6).

Open: Mon 12:30pm–7pm, Tues–Fri 8am–7pm, Sat–Sun 8:30am–3pm.

The Agora

We can still stay within the orbit of the Acropolis and feel its presence over our shoulders. The second most important corner of antiquity is the region around the Agora, at the base of the Acropolis on the northwest side. In ancient Athens, the Parthenon was the center of religious life, but the Agora was where the business was done and the fun was found. One of the former arcades, the **Stoa of Attalos,** has been rebuilt (by the efforts of the American School of Classical Studies) and now houses a museum filled with the bits and pieces found around the Agora, including models of the Acropolis and the Agora, which will help you understand both sites better—so go there first. Originally, the stoa was the market, and it housed some of the first government offices of a democracy. The dominant feature here, however, is the majestic **Temple of Hephaestus,** usually referred to as the Theseum (*Thissíon* in Greek). It's as old as the Parthenon, and unquestionably it's the best preserved of all Greek temples. The Ancient Agora Museum in the Stoa of Attalos, to use its full title, is open daily from 8am to 3pm. The museum, but not the site, is closed Monday. Admission is 400 Drs ($2) each for the site and the museum (free on Sunday). For information call **321-0185.**

Other sites in this neighborhood include the old **Dipylon Gate,** which used to be the first landmark on the road from Athens to Thebes; the Keramikos, the cemetery of ancient Athens, where you can still see some old sculptured memorials and stelae in the graveyard itself along with funerary tablets and ceramics dating from the 11th century B.C. in the adjoining museum. The Keramikos Archeological Museum (☎ **346-3552**) is open Tuesday to Sunday from 8:30am to 3pm. Entrance fee is 400 Drs ($2).

Still in this general region, but not in the Agora itself, is the so-called **Tower of the Winds,** a clock built in the Roman period in the shape of an octagonal tower, with figures of the winds, a weather vane, and a unique hydraulic mechanism.

Farther to the east, between the Acropolis and the National Garden, is the **Temple of Olympian Zeus** (what a resounding name!), at the junction of two avenues—Amalías and Ólgas—facing the southern entrance to the National Garden. Begun in the 6th century B.C., the temple was built on a terrace 225 yards long, but today it's very much a ruin that's most impressive when it's floodlit in the evening. The best place to admire it is not the site itself but from the lounge of the Royal Olympic Hotel or the roof of the new Athens Gate Hotel. The temple site is open Tuesday to Sunday from 8:30am to 3pm. Admission is 400 Drs ($2). Nearby is **Hadrian's Arch,** built by the Roman emperor Hadrian in the 2d century B.C., which marked the boundary between the ancient quarter of the city and the new Athens, or Adrianople, as it was then called.

2 More Attractions

City Sights

Two of the more popular destinations for tour buses are the Panathenaic Stadium and the Presidential Palace, both within a couple of blocks of each other, beyond the National Garden. The white-marble stadium was built on the site of an ancient 4th-century B.C. stadium for the first modern Olympic Games in 1896. The Royal (now Presidential) Palace was the home of young King Constantine II before he went into exile in 1967; it's a handsome, French-style château, but you can't see much of it behind all the trees. Most people go there to see the *evzones'* changing-the-guard ceremony. Don't expect to see anything like the ceremony at Buckingham Palace; in fact, don't bother visiting the Presidential Palace and the stadium unless you have oodles of time.

Surrounding the Parliament Building, back at Sýntagma Square, is the National Garden. It's a formal garden, with a remarkable mixture of trees, shady nooks, swan lakes, duck ponds, terrace cafés where orchestras play Viennese waltzes, and a beautiful palacelike building called the Záppion, which is used for temporary exhibitions and European Community meetings.

One place you should visit, though, even if only briefly, is the cathedral, or Mitrópolis, of Athens, halfway between Sýntagma and Pláka. A red pile in Byzantine style, the cathedral's interior is draped with icons, which in turn are draped with silver votive offerings, like necklaces on an ample-bosomed dowager. The votive offerings are usually small effigies of people who have been blessed or cured by a particular saint. The cathedral genuinely looks like a place of worship, even down to the black-garbed priests shuffling around in the rear.

The baby cathedral right next to it, the church of Ághios (or Saint) Elefthérios, dating from the 13th century, is as austere as the cathedral is ornate. This is a gem of Byzantine architecture, but it was built from marble and stone filched from pagan temples of the classical period. There are many of these venerable Byzantine churches around Athens. Your favorite may well be the minuscule 11th-century church of Aghía Dýnamis (Divine Power), squatting in the middle of the sidewalk, beneath the arcade of the modern Ministry of Education, on Odós Mitropóleos, or the church of Ághios Kapnikáreos, in the middle of the street halfway down Odós Ermoú.

Museums

The following notes should be of interest to the serious museum-goer.

ADMISSION

Admission to all state museums is *free* on Sundays and working days unless otherwise noted (but again, double-check). Naturally, this means that museums are busiest on those days, and if you want peace and quiet you'd better be prepared to pay some drachmas.

People who can prove that they belong to the following categories are allowed into museums free of charge: directors of studies and students of foreign archeological schools; foreign archeologists, architects, and artists on a study visit; foreign interpreters and guides; foreign professors of classical studies; foreign students of classical studies (high school or university level); and children up to age 6. To get your free pass for museums in Athens, contact the office of the **Directorate of Classical and Prehistoric Antiquities,** Department of Museums, Odós Aristídou 14 (☎ **321/8555**). The office is open Monday and Friday from 11am to 1pm only. Or pick up a pass at the Acropolis Archeological or National Archeological Museum. Take along your passport, plus proof of who and what you are. For museums outside Athens check with the GNTO for local offices. On second thought, it might be easier just to pay.

CAMERAS

There are some curious rules here: If you pay the equivalent of the general admission charge, you may take pictures, provided you don't use a tripod or flash cubes. But you *may* use a tripod in museums if you pay an extra fee; similarly, you may use a tripod in archeological sites if you pay a fee (**note:** the Acropolis is classified as an archeological site). If you're using a tripod, however, you may not photograph "a person or persons together with an antique object." Use of a video camera is sometimes permitted (at, of course, an extra charge). Check first.

HOURS

Hours are subject to change. If you can, check with the Greek Tourist Organization (EOT) or with your hotel receptionist. Unless indicated otherwise, all museums are closed on Tuesday.

PUBLIC HOLIDAYS

Museums and archeological sites are closed on New Year's Day, March 25 (Independence Day), Good Friday (after noon), Easter Sunday, May 1st, Christmas Day, and December 26. For other holidays, check with the Greek Tourist Organization.

Benaki Museum, Odós Koumbári 1 (corner of Leofóros Vassilíssis Sofías). ☎ 361-1617.

It is, of course, almost *de rigueur* to visit the National Archeological Museum in Athens. If you're a classical scholar you'll be excited by its thoroughness; if you're not, it may stagger you with its size. The Benaki, on the other hand, is a manageable museum. It's more human, which is probably how its founder, the late Anthony Emmanuel Benaki, a wealthy Greek from Alexandria, Egypt, would have liked it. This mansion was, in fact, his home, and most of the exhibits are part of his own collection, which his family turned over to the state after he died, in 1954. Judging by the exhibits, Benaki must have been a man of wide-ranging interests, because here you'll find relics of the Greek War of Independence, ecclesiastical treasures, textiles, ceramics, glass, costumes, and furniture of Greek, Turkish, and Islamic craftsmanship.

The museum is on three floors (first-floor galleries are temporarily closed), and the room arrangement is rather odd, so buy the 1,330-Dr ($5) guidebook in English. These are some highlights: the portable writing desk of Lord Byron (who fought in the War of Independence and died at Messolónghi in the Peloponnese, in 1824); antique pistols and rifles impeccably decorated with silver and engravings; an intricately carved wooden door from Baghdad (9th c.); a virtually complete 17th-century reception room from Cairo with mosaic floor, fountain, basin, and tiled pilasters; a pair of early works by El Greco; some fascinating Coptic fabrics and embroidery; a whole roomful of Egyptian, Roman, Mycenaean, and French silver and gold jewelry; and one-third of a magnificent collection of Chinese art that once belonged to another wealthy Greek (the remaining two-thirds is in London) and consists of works from the Han, T'ang, Sung, Yuan, Ming, and Chin dynasties. There are also collections of household embroideries and festive costumes from the islands, golden embroidered coats from Epirus (Ipiros), liturgical seals, distaffs, and musical instruments.

Admission: 400 Drs ($2).

Open: Wed–Mon 8:30am–2pm. **Directions:** It's a short walk up from Sýntagma Square or down from Kolonáki Square. **Bus:** yellow bus no. 3, 13, or 8; blue bus no. 224 or 214.

Byzantine Museum, Leofóros Vassilíssis Sofías 22. ☎ **721-1027.**

The museum is at the far end of a pleasant courtyard lined with fountains and sculpture fragments, and it is rather like a Florentine palazzo. It has two floors of mosaics, sculpture, fragments, altars, garments, archbishop's staffs, and Bibles. The descriptive signs are in English as well as Greek. Call first, as there is some restoration work going on.

   Admission: 500 Drs ($2).

   Open: Tues–Sun 8:30am–3pm.

Center for Folk Art and Tradition, Odós Angheliki Hatzimicháli, in Pláka. ☎ **324-3987.**

Opened in 1981, the center is in the refurbished town house of a wealthy Athenian family—and feels lived-in, as though the family had just left to vacation on Skiáthos. Door frames, mantels, and window seats are of dark wood, elaborately carved in classic and folk designs of ships, birds, and mythical creatures. Exhibits include tiled fireplaces, Skýros plates, hand-woven fabrics, stained-glass windows, and family portraits.

   Admission: Free.

   Open: Tues and Thurs 9am–9pm, Wed and Fri–Sat 9am–1pm and 5–9pm, Sun 9am–1pm.

City of Athens Museum, Odós Paparigopoúlou 7 at Klafthmónos Square. ☎ **323-0168.**

Halfway along Odós Stadíou, this new museum is in a refurbished "palace" once occupied by King Otto I. You'll see paintings, prints, royal memorabilia—and a striking scale model of Athens as the city appeared in 1842.

   Admission: 200 Drs (80¢); free on Wed.

   Open: Mon, Wed, and Fri–Sat 9am–1:30pm.

Historical and Ethnological Museum, Odós Stadíou 13 at Kolokotróni Square. ☎ **323-7617.**

This is modern history's equivalent of the National Archeological Museum—the story of Greece from the Balkan Wars (1912–13) through more or less the present day.

   Admission: 200 Drs ($1); free on Thurs.

   Open: Tues–Fri 9am–2pm, Sat–Sun and holidays 9am–1pm.
   Closed: Aug.

Kanelopoulos Museum, at Odós Theorías and Odós Pános, in Pláka. ☎ **321-2313.**

In a private neoclassical home, this private collection of classic Greek artifacts includes vases and figurines, Byzantine icons, religious embroideries, and Persian *objets d'art* in gold and crystal.

   Admission: 400 Drs ($2).

   Open: Tues–Sun 8:30am–3pm.

Museum of Cycladic Art, Odós Neophýtou Douká 4. ☎ **724-9706.**

Located off Leofóros Vassilíssis Sofías, just beyond the National Garden, is the world's first museum devoted solely to art from the

Cycladic islands. And a beauty it is, in its own striking, modern building of glass and marble, endowed by the foundation of a former shipowner, Nicholas P. Goulandris. The permanent exhibition, beautifully displayed against midnight-blue suede, features statuettes, figurines, jewelry, and vessels in clay or translucent marble, covering a period of 5,000 years—from as far back, in fact, as 3300 B.C.—yet extraordinarily "reminiscent" of much modern art and sculpture. The lobby gift shop has stylish replicas of the exhibits (the jewelry is particularly attractive), and there's a pleasant coffee shop in the annex—a restored turn-of-the-century mansion.

Admission: 250 Drs ($1).

Open: Mon and Wed–Fri 10am–4pm, Sat 10am–3pm.

Museum of Greek Folk Art, Odós Kydathinéon 17, in Pláka. ☎ **321-3018.**

Folk art here includes vestments, embroidery, pastoral wood carving, icon stands, reliquaries, carnival costumes, and a roomful of murals from Lesbos (Mytilíni). The museum's collection of folk ceramics is displayed in a former mosque at Odós Áreos 1 in Monastiráki Square.

Admission: 200 Drs ($2).

Open: Tues–Sun 8:30am–3pm.

National Gallery, Leofóros Vassiléos Konstantínou 50. ☎ **723-5937.**

The Ethnikí Pinakothíki and Moussío Alexándrou Soútsou, or simply National Gallery, is the gleaming building opposite the Athens Hilton. The National Gallery was established in 1900; its new home, however, was inaugurated in 1976, and it's a beauty. The collection includes a Goya (*Fiesta*), a Correggio (*Guardian Angel*), a Poussin (*The Holy Family and St. Anne*), a Van Dyck (*Portrait of a Nobleman*), and half a dozen El Grecos. Unfortunately, they're not always on view. A large gallery is given over to temporary exhibits, and there's a sculpture garden at the rear.

Admission: 200 Drs ($1).

Open: Tues–Sat 9am–3pm, Thurs–Wed 5pm–9:30pm, Sun and holidays 10am–2pm.

War Museum of Greece, Odós Rizári 2, at the corner of Leofóros Vassilíssis Sofías. ☎ **729-0543.**

"War" in this fabled corner of the world means Achilles vs. Hector, Greek vs. Persian, and Alexander the Great vs. the East, as well as the conflicts of more recent periods, such as the War of Independence (1821), the Balkan Wars (1912–13), World Wars I and II, and the Korean War, in which Greece sent troops under the flag of the United Nations. The collection, therefore, includes Neolithic cudgels, obsidian hammers, Corinthian helmets, diagrams of ancient battlefields, paintings, uniforms, ship models, a glittering armory of swords and sabers, and in the courtyard, an exhibition of howitzers, torpedoes, and antique fighter planes. There is a refreshment corner in the basement.

Admission: Free.

Open: Wed–Mon 9am–2pm.

Panoramas

Athens has several vantage points, besides the Acropolis, from which you can get superb views of the city. **Lykavittós Hill** is really a limestone rock reaching almost 1,000 feet into the once-crystalline Athenian sky. In the evening the top half is floodlit, and from the Acropolis it looks something like a giant soufflé. By day it's a green-and-white hill topped by a tiny, glaringly white church, Ághios Gheórghios. It's a nagging challenge, and sooner or later you're going to want to climb it. Don't try to walk up (pilgrims used to, but it's an Everest for the faithless); and don't try to take a cab, because it goes only halfway and you still have quite a hike to get to the top. Take the 2-minute funicular up the southeast flank. To get there, follow the TELEPHERIQUE signs to the corner of Kleoménous and Ploutárchou Streets, between Kolonáki Square and the Athens Hilton. The fare is 500 Drs (about $2) round-trip. The panorama from the top is priceless—all the way to Mt. Parnes in the north and west to Piraeus and the Saronic Gulf, with the Acropolis sitting like a ruminant lion halfway to the sea. There's also a café/restaurant up there, described in Chapter 5.

Philopáppos Hill is the big hill west of the entrance to the Acropolis. It gets its name from the monument to a versatile fellow (a Syrian prince, Roman consul, and Athenian magistrate) that was erected there around A.D. 115. On some maps you'll see a sign on the northwest flank saying PRISON OF SOCRATES. It's a cave, and maybe it was and maybe it wasn't the philosopher's prison.

Lower down this great outcropping of rock, you come to the hill known as **Pnyx** (pronounced *p-nicks*). You may visit it some evening, because it's now used as the auditorium for the *son-et-lumière* (sound-and-light) show at the Acropolis, but you may not have time to reflect on what a hallowed spot it is. Free speech was born here. During the days of Pericles, the Athenian Assembly met here; called Ecclesía, it was essentially a quorum made up of as many of the city's 150,000 free citizens as felt like attending. The Ecclesia gathered about 40 times a year and listened to the great orators who addressed the Athenians from the speaker's podium (or *bema,* which you can still see). The amphitheater seated 18,000; and to make sure it was well filled even when the Ecclesia was discussing something tedious, the police went around with ropes dipped in wet paint and herded the citizens up the hill to the Pnyx. Some of the most fateful decisions in Athenian history were made on this beautiful hillside; some of history's most rousing speeches were delivered right here on the speaker's podium.

Still another historic hill, to the northeast of the Pnyx and closer to the Acropolis, is the **Areopagus.** The name means "Ares Hill," and according to legend this is where Ares (that is, Mars, the god of war) was tried for murdering one of Poseidon's sons. He was acquitted. So was Orestes, when he was tried here for murdering his mother (read all about it in Aeschylus's award-winning trilogy *Oresteia*). And it was probably on this hill, in the spring of A.D. 54, that St. Paul delivered his sermon to the Athenians. Nowadays, when you walk past here on a soft Athenian evening, the great hill is suffused with the silhouettes of young lovers and travelers.

How do you get to these hills? You can, of course, take a taxi. But to absorb the full significance of paths that have known the footfall of so many Olympian personalities, you really have to walk. Slowly.

3 Cool for Kids

The great antiquities and classical sites that lure adults across the oceans are likely to be a downer for kids. The youngest among them will enjoy scrambling over the tumbled ruins of the Acropolis and elsewhere, but the city's museums are likely to induce a bad case of the fidgets, except for the most erudite and precocious kids. Athens is not a kids' city, on the whole, but here are a few attractions and activities that may excite their curiosity:

- A trip on the funicular up Lykavittós Hill, and a walk down.
- A rock or pop concert at the Lycabettus Theater (see *The Athenian* magazine for details).
- A trip on the hydrofoil to Aegina.
- The changing of the guard at the Parliament Building.

4 Nearby Attractions

The Acropolis is 5 miles from the sea, and in the days of Pericles it was quite a hike across the countryside to reach Fáliro (Phalerum) Bay. Now it's a short bus ride, and the suburbs of Athens reach all the way to the edge of the sea. But the entire coast—from Piraeus in the north, all the way south past the airport to Glyfáda, and even as far as Lagoníssi—is virtually an extension of Athens. In summer the downtown nightclubs move out there; Athenians go to the seaside for dinner, and wealthy Athenians flock out to the luxury hotels and beach houses—and stay put until September.

So, you haven't really seen Athens until you've seen something of its seaside satellites. In fact, if you're planning to be in these parts in midsummer, you might even consider checking into a hotel by the sea and making your sightseeing excursions into town from there. Glyfáda is only 20 minutes by car from downtown Athens; Vouliagméni is 30 minutes from downtown; and Piraeus is about 15 minutes from downtown.

Piraeus

The port of Piraeus (in Greek *Pireéfs* or, more commonly, *Pireás*) is about 6 miles from Sýntagma Square. In 461 B.C., Themistocles linked the two cities by his Long Walls, but now they're intertwined by their sprawling suburbs.

Two outstanding events have taken place in the history of Piraeus. Themistocles chose the site as the home port for the Athenian fleet he was about to build—the "wooden walls" that would protect Athens against the Persians, as predicted by the oracle at Delphi. After the Peloponnesian War between Athens and Sparta, it slumped back again to a fishing village; and when in the 19th century, Greece became independent and Athens became the capital, Piraeus was a ragtag hamlet on the edge of the water.

After the turn of the century, it slowly emerged as one of the major ports of the Mediterranean, thus preparing it for its second outstanding event—when Melina Mercouri made a movie called *Never on Sunday* (1959), which has since introduced the waterfront of Piraeus and its boisterous bars to the whole world. The waterfront still looks like the movie here and there, but Piraeus has blossomed in recent years; on your way to or from your cruise ship, you may want to spend an hour or two among its flower-decked boulevards and terrace cafés.

The dedicated archeologist can find many remnants of antiquity here, including traces of the Long Walls (the subway track follows roughly the same route). The city's museums of archeology and naval history are worth peeking into.

In the past few years, the city's gung-ho council has pushed ahead a rejuvenation program that included new beaches and beach facilities and, especially, the big new marina at Zéa. You may be coming here at some point to catch a small ferry or hydrofoil to some of the islands, but if not, come anyway and take a look at the luxury yachts and three-masted schooners and other toys of the Mediterranean jet-set. There's a new, completely equipped marina with restaurants, hairdressers, ship brokers, ship chandlers, and other appurtenances of seagoing. The large cruise ships, by the way, leave from the docks around Aktí Miaoúli and Aktí Xaveríou in Piraeus port, over the hill, or around the bend.

On the opposite side of the bay is the hilly peninsula known as **Castella** (which was the site of ancient Munichia and another acropolis). It's mostly residential (very desirable, with views over the harbor and the Royal Hellenic Yacht Club next door), and there are several good restaurants and cafés up there.

Around another bend is another bay and a circular harbor bobbing with more yachts and sailboats, the entire waterfront ringed with blue, yellow, and red awnings of the restaurants across the street. This is Mikrolímano, which you read about in Chapter 5. In the morning, it's a typical little fishing village, with the fishermen mending their nets and drying them in the sun; in the evening, it's Athens's dining hall. It's one of the most romantic places for dining out along the entire coast (yet only 20 minutes by car from Sýntagma Square or by subway from Omónia Square to the Néo (New) Fáliro stop). There are tables all along the waterfront, their matching restaurants across the street. After dinner, you can take a half-hour trip around the harbor with a gnarled old Greek seafarer in his calïque. Around midnight you still won't want to head back into town, so take your car or a taxi farther down the coast to one of the nightclubs by the sea.

The Apollo Coast

The next spot along the shore, known by the tourist authorities as the "Apollo Coast," is **Fáliro,** which way back used to be *the* harbor of Athens; then comes **Kalamáki,** which is a continuation of the nightclubs, restaurants, and tavernas of Palió (Old) Fáliro. The no. 132 blue bus, marked EDEM, will take you from Sýntagma Square to Fáliro, and the no. 103 bus, marked AGHIOS KOSMAS, will take you to Kalamáki, both for less than 30¢.

Ághios Kosmás is a new beach development and sports center. It has two soccer fields, eight basketball courts, eight volleyball courts, two tennis courts, and a beach for 3,000 bathers.

Glyfada

Glyfáda is the first of the big resorts, and it's only 10 miles from Athens: You can catch a no. 129 bus from Leofóros Vassilíssis Ólgas—the fare is only 75 Drs (30¢). The main road to Soúnio passes through the center of town; but if you're driving, turn off at the big green nightclub Dionysios onto the marine drive, where you'll pass an unending stream of cafés, restaurants, tavernas, hotels, and marinas. The café/restaurants on the beach side are mostly modern places where you can have anything from pizza to freshly caught barboúnia (red mullet), and your dinner bill needn't go above 3,000 Drs ($12).

WHERE TO DINE

One of the most famous restaurants along here is **Psaropoulos** (telephone for a reservation: 894-5677), popular with politicians and high society, but rather expensive by Greek standards—say, 4,000 Drs ($21) and up per person, with wine.

All the way at the end of this marine drive, you'll come to a restaurant on both sides of the street, with tables right at the edge of the marina. This is **Antonopoulos** (☎ **894-5636**). An order of prawns (big ones, but only three of them) costs about 2,500 Drs ($10); red mullet is also about the same price. Right next to it, behind the trees and right on the beach, is the **Asteria** nightclub and taverna (☎ **894-5675**). It's part of the big Astir Beach development that includes restaurants, snack bars, a bookstore, and a public beach (200 Drs, or about $1, admission). This area is also the best place to stay in Glyfáda.

MOVING ON

There are two more public beaches, with entrance fees of 200 Drs (about $1), in the next village, Voúla, but keep going another 5 miles to two of the stars of the coast, Kavoúri and Vouliagméni.

Kavoúri & Vouliagméni

These two are the liveliest and loveliest of the resorts within 15 miles (and a 75 Dr or 30¢ bus fare) from Athens.

They're on either side of a cape covered with pine trees, separating the bay, one half facing the sea and the other half on the bay. The scenic beach faces a flotilla of gleaming white yachts (there are still more of them tucked away in a marina farther down the cape); the restaurants are stacked above the beaches with terraces overlooking the sea, and new hotels and apartments are stacked up behind the restaurants. There are so many new hotels going up, there's no point in saying which is the best, but among the best are still the Astir Palace Hotels.

WHERE TO STAY

The **Astir Palace Hotels** complex was one of the grand resorts of Europe, the playground of the shipping tycoons, filling a private peninsula a few miles south of the airport; but in recent years it has hit a rough spot. As of summer 1994, the three government-owned hotels—Arion Astir, Nafsika Astir, and Aphrodite Astir—were about to be taken over by Barron Hilton's Conrad Hotels, with the likelihood that they would be allowed to operate a casino on the property. What Conrad Hotels planned to do was still up in the air at press time, but if they can sharpen up the attitude of the staff, their arrival could well restore the palatial Astir hotels to the forefront of European resorts. Have your travel agent bring you up to date on the situation there.

WHERE TO DINE

The restaurants in the Astir complex are international in scope and price; if you want something simpler and more typical, head for the far end of town (en route to Soúnio) and the last restaurant on the right, **Taverna Lambros.** It sits within a park, on a bluff above the sea, and nobody speaks English, but you can go into the kitchen and point to what you want—mídia fassólia saláta, tzatzíki, dolmadákia, barboúnia, and souvláki moscharísio, all for 2,800 Drs ($11), together with mineral water. The moonlight is free.

South to Sounio

But the best is yet to come. From Vouliagméni to Cape Soúnio (about 40 miles from Athens), the coastline twists and turns around beaches and rocky coves; a beautiful scenic highway winds alongside, sometimes by the edge of the sea and sometimes up on the cliffs. This is the true "Apollo Coast." And from the point of view of sunning and swimming, it's worth the extra miles and minutes from Athens, because there you'll find less pollution and less noise from the aircraft landing at Ellinikón Airport. Try, for example, the town of Várkiza, where the beach has small bungalows rentable by the day (about 5,000 Drs or $20, no reservations required), and a good, inexpensive, self-service cafeteria. For a hotel, try the 32-room Class B **Várkiza** or the Class A **Glaros.**

South of Várkiza are half a dozen small towns, most of them being spruced up and "resortified," so that you now have a choice of about a dozen hotels in these parts. The most popular of these towns is Lagoníssi, 25 miles from Athens, but you'll find the most attractive hostelry along these shores in Anávissos—the government-owned **Xenia Ilios Hotel,** its dun-colored contemporary lines stepping down the hillside. Each of the 102 guest rooms enjoys views of sea, shore, and passing ships. In winter the Ilios serves as a hotel training school; in summer the students polish their skills on paying guests. The summer service may be better than usual, and the rates are not formidable (reservations: call **02/913-7024**).

But your final goal is Cape Soúnio—specifically, the romantic temple of Poseidon, perched high on the cliff above the sea.

Cape Soúnio

You get your first glimpse of the **Temple of Poseidon** on Cape Soúnio (also Soúnion, Sunium) from the coastal road, several twists and bays before you actually get to the cape. First you see it, then you don't; finally, you're there. The temple was built in 444 B.C., probably by the architect who designed the temple of Theseus in Athens. Only 15 of its original 34 Doric columns remain, but it's still one of the most dramatic sights of Greece. Lord Byron was so carried away by it that he carved his name on one of the columns. (You try that today and *you'll* be carried away.) The site is closed on Tuesday. Admission is 600 Drs ($2). After you've tramped around this sea-girt acropolis, go down to the bay for a swim (the beach is nothing special, but the water and the view are) or lunch at one of the waterfront tavernas.

WHERE TO STAY

If you decide to stay overnight, you have a choice of two Class A hotels in Soúnio: the 45-room **Egeon** charges 18,000 Drs ($72) for two with half board; and the 152-room **Cape Soúnion Beach Hotel** 14,200 Drs ($57) for two with half board.

EN ROUTE BACK TO ATHENS

There's an alternative, picturesque route back to Athens from Soúnio, following the valleys and wine villages of the interior. It's a tough decision which to take—coastal or inland. Bets are you'll want to enjoy the constantly changing shore, the sparkling water that changes from deep blue to turquoise from bay to bay, and the islands and sailboats and fishing boats along the way. In any case, most people want to stay at Soúnio until the sun sets beside the temple of Poseidon, so you may drive back in the dark anyway. In which case, stop off for dinner at the Astir Palace in Vouliagméni, or one of the fine seafood restaurants and beachside tavernas along the coast if you're less than impeccably dressed.

5   Special-Interest Sightseeing

Most special-interest sightseeing (for example, archeological or classical) has already been set up as organized tours. For other, irregularly scheduled sightseeing walks or lectures, check the listings pages of *This Week in Athens.*

6 Organized Tours

One of the simplest, most relaxing ways to get around the sights of Athens is to call a tour operator, make a reservation for the next morning, and have the bus come and pick you up at your hotel.

The company will pick you up in an air-conditioned coach, a comfortable 52-seater, with a guide who'll speak English plus one other language. The companies offer a choice of four or more sightseeing tours in Athens. Here are two examples:

The **Morning Half-Day Tour** (from 9am to 1pm) includes the National Archeological Museum (except on Tuesday when it substitutes the Benaki Museum), National Library, university, Athens Academy, Presidential Palace, Panathenaic Stadium, temple of Olympian Zeus, Hadrian's Arch, Metropolitan Cathedral, and church of Ághios Elefthérios. The price is 6,950 Drs ($28).

The **Athens by Night Tour** is more fun than usual because in winter it includes a drive past the floodlit Acropolis, then along the edge of the sea to Castella (Piraeus), with a visit to a taverna for dinner and a floor show. In summer the tour starts off with the *son-et-lumière* (sound-and-light) show at the Acropolis and ends with dinner and a taverna show in Pláka. These tours last from 8:30pm until 12:30am and cost from 9,600 Drs ($38) with dinner.

An alternative evening choice is the sound-and-light spectacle (English-language commentary) plus Greek folk dances. This tour, available nightly from May through September, lasts from 8:30pm until midnight; the cost is 6,650 Drs ($26).

For information on these and other tours, contact **American Express,** Odós Ermoú 2, on Sýntagma Square (☎ 324-4976); **Viking Tours,** Odós Artemídos 1, Glyfáda (☎ 898-0829, fax 894-0952; in the U.S., toll free **800/341-3030**); **Key Tours,** Odós Kalliróis 4 (☎ **923-3166,** fax 923-2008); or **CHAT Tours,** Odós Stadíou 4 (☎ **322-3137,** fax 323-5270).

7 Sports & Recreation

Spectator Sports

The Hellenic Yachting Federation (☎ **413-7351**) has information about sailing events. The Touring and Automobile Club of Greece (or ELPA, ☎ **779-1615**) will provide information about road rallies and auto races. For sporting events at the Olympic Stadium, check with the Greek Tourist Organization (EOT, ☎ **322-2545** or **323-4130**).

Recreation

CAMPING

Inquire at the Greek Tourist Organization, Odós Karagheórghi tís Servías 2 (☎ **322-2545** or **323-4130**), on Sýntagma Square (in the National Bank of Greece). If you want information before you go to Greece, contact one of the Greek Tourist Organization's offices in the United States or Canada (see "Information, Entry Requirements, and Money" in Chapter 2). There are a dozen camping sites in and around Athens and more than 100 throughout Greece. You can now rent fully equipped campers; for details, contact Camper Caravans, Odós Níkis 4 (☎ **323-0552**).

MASSAGE & SAUNA

The Hilton's resident masseuse charges 5,600 Drs ($22) for a 30-minute massage; sauna is 2,000 Drs ($8). Call **725-0201** (ext. 685), from 11am to 9pm. Or try the Athenaeum Inter-Continental (☎ **902-3666**), where rates are similar. At the Caravel Hotel (☎ **729-0721**), a sauna-plus-gym package is available at just 4,000 Drs ($16).

SWIMMING/BEACHES

There are no public pools in town. (You can pay to swim at the Hilton and some of the other hotel pools.) Your best bet is to head directly for the Apollo Coast and establish a base of operations there. Keep in mind that Piraeus is a very busy port and that at Glyfáda and Vouliagméni you have the problem of aircraft noise. The place you may want to head for, as do most Athenians, is Várkiza, about an hour from the city by bus (which leaves from Leofóros Ólgas, near the Záppion, but you may be able to join other beachgoers and share a taxi inexpensively). At all the beaches along the shore where you pay an admission fee, there are changing facilities and showers, and the beaches themselves are cleaned every morning; most of them also have snack bars or restaurants. Rates average 250 Drs ($1); Várkiza is in the top range and costs 700 Drs ($3). There are often beach cabins available for an additional 1,200 Drs ($5).

Swimmer beware: If you swim from rocks rather than sand, watch out for sea urchins. The Greek sun is hot and piercing; if you overdo it and catch a burn, rub on yogurt.

7

Strolling Around Athens

off

SOME 30 YEARS AGO, WHEN I FIRST VISITED ATHENS, WANDERING AIMLESSLY about the city and idling in cafés were two of my favorite pastimes here. They still are—but my walking and café-hopping are now confined to a few areas where cars and buses don't dominate the scene. One of the most appealing places for walking is the residential district of Kolonáki, although even here Athens is succumbing to an overabundance of cars; the streets, narrow to begin with, are made even narrower by parked cars, and the sidewalks are often obstacle courses because cars and motorcycles are parked half on, half off the pavement. Nevertheless, because of the deficiencies of the city's transportation system, walking is the quickest way to get to your destination. And as in any city, it is still the best way to get a feel for the place, to immerse yourself in the sights and sounds and smells of this vibrant, energetic metropolis that offers to the visitor a unique blend of Western and Near Eastern cultures.

The walking tours described below cover the center of Athens. The first, beginning and ending in Kolonáki, is a wider tour of museums, architectural sights, shops, and geographical points of interest. The second tour is a walk from Sýntagma Square, the heart of the city, to the area of Monastiráki, with its popular flea market, then on to Pláka, and ending at the National Garden, right across from Sýntagma Square.

Walking Tour 1
Around the City's Center

Start   Kolonáki Square.
Finish   Kolonáki Square.
Time   The walk only, 2 hours; add 1–2 hours more for museums.
Best Time   Early morning or late afternoon.
Worst Time   Noon, when the Athens sun is at its fiercest (**note:** noon is also not a good time to be atop Lykavittós Hill if you want to shoot photos or videos).

The best plan is to settle into a café chair beneath a canvas awning, get out your map, and study your route. I usually begin at Café Lykavittós, on the corner of Odós Anagnostopoúlou, at the top end of Kolonáki Square. The square tilts, northwest to southeast, with a leafy garden in the center and with terrace cafés and boutiques on

IMPRESSIONS
Athens, the eye of Greece, mother of arts and eloquence.
—Milton, *Paradise Regained,* 1671

In Athens I saw . . . a spirit . . . which a thousand years of misery had not squelched.
—Henry Miller, *The Air-Conditioned Nightmare,* 1945

Athens leaves me cool.
—Henry Adams, 1898

two sides. Don't be sidetracked by the glimpses of boutiques and emporia along each side street—you'll be returning to Kolonáki Square, so leave your shopping until then.

Diagonally across the square is Odós Koumbári. Walk down it about 100 yards to the corner of pell-mell Leofóros Vassilíssis Sofías. Across the avenue is the National Garden. On your right, at the corner, is the:

1. **Benaki Museum.** Admission is 400 Drs ($2). Anyone who is an enthusiast of things Byzantine will probably want to return later for a more comprehensive visit, but for travelers on a tight schedule this is the time to go in. Don't miss the folk art exhibit downstairs—it's not well signposted and it could easily be overlooked. What can't be overlooked is the interesting gift shop just to the right, inside the main entrance.

   Leaving the Benaki, go left along Vassilíssis Sofías two blocks, to Odós Neophýtou Douká, where you'll see the oddly modern, glass-sheathed facade of the:

2. **Museum of Cycladic Art,** part of the Nicholas J. Goulandris Foundation (admission 250 Drs or $1). Its four floors (one of them given over to temporary exhibits) have been augmented by an annex in an adjoining town house, where you will find your first possible refueling stop— which just happens to be one of the loveliest in the city.

Refueling Stop

The mini–coffee shop in the new wing of the museum—in the conservatory-style rotunda surrounded by tall windows of art-deco glass, floors of gray marble inlaid with mosaics, and a marble statue of an Athenian boy dating from 310 B.C. A latter-day Athenian youth will bring you coffee and orange cake on a silver tray, with a tall glass of water and paper napkins carefully arranged on both the plate and the saucer—for about 1,000 Drs ($4).

Leaving the museum by the main entrance, go left on Neophýtou Douká back to Leofóros Vassilíssis Sofías, then left again three blocks, to Odós Ploutárchou. This walking tour can easily take in the **Byzantine Museum** and the **War Museum,** both on the other side of Vassilíssis Sofías, but this is the place to cross—the intersection has traffic signals and a pedestrian crosswalk. Otherwise, turn left, look ahead, and take a deep breath: For the first four or five blocks, Ploutárchou rises in a steady incline but thereafter it becomes positively precipitous, ending in flights of steep stairs. Take a deep breath again and forge ahead. After a few paces, on the left, you'll come to the:

3. **British Consulate,** an ungainly modern building easily identified by its guardhouse and the clutter of metal

obstructions on the sidewalk—to prevent cars from parking or, presumably, ramming the entrance. (The **British Embassy,** facing the next street at the end of the garden, is a much more dignified turn-of-the-century mansion. On the right side of the street is a bakery shop called:

4. Complet, at Ploutárchou 11. It is a convenient place to pause if you plan to picnic atop Lykavittós Hill, for here you'll find a variety of fresh breads, rolls, and cakes in various shapes and sizes. Their appealing look and blend of intoxicating aromas will give you an appetite right on the spot.

If, however, you are not in the mood for a picnic and a long hike up Lykavittós, proceed a few paces more until you come to a pleasant little ouzerí with a Turkish name and a Mediterranean menu.

Refueling Stop

Yali Kafines, at Odós Ploutárchou 18, is one of the new breed of ouzerís/ *kafenía,* with contemporary decor and a few tables set up under the acacia trees on the sloping sidewalk. The place is open from noon onward. Find a seat, order a drink (ouzo or something lighter), and ponder your choice of midday meal—tabbouleh salad, Cypriot meatballs, or codfish croquettes with garlic sauce (go easy with the sauce if you intend to continue with the tour).

At Odós Kafneádou the first of the gift-and-souvenir shops appear; at Odós Patriárchou Ioakím the steps and the huffing and puffing begin. On the left is:

5. Bajazzo, a bar and restaurant in a handsome mansion in Mets, near the Olympic pool.

At the corner of Odós Kleoménous two stores will catch your attention. The first is:

6. Okeania, at Odós Ploutárchou 43. It specializes in pottery (including some attractive blue-and-white candleholders) and in silver brooches, earrings, and pendants based on Victorian-era designs (prices start at 1,500 Drs or $6; no credit cards). The other store is:

7. Paniyiri, two doors along at Odós Kleoménous 25. It's a cubbyhole of a store specializing in boats made from driftwood, handcarved and hand painted in a naïf style and priced from 5,000 Drs, or $20 and up (no credit cards). A little farther along the way is a private workshop called:

8. Poseidon at Odós Ploutárchou 64. The workshop, at the top of the stairs, overflows onto the sidewalk with an array of handcrafts—figurines, ceramic chess sets, dolls, jewelry, and assorted gift items. It's a diverting spot to spend a few minutes before crossing the street, past the orange trees, to the entrance-way for the:

9. **Lykavittós Hill funicular.** You could, of course, walk up the hill (about a 30- to 40-minute hike from the St. George Lycabettus Hotel), but the funicular will haul you up in 3 minutes or so for 500 Drs ($2). Don't make too much fuss about where you sit—most of the journey takes place inside a tunnel. When you step off the funicular, at the summit of:

10. **Lykavittós Hill,** you're just a few paces from the highest point in Athens, at an elevation of 909 feet. The hill is crowned by the tiny white chapel of St. George, which looks more like a smooth-lined island church than like the Byzantine churches you've seen down below in Athens; its interior is piously crammed with icons, murals, and candles. From the observation decks, you can see all the way to the sea and the sometimes hazy silhouettes of tankers, cruise ships, and ferryboats gliding across the waters. From up here you can look down on the distant Acropolis, a view that unfolds the layout of the complete hilltop site. To descend Lykavittós either take the funicular or, if you still have the energy for a little exercise (this is, after all, a *walking* tour), follow the:

11. **Footpath,** from the side of the chapel, that leads down the hillside through pines and acacias, the shrubbery brightened occasionally by swatches of blossoms. The path is easy to negotiate—in good walking shoes. The first exit lets you out at Odós Loukianoú; keep walking a few more yards to:

12. **Dexamení Square,** which you reach by walking down the road past the St. George Lycabettus Hotel (on the left), past the hotel's outdoor café terrace (on the right), and then by making a sharp right turn down a sort of *allée* with tables and chairs set up beneath the trees. Continue across the open plaza at the bottom to a flight of marble stairs; go down the stairs, across the street, and down another flight of stairs; then cross Odós Fokilídou to the next intersection. From there proceed left on Odós Anagnostopoúlou and you'll be back in Kolonáki Square 2 minutes later—unless you stop to browse in the boutiques.

Refueling Stop

The **Dionysos-Zonar's restaurant** on top of Lykavittós has both indoor and outdoor dining rooms and a spacious umbrella-shaded terrace for snacks and light meals. The terrace faces northeast: The view from your table is down Kolonáki Square, across the roofs of the U.S. Embassy, the new Athens Concert Hall, and the Hilton Hotel to the slopes of Mt. Hymettus. Halfway down the footpath there is an ouzerí with an arbor-covered terrace overlooking the city.

Walking Tour—Around the City's Center

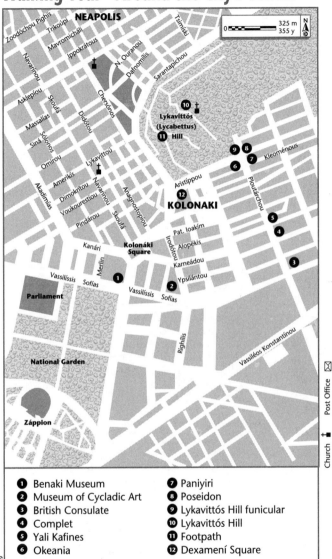

0 ━━━━━ 325 m
      355 y

NEAPOLIS

Zoodóchou Pighís · Trikoúpi · Mavromicháli · Ippokrátous

Navarínou · Asklepíou · Skoufá · Massalías · Solónos · Siná · Omírou · Amerikís · Akadimías

N. Ouranoú · Dáfnomílis

Sarantapíchou · Tsimiskí

Chesónos · Didótou

Lykavittoú · Navarínou · Dimokrítou

Anagnostopoúlou · Youkourestíou · Pindárou · Skoufá

❿ Lykavittós (Lycabettus) Hill **⓫**

Aristíppou

⓬ **KOLONAKI**

⑨ ⑧
⑦ Kleoménous
⑥

Ploutárchou

Pat. Ioakím · Irodótou · Alopékis · Karneádou

Kanári · **Kolonáki Square**

Merlín · **❶**

Vassilíssis Sofías

Parliament

Vassilíssis Sofías **❷** Ypsilántou

⑤
④

③

Righílis

Vassiléos Konstantínou

National Garden

Záppion

Vassiléos Konstantínou

Post Office ⊠

Church ✝■

❶ Benaki Museum
❷ Museum of Cycladic Art
❸ British Consulate
❹ Complet
❺ Yali Kafines
❻ Okeania
❼ Paniyiri
❽ Poseidon
❾ Lykavittós Hill funicular
❿ Lykavittós Hill
⓫ Footpath
⓬ Dexamení Square

9389

Walking Tour 2
Pláka & Monastiráki

Start   Sýntagma Square.
Finish   Pláka or Sýntagma Square.
Time   Allow 2 hours, not counting shop browsing or museum time.

Best Time   Sunday morning.

Worst Time   Monday through Friday, 12–2pm when shops are closed.

The best way to start your walking tour is by picking up a map at the office of the nearby Greek Tourist Organization (EOT). Cross the street to Sýntagma Square and—sit down. Have a cup of Greek coffee. Check out your map route; check out the square itself; best of all, check out the people of Athens. When you're ready, head down Odós Mitropóleos. You will soon come to the "little church in the sidewalk" called:

1. **Aghía Dýnamis** (Holy Strength), at the corner of Odós Mitropóleos and Odós Pendélis. It holds its own against the Metropolis Cathedral. Carry on straight down Mitropóleos and you'll come to:

2. **Cathedral Square** (Platía Mitropóleos), where the Metropolitan Cathedral sits, and so can you. The church of Ághios Elefthérios, to the side of the cathedral, is a beautifully ornate building. Inside, you'll find heavily tooled silver icons with wood-painted faces, and smaller icon offerings. When you leave the square, turn left and head for:

3. **Odós Pandróssou.** This is the famous bazaar street of Athens. Every kind of tourist souvenir hangs in open-air stalls; bouzouki tapes play full blast as bargain hunters attend to their mission. Be sure not to miss:

4. **Melissinos',** at Pandróssou 89. Stavros Melissinos is Athens's famous poet, sandal maker, and goodwill ambassador. The world needs more Stavroses (and you may find you need a pair of his sandals, a bargain).

Refueling Stop

The Center of Hellenic Tradition, at Odós Mitropóleos 59. Step into a cool, tiled arcade right in the middle of bustling Odós Pandróssou and you'll find a rich collection of Greek handcrafts housed in a pleasant café with wooden ceiling and good Acropolis views. Antique maps, framed political cartoons, and old photos of stern-faced wedding couples line the walls, along with hand-painted tapestries, brass doorknobs, and religious icons. A good stop for a refreshing coffee frappé or an ouzo cum *mezédes* (appetizers).

Rested and fortified now—and having perhaps addressed some more postcards to friends back home (how many ways can you describe the Acropolis?)—continue along Odós Pandróssou. The street soon spills into:

5. **Monastiráki Square,** site of Athens's flea market, which is as popular with tourists as it is with Athenians. There is a little monastery in the square, but it almost gets lost in the flea market, traffic roundabout, and subway entrance. The

Walking Tour—Pláka & Monastiráki

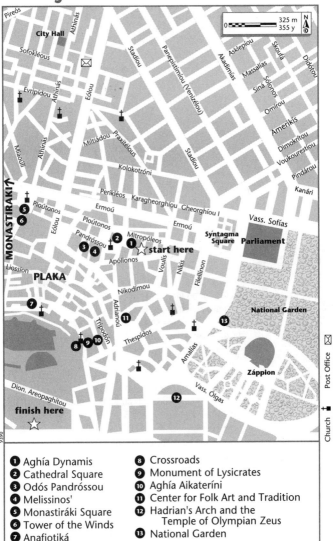

1 Aghía Dynamis
2 Cathedral Square
3 Odós Pandróssou
4 Melissinos'
5 Monastiráki Square
6 Tower of the Winds
7 Anafiotiká
8 Crossroads
9 Monument of Lysicrates
10 Aghía Aikateríni
11 Center for Folk Art and Tradition
12 Hadrian's Arch and the Temple of Olympian Zeus
13 National Garden

flea market is particularly lively on Sunday mornings. From here head left toward the Acropolis and you'll enter the street maze that is Pláka. Here, you classical-ruin buffs will find the:

6. Tower of the Winds (Aerides), an octagonal, almost whimsical marble tower from the Roman period; it once had a working mechanical clock inside. The tower fronts the Roman Agora, at the junction of Odós Eólou and several little side streets. Keep the Acropolis in front of you and head up to a part of Pláka known as:

7. **Anafiótika.** A neighborhood settled by immigrants from the island of Anáfi, in the Cyclades, it consists of a small cluster of low, whitewashed homes that seem to cling to the bottom of the Acropolis outcropping. Stroll through the winding streets here (many are unmarked, but they all eventually lead back to one of Pláka's main streets) and you'll get a flavor of what the little villages of the Cycladic islands are like. Whatever street you're on will lead you to a:

8. **Crossroads,** from which you could either head up to the Acropolis for a full afternoon of sightseeing or wind back down through Pláka. If you choose the latter, head down via Odós Thespídos to the:

9. **Monument of Lysicrates,** being excavated at the corner of Odós Epimándou and Odós Výronos. Then round the corner to the church of:

10. **Aghía Aikateríni,** which is in its own little palm-lined square. If you return to Odós Thespídos, make a right; it will turn into Odós Kydathinéon, one of the main streets of Pláka. From there you can go to the:

11. **Center for Folk Art and Tradition,** at Odós Angheliki Hatzimicháli 6 (off Kydathinéon). It's a good place to visit to get a feel for what Pláka life must have been like once, in all its 19th-century elegance. When Kydathinéon hits Odós Filellínon, make a left, then turn right onto Leofóros Amalías, another crossroads. Across the avenue you'll find:

12. **Hadrian's Arch and the Temple of Olympian Zeus.** Both of these colossal monuments bear silent witness to the ancient glory of Greece—before there were all those cars, mopeds, and buses speeding noisily, and noisomely, past the entrance to the site.

 For deliverance from the noise and noxious fumes that offend ruin and tourist alike, make your way to one of the few green oases in Athens, the:

13. **National Garden.** The main entrance is on Leofóros Amalías. Wander through the lush walkways, listening to the birds, or just sit on a bench and relax. If you choose to stay until after sunset, go to the outdoor café near the Záppion exhibition hall, find a table, order something refreshing, and sit back to enjoy the entertainment offered by Greek and foreign cabaret artists.

8

Shopping A to Z

People don't go to Athens for a shopping spree as they might to London or Amsterdam or the Caribbean. But there are stores enough and temptations enough in Athens to lure you from ogling the antiquities, so be sure to bring along some spare cash for gifts and souvenirs—especially since there are so many attractive items that you can buy only in Greece.

1 The Shopping Scene

Best Buys

What are the favorite buys in Athens? That's hard to pin down; but generally speaking, Americans are impressed by the jewelry (especially gold items and the reproduction of the patterns and designs of antiquity), flokati rugs, hand-knit sweaters (made by village women in winter, priced in some cases less than the wool alone back home), leather goods, hand-woven and hand-embroidered blouses and dresses, local pottery from the islands, *tagária* (beach bags of cotton or wool), furs, and icons. There are many more, as you'll see when you wander around the streets of the city—or when you skim through the roundup following.

Store hours are officially from 9am to 5pm, Monday through Friday; to help relieve traffic congestion and thereby pollution, the government decided to declare an end to the traditional Greek "siesta." However, this was not a universally popular decree and many shops continue to close around 2pm, reopening from 5 to 7pm. Kiosks and the flea market are nearly always open; shops in Pláka usually stay open late to catch the revelers; most stores are open until 2pm on Saturday.

Main Shopping Areas

The main shopping centers in Athens are concentrated in the streets around Sýntagma Square, around Kolonáki Square, and the side streets between Stadíou and Panepistimíou Streets. To generalize, you might say that the gift and souvenir stores are more numerous around Sýntagma; that the Athenians' everyday shopping is done around Stadíou and Patissíon Streets (this is where some of the major department stores are to be found) or on bustling Ermoú Street, between Sýntagma and Monastiráki; and that cosmopolitan Athenians shop in the streets between Sýntagma and Lykavittós Hill. But these are only generalizations, and you'll find quality shops in the most unlikely neighborhoods.

Of course, the most interesting shopping streets can change from year to year. Right now, for example, **Tsakáloff Street,** running off Kolonáki Square, is turning out to be one of the most interesting shoppers' streets in the city. Two blocks of Tsakáloff have been cleared of traffic and decked out with café tables and umbrellas; its procession of fashion boutiques, jewelry stores, and furniture and fabric shops were augmented in 1990 by a swank, award-winning *galleria* in a former town house (no. 5)—four stories of goodies, including a

Shopping Around Sýntagma Square & Pláka

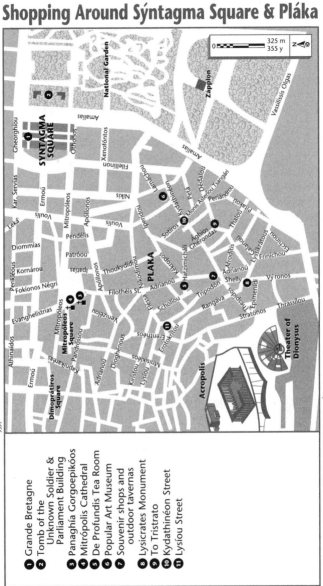

1. Grande Bretagne
2. Tomb of the
   Unknown Soldier &
   Parliament Building
3. Panaghía Gorgoepikóos
4. Mitrópolis Cathedral
5. De Profundis Tea Room
6. Popular Art Museum
7. Souvenir shops and
   outdoor tavernas
8. Lysicrates Monument
9. To Tristrato
10. Kydathinéon Street
11. Lysíou Street

branch of **Pentheroudakis,** the jewelers, a branch of Gucci, a dinky shop selling handcrafted decorative glassware, and a smart little white-on-white café with tables in the street; or for women's designer clothes: Trussardis at Odós Tsakáloff 15; Ritz at Tsakáloff 13; and Kathy Heyndel's at Odós Alopékis 21. Other browsers' streets in this neighborhood are **Skofias, Soudias, Milioni,** and **Patriárchou Ioakím**—but almost all the Kolonáki streets, even the most precipitous, are worth a stroll for isolated boutiques and shops.

The *original* pedestrian-mall street in this area, however, is still one of the city's most fashionable shopping streets—Odós Voukourestíou, 2 blocks from Sýntagma Square, between Odós Panepistimíou and Lykavittós Hill, a mall decorated with potted plants and globe lamps and lined with some of the city's swankest jewelers and fashion stores.

Bargaining

Should you bargain in Athens? Before you run out and start haggling, be warned that not all the city's shopkeepers take kindly to it. You can tell by the look of the place whether you can or cannot. Save your bargaining for the streets, especially the flea market—but when you do it, do it with gusto.

Some Rules: Take your bargaining seriously—don't have the family gawking in the background. Totally disregard the vendor's first offer; reject out of hand his second. If you have a Greek friend, let him or her do the bargaining for you. And never rush. If you like something with a special passion, begin bargaining for the item next to it, then "settle" for the one you want. When in doubt, don't buy. What you want is probably cheaper next door.

Tax-Free Shopping

The tax-free shop at the airport is very limited in its choices: Don't put off serious shopping until you get there, other than small gifts, perfume, cigarettes, liquor, and souvenirs.

2   Shopping A to Z

Antiques

Antiqua, Leofóros Amalías 4. ☎ **323-2220.**

This is a proper, elegant antiques shop owned by a family that knows and loves its wares. The store is filled to the brim with clocks, jewelry, paintings, ancient Greek votive dishes, ivory statues, icons, Chinese vases and carvings, and French and Venetian furnishings. The shop is a bit off Sýntagma Square, and the prices range from 5,000 Drs to 1 million Drs ($20 to $4,000).

Gallerie Antiqua, Leofóros Vassilíssis Sofías and Odós Messoghíon 2. ☎ **770-5881.**

This elegant shop houses the works of noteworthy Greek and foreign painters, exquisite art objects, and furniture of high quality and good taste. It's near the U.S. Embassy.

Tassos T. Zoumboulakis, Odós Kriezótou 7. ☎ **363-4454.**

Founded at the beginning of the century, this gallery collaborates with several of the finest art dealers in Europe and the United States, so it's not restricted to works by Greek artists. Nevertheless, those are the works that will probably interest you most, and here you'll find a selection by Greek artists who are known only within their homeland and others who have earned reputations abroad; among them are Tsazouchis, Chryssa, Matta, Alan Davie, and Fassianos. Furthermore, the gallery occasionally exhibits works by international contemporary artists.

Art Galleries

These are four galleries where you will see rotating exhibits of works by local and international artists: **Athens Gallery,** Odós Glýkonos 4 in Kolonáki (☎ **721-3938**); **Desmos,** Odós Akadimías 28 (☎ **360-9449**); **Jean Bernier Gallery,** Odós Marásli 51 (☎ **723-5657**), which is open Tuesday to Friday 11:30am to 8:30pm, Saturday 11:30am to 2pm, and has international contemporary art; and **Hydrohoos Art Gallery,** Odós Anapíron Polémon 16 in Kolonáki (☎ **722-3684**).

Books

Les Amis des Livres, Odós Valaorítou 9.

This shop is everything its name promises to lovers of books—rare books, prints, and engravings of Greek scenes. Open Monday to Saturday 9:30am to 3pm in winter; closed Saturday in summer.

Compendium Bookshop, Odós Níkis 28. ☎ **322-1248.**

Compendium, near Sýntagma Square, has an extensive selection of foreign-language books and magazines.

Eleftheroudakis, Odós Níkis 4 (☎ **323-1401**) and the Athens Tower (☎ **770-8007**).

Eleftheroudakis (the accent goes on *-dákis*) has a variety of English-language books, from popular works of fiction to scholarly studies, as well as a vast collection of books in Greek and some in other languages.

Pantelides, Odós Amerikís 11 (☎ **362-3673**).

Here you'll find local lore and classical history. The bookstore carries lots of Penguins.

Crystal & China

Studio Kosta Boda, Odós Stadíou 19.

This shop has two floors devoted to crystal and china ware by makers such as Noritake, Kosta Boda, Royal Copenhagen, and Arabia.

Department Stores & Supermarkets

The three major emporia (at least those that come closest to the American concept of a department store) are the **Athenée,** halfway along Odós Stadíou, at nos. 33–35; **Lambropouli,** at Eólou and Lykoúrgou Streets; and **Minion,** the "Macy's of Greece," at Odós Trítis Septemvríou 10, near the National Archeological Museum. The **Prisunic Marinopoulos** stores are a combination department store and supermarket, where you can buy Marks & Spencer's knitwear or pick up some useful inexpensive items and the makings of a great picnic; these stores are identified by a large orange **M**—the closest one to Sýntagma is at Odós Kanári 9, just off Kolonáki Square. Two supermarket chains with a wide range of European delicacies are **Vassilopoulos** and **Sklavenitis.**

Fabrics

Argaliou Brailas, Odós Filellínon 7.

Argaliou means "loom" and *Brailas* is the name of a family that looms, so this is the place to head for top-quality hand-woven silks. *Even the threads are hand-spun.* Prices range from 13,500 Drs ($54) for a meter of heavy silk to 10,400 Drs ($42) for cotton silk. Made-up items include hand-woven capes from 30,000 Drs ($120), and reversible hand-woven handbags with shoulder straps (hand-crocheted finish) for less than 8,200 Drs ($33). They'll also make up anything for you, carefully tailored, within 2 to 3 days.

Tsantilis, Odós Ermoú 23–25. ☎ 323-9401.

This shop presents a dazzling array of fashion fabrics and ready-made clothing; a branch boutique is at Odós Stadíou 4.

Fashions

FOR WOMEN

This is a subject that you have to look at from two angles: local designs and fabrics on the one hand, high fashion and international chic on the other. Sometimes they overlap, with intriguing results. Generally speaking, shopping is more varied and rewarding in Athens now that Greece is a full-fledged member of the European Union, and nowhere is this truer than in matters of fashion. Hitherto, many of the designer shoes on sale in fine stores in Paris or Rome or New York were actually made but not sold in Greece; now they are, at prices way below what you'd pay elsewhere. Fashions (for both women and men) are rapidly shrugging off their traditional gray-serge conservatism for flashier colors and linens.

Yannis Travassaros, in the Athens Hilton, Leofóros Vassilíssis Sofías. ☎ 722-0201.

Yannis Travassaros has his main boutique in the Athens Hilton. He designs virtually everything he sells, and in most cases he also weaves his own fabrics, or trims coats or dresses with old embroidery and authentic *bibiles* (needlework borders) from his own collection of old Greek costumes. His collection of haute couture is also well known by many Athenians.

For more women's fashions, less pricey than those in the boutiques of Kolonáki, check out the windows of the following stores, all on Odós Ermoú: **Sinanis** at no. 9 (with a branch at Odós Voukourestíou 23), and **Agenda** at no. 47.

Just around the corner from Sýntagma Square, at Odós Voukourestíou 12 and Odós Panepistimíou 6, the **Contessina** boutique has an interesting array of fashions and gifts.

Lizard, at Odós Kriezótou 14, **Thiros,** at Odós Tsakáloff 8, and **Gianari Gallani Boutique,** on the corner of Kolonáki Square and Odós Skoufá, have elegant selections of leather goods.

FOR MEN

If you want to look over suits, jackets, and shirts by Europe's top-flight designers (particularly Italian), the appropriate stores seem to be concentrated near the intersections of Odós Akadimías with Odós Pindárou, Odós Voukourestíou, and Odós Amerikís (for example, Simbolo, at no. 18). A few of the trendiest men's boutiques have set up shop in Kolonáki, mainly along Odós Tsakáloff.

Ascot, Odós Níkis 29, just off Sýntagma Square 62. ☎ **324-6551.**

Ascot, with another branch at Odós Omírou 62, features a wide selection of suits, sportcoats, slacks, shirts, sweaters, ties, and toiletries.

Gianfranco Ferre, Odós Anagnostopoúlou 4. ☎ **722-9738.**

Italian styling—shoes, suits, shirts—and prices that will make you think twice about spur-of-the-moment purchases.

Emporio Sportiv, Odós Tsakáloff 17.

The place to stock up on casual clothing before you fly off to the isles. Moderate prices.

Perla, Odós Stadíou 5. ☎ **323-9854.**

With a classy branch in the arcade here and other stores throughout the city, Perla also has a fine selection of men's shoes and assorted menswear. There's also a branch of Perla at Odós Akademías 27, for men and women.

Gifts

For gifts for sons, daughters, grandchildren, nephews, and nieces, head for one of these toy shops: **Panhellinios Agora,** Odós Stadíou 9; **El Greco,** Odós Kréontos 30–32; or **Tsokas,** Odós Eólou 52.

Bambino Kontossi, Odós Ermoú 39.

At Bambino, you'll find clothing for kids of all ages, as well as for mothers-to-be.

Personality Kids, Odós Sólonos 21.

Exactly as it sounds, with clothing in the bright colors of the Greek islands.

Zouzou, Odós Voukourestíou 26.

The windows here overflow with stuffed animals, games, and toys from all over Europe and the United States.

Handcrafts & Souvenirs

You'll find the handcraft/jewelry/souvenir/"Greek art" type of shop everywhere in Greece, and it often doesn't make much difference which one you step into. The prices and merchandise, all "typically Greek," are similar at most of them. In this section, however, the listing concentrates on shops selling handcrafts that are of better quality than the usual souvenir-type trinket.

In addition to the following listings, other handcraft and Greek art shops include **Stathis,** at Odós Venizélou 2 (just off Mitrópolis Square); and **Cleo's** in the Hilton arcade (bags, dresses, necklaces, bracelets, leather pitchers, and rings).

ADC, Odós Valaorítou 4.

ADC, short for "Athens Design Center," is a small outlet for the works of a group of designers in ceramics, silver, bronze, and pottery. Its displays include saucers, cups, plates, bowls, flowerpots, and one-of-a-kind ceramic sculptures. Unusual pottery pieces include turtle doves and boxes, an interesting collection of silver-and-bronze jewelry, and unusual bronze candleholders for as little as 3,400 Drs ($14).

Cantoros, Odós Voukourestíou 28. ☎ 361-2536.

Cantoros specializes in ceramic lamps and bangles and assorted household items—ideal gifts at reasonable prices.

Greek Corner [Sam Pessah & Son], Odós Karagheórghi tís Servías 10. ☎ 322-2327.

The Greek Corner is bursting with every sort of "authentica" available, including silver and gold jewelry, ceramics, coins, and icons anywhere from 3,200 Drs to 250,000 Drs ($13 to $1,000) in price.

Mati, Odós Voukourestíou 20. ☎ 362-6238.

Here you can buy "mati" stones for keeping the evil eye away as well as old monastery lamps, candlesticks, glass and silver, and all sorts of *unexpected* things.

National Welfare Organization, Leofóros Vassilíssis Sofías 135. ☎ 646-0603.

The NWO (also known as the Hellenic Folk Art Gallery) channels the work of poor families and schoolchildren from all over Greece; it supplies the designs (invariably adapted or copied from museum pieces) and the families do the rest. Their handwork makes excellent gifts that are easy to pack and easy to carry; and some are easy on the wallet: a package of two embroidered linen guest towels for under 2,000 Drs ($8), sets of four napkins and placemats for 25,000 Drs ($100) and up, and hand-embroidered tablemats for upward of 10,000 Drs ($40) each. These prices are about one-third less than what you'd pay for comparable articles in New York, and all profits go to charity. The NWO has another shop at Odós Ipatías 6 (☎ 324-0017). Open Monday to Saturday 8am to 3:30pm, with no lunch break.

Pandora, Odós Voukourestíou 12. ☎ 361-2821.

Pandora is one of the more attractive shops along Voukourestíou, selling artifacts, jewelry, women's wear, and gifts. It's clean and well laid out, and its owner quite clearly takes pride in the place.

Tanagrea, Odós Mitropóleos 15. ☎ 801-8592.

Located at the corner of Voulis and Mitropóleos Streets (near the little church in the middle of the sidewalk), this shop sells "Les Falences de la Grèce, all handmade items," in classic and contemporary designs from all the islands and areas of Greece.

To Anoyi, Odós Sotíros 1. ☎ 322-6487.

One of the most delightful handcraft shops in Athens is one floor up in a quaint little Pláka house. When you climb the stairs to iconographer Katherine Apostolou's workshop, you may find her painting to the music of Mahler. Her dazzling display of crafts includes attractive enamel ashtrays with delicate designs of boats and animals, bronze candleholders, hand-blown glass, Greek pottery, cotton scarves with traditional regional designs, and decorative wooden eggs in traditional designs. There's something here for every taste and every budget, including the most modest.

Jewelry

This is one of the most popular shopping items in Greece. The range of merchandise runs from souvenir trinkets based on ancient designs to chic avant-garde creations in gold and precious stones.

Some of the city's finest small jewelry stores are on the Odós Voukourestíou pedestrian mall. Among them are **Anagnostopoulos** at no. 13 (☎ **360-4426**) and **Vildiridis** at no. 14 (☎ **363-5145**). **Athiniotakis** at no. 20 and **Petra Nova** at no. 19 both feature *petrádia,* or semiprecious stones (amethyst, tiger's eye, lapis, turquoise, and sodalite are the most popular), set in imaginatively designed pins, necklaces, rings, earrings, and pendants, at prices ranging from 20,000 Drs ($80) to well over 500,000 Drs ($2,000).

La Chrysotheque Zolotas, Odós Panepistimíou 10. ☎ 361-3782.

Neck and neck, so to speak, with Lalaoúnis (see below) in quality and price is the other great name in Greek jewelry—with branches in several deluxe hotels and museums throughout the islands and mainland.

Gold Coin Jewelry, Odós Stadíou 17. ☎ 322-0600.

This place actually sells *you* money—a unique collection of unusual coins, all of them copies of ancient Greek currencies.

Lalaounis, Odós Panepistimíou 6. ☎ 361-1371.

Some of the most original and imaginative gold jewelry in the world is designed by Ilias Lalaoúnis and handcrafted by his artisans in a workshop in the shadow of the Acropolis. Lalaoúnis introduces two new collections a year (sometimes more when he receives a special commission from a sheik). A typical collection might include a dazzling array of gold necklaces, bracelets, and rings evolved from the shapes of aboriginal and prehistoric tools and statuettes, priced in the thousands of dollars. However, visit any of the Lalaoúnis stores and you'll find items costing as little as 12,000 Drs ($50). The main store has branch boutiques in the lobbies of the Athens Hilton and Athens Tower, at the airports on Corfu, Mýkonos, and Rhodes, and in 15 different locations abroad.

If you admire the Lalaoúnis concepts but cannot afford the price of gold, visit a store called **The 4 Lamda** in the Athens Tower skyscraper. It's actually another branch of Lalaoúnis, with the same imagination and flare in design, but most of the items are crafted in silver, with scores of gifts ranging from 7,800 Drs to 14,500 Drs ($30 to $60), as well as more substantial items.

Maria Antoniades, one floor up at Odós Apóllonos 6.

There are more museum copies at the showroom of archeologist Maria Antoniades, as well as original modern designs in gold, silver, and precious stones. Prices range from a few hundred dollars to 950,000 Drs (about $3,800).

VIP, Odós Níkis 10. ☎ **323-2262.**

VIP stocks Byzantine seals and brooches copied from originals in the National Archeological Museum, mostly from the Mycenaean and Alexander the Great periods. Most of the items are priced above 19,000 Drs ($76).

Kiosks

If you can't find it anywhere else in Athens, you'll probably find it at one of the numerous sidewalk kiosks (*períptero,* plural *períptera*), a unique Greek institution. They're open 18 hours a day (in some cases, around the clock, although you may find kiosks outside the center of town closed on Sunday afternoons). Kiosks sell an incredible assortment of goods: chocolates, magazines, newspapers, dolls, postage stamps, cigarettes, cakes, pharmaceuticals, chewing gum, film, pens, light bulbs, detergents, cosmetics, books, among sundry other items that you may suddenly find yourself out of. And you can use their telephones for local calls for just a few drachmas.

Knitwear

For handwoven, hand-knitted sweaters, go to **Helen de Luca** at Odós Hatzimicháli 4 (two doors down from the Hotel Nefeli).

Leather Goods

There's more leather—wallets and luggage—at **Magasin Scourletis,** Odós Speusíppou 8, in Kolonáki, and **Louis Vuitton,** at Odós Voukourestíou 39.

Markets

Centering on Odós Pandróssou and spreading out to surrounding streets, the **Flea Market** is just what you'd expect it to be: a monumental assortment of castoffs, some of it junk, the treasures or otherwise from the attics of Attica. You might like some of the brass and copper ornaments, jewelry, 1930 Victrolas, icons, lamps, woven bags, or old used clothing. Make a special point of visiting the crafts shops in the restored arcade at Pandróssou 15 (watch for the Hermion Café sign). A visit to the Flea Market can be quite exciting, especially if you try your hand at bargaining. Save this trip for a Sunday, but go early—the colorful pushcarts push off at 1pm.

If the Flea Market should put you into a general market mood, then head for the **Meat Market,** at Odós Eólou 81. A tiny entrance beckons the unsqueamish into a passageway of butchers' stalls, with red meat hanging everywhere. Twenty steps in, the passageway is transformed into a giant cross of stalls. The **Fish Market** is here, too.

On the other side of the Meat Market is Odós Sofokléous, home to dozens of little cheese, olive, and grocery stores. Go there for a lunch of feta cheese, black/brown olives (they're loaded with vitamins A and C), a loaf of bread, and your choice of wine.

Note: The Meat and Fish Market area has been under renovation for several years. What's supposed to emerge is a brand-new open market with new stalls and passageways. What's actually emerged so far is a concrete shell that gives the old market a very shopworn feel. A few blocks have also become a market for illegal businesses of the drug and flesh sort. An area still worth a visit, but keep your eyes open.

In addition to these markets, there are several street markets (called, collectively, *laïkí agorá*), following a tradition that dates back to the Middle Ages. Stalls are piled high with fruits and vegetables, as well as with clothing and country wares brought into town by itinerant merchants. These markets are held in different neighborhoods on different days (invariably from early morning until 2pm); ask at the hotel reception desk for the day or location of the market nearest your hotel.

Museum Shops

Some of the most interesting, most *Greek,* shopping is to be found in the shops of the city's museums—including the **National Archeological Museum** at Odós Tossítsa 1 (reproductions of vases, figures, statues) and the **Benaki Museum** at Odós Koumbári 1 (jewelry, table linens, prints, matchbooks, among other items). But one of the most stylish collections is in the Nicholas P. Goulandris Foundation's **Museum of Cycladic Art** (at Odós Neophýtou Douká 4). There, you'll find tasteful copies in resin of, say, a 4th-century B.C. handshake, vases, lamps, and figurines; copies in silver of a 14th-century B.C. sword and a 6th-century A.D. Byzantine lamp with cross; and silver jewelry—brooches, earrings, and pendants featuring adaptations of violin-form figurines and Cycladic motifs. The Benaki's museum pieces are complemented by a varied collection of books, cards, gift items, and videocassettes.

Optical Needs

Optical, Odós Ermoú 6 (☎ **323-6792**) and Odós Patriárchou Ioakím 22 (☎ **724-3564**).

If you want to check out the latest sunglass designs being worn around the Mediterranean resorts—or if you need repairs to your own spectacles—this is a reliable address.

Rugs

There's a bewildering choice of designs and colors in Greek rugs: Horassa, Hamadan, the Lobanof with its playful lions, Greek designs from the Acropolis, blue-and-yellow Byzantine designs, the Skyrion (based on motifs taken from a village cemetery near Corinth), the Greek classical designs with their stark blues and whites and subtle flecks of ocher, and some Asian designs that look like woolen Jackson Pollocks (and beautiful enough to hang on a wall).

Flokati rugs are among the most popular purchases for visitors to Greece, and most visitors flock to **Karamichos-Mazarakis Flokati** on the corner of Voulís and Apóllonos Streets (☎ **322-4932**).

Flokatis come from the city of Tríkkala in central Greece; they're made from New Zealand wools, softened under fresh spring waterfalls in Tríkkala before being woven by hand or machine to make thick, close piles. Both showrooms display a variety of flokati rugs in natural tones or kaleidoscopic patterns; at Karamichos-Mazarakis you'll even find wool rugs patterned after rare Salvador Dalí paintings from private collections. Prices range from 7,500 Drs ($30) for a 2-by-5-foot rug in natural colors. Karamichos-Mazarakis will pack, insure, and mail your purchases.

Shoes & Sandals

Mouriades, Odós Stadíou 4.

If you didn't pack adequate shoes for clambering over all those ruins and archeological sites, try this store. It has branches throughout Athens, and most people consider it the best shoe shop in the city, with prices from $14,000 Drs to 72,000 Drs ($56 to $300), including some Bally models.

Stavros Melissinos, Odós Pandróssou 89. ☎ 321-9247.

Here you'll find the "poet sandal maker" of Athens, Stavros Melissinos. Look in the dusty window and you'll see several yellowing newspaper articles about this remarkable man, in among the sandals, straps, and tools of the trade; inside the small shop, you'll find up to 30 different styles of sandals, ranging in price from 1,500 Drs to 3,000 Drs ($6 to $12). If your feet are bigger or smaller, Melissinos will make you a special pair. He counts among his clients various celebrities, and framed certificates above his workbench testify that Harvard, Oxford, and even the White House have copies of his books of poetry in their collections. (You could buy one for your collection, too; just ask its author.) An unaffected, gentle, and friendly man, Melissinos will chat about his poetry with you while helping you choose your sandals.

Tony's Sandals, Odós Adrianoú 52.

Tony's, near the Roman Agora, is the place to go when you want a comfortable pair of shoes or boots—casual style. Tony is the brother-in-law of Stavros Melissinos.

Sponges

Sponges might seem an unlikely purchase, but they're on sale on street corners all over the city. These are natural sponges fetched out of the nearby sea by hardy divers. They come in all sizes and range in price from 950 Drs ($4) all the way up to somewhere around 3,800 Drs ($15)—but you'd pay several times the amount back home.

Worry Beads

"Worry beads," or *kombolóia,* as they're called in Greek, are Greece's answer to tranquilizers, but try twiddling them yourself and you may find they have just the opposite effect—it's not as easy as it looks. Fortunately, they don't cost a fortune. You'll find selections in most "Greek art" shops.

9

Athens Nights

A THENIANS DON'T PAINT THE TOWN RED—THEY SAY "LET'S GO BREAK SOME plates!" It's an old Greek custom. When the audience is enjoying itself, it's expected to show its appreciation exuberantly. Greeks used to do this by smashing plates or glasses or throwing flowers on the stage. The plate- and glass-smashing is now banned by the police, so the audiences throw flowers or plastic baubles instead; but you'll still find occasions when the music, the stars onstage, the stars above, and Dionysus combine to rouse the audience to smashing pitch. Just in case it happens some night when you're around, don't insist on a ringside table. Sit well back of the middle of the floor. (And don't break any plates because the taverna will charge a hefty premium for them.)

Athens itself is, of course, the greatest show of them all. The way to enjoy it is simply to go to the nearest café, find a table, and watch the performers—the lottery sellers, the sponge sellers, the souvláki vendors, the taxi drivers, and the stately old women all dressed up for a gala at the Grande Bretagne.

If you insist on a more active nightlife, you can find it easily in Athens. This ancient and modern city offers possibilities for evening entertainment as probably no other capital in Europe does. Take your pick: You can watch ancient Greek drama in a theater dating from the time the play was written; you can relive the history of the Acropolis in the awesome *son-et-lumière* (sound-and-light) spectacle; you can sit on a roof garden beneath the floodlit Acropolis and watch a folklore show—or you can get up and dance a Zorba-like *syrtáki;* you can listen to a world-famous orchestra playing Beethoven or jazz in a 2,000-year-old amphitheater. The possibilities are indeed many.

Whatever you decide to do, you'll soon discover one of the most appealing features of nightlife in Athens. Not only is it varied, not only is it unique, but also it's priced so low that you can enjoy almost everything it has to offer—even if you're on a tight budget. The only restraint on living it up right through the night is the thought that tomorrow you still have so many ancient wonders to see.

The entertainment pages of *Athens News* and *The Athenian* are the best guides to local events in Athens, what's playing in theaters, concerts, operas, cinemas, nightclubs, tavernas, and restaurants.

1 The Performing Arts

Concerts, Opera & Ballet

The best thing to have happened to Athens in years, maybe centuries, is the completion of the new **Athens Concert Hall** (Mégaro Moussikís Athinón), a theater/conference hall project that has been under way in fits and starts since 1956. The hall's pillared, Doric-inspired facade of Dionysos marble encloses spacious chandeliered promenades, exhibition space, a 500-seat recital hall, and a 2,000-seat multifunction, high-tech auditorium that can serve as a concert hall, opera house, cinema, or meeting hall simply by adjusting its wooden walls and ceilings. The consensus is that this modern concert hall has outstanding acoustics. The official opening of the hall in spring 1991 was a ceremony at which former U.S. President Jimmy Carter was awarded the Alexander S. Onassis Foundation's Aristotle Prize; in its first seasons as a music center, it has hosted such distinguished international musicians as the Royal Philharmonic Orchestra, violinist Pinchas Zuckerman, and soprano Agnes Baltsa. The Athens Concert Hall is at Odós Vassilíssis Sofías 89, adjacent to the U.S. Embassy, reachable by bus no. 3, 7, or 13 from Sýntagma Square. For tickets (from 1,000 Drs or $4 to 10,000 Drs or $40), call **728-2333.** Unfortunately, although the hall is fully air-conditioned, it is closed during July and August.

Other performing-arts events include opera and ballet, at the **Olympia Theater** (Odós Akadimías 59, ☎ **361-2461**), as well as chamber music and recitals, at the **Gloria Theater** (Odós Ippokrátous 7, ☎ **362-6702**). The best sources for information on performing-arts events throughout the city are *The Athenian* and *Athens News*. Another source is the receptionist or the concierge of your hotel, who may even be able to acquire tickets (for a small fee or tip).

Athens Festival

Inaugurated in 1955, the Athens Festival is a summer-long series of cultural events held at the **Herod Atticus Odeum,** an impressive outdoor theater, at the foot of the Acropolis, built in A.D. 161 and largely restored after World War II. The festival, which has achieved world renown, stages ancient Greek plays, concerts, ballets, and modern dance performances. The program changes each year. Among the internationally known artists who have appeared at the festival are Luciano Pavarotti and Frank Sinatra, along with such acclaimed orchestras as the New York Philharmonic and the Amsterdam

---

Major Concert/Performance Halls

Athens Concert Hall, Odós Vassilíssis Sofías. ☎ **729-0391.**

Opened in 1991, the Concert Hall is one of the newest and finest halls in all Europe. It hosts opera, theater, and classical as well as modern music performances.

Odeum of Herod Atticus, Odós Dionýsou Areopaghítou, below the Acropolis. ☎ **323-2771.**

This is among the most ancient (A.D. 161) and most dramatic of all performing venues in the world. At the odeum (odíon in Greek), the Athens Festival presents a wide range of theatrical, dance, and music performances during the summer and early fall. It's an easy taxi or bus ride from Sýntagma Square, beyond the Hilton Hotel and next to the U.S. Embassy. **Pallas Theatre**, Odós Voukourestíou 1. ☎ **322-8275.**

Most of the major jazz and rock concerts are held here, as well as classical music performances.

Concertgebouw. The Bolshoi Ballet and the Martha Graham Dance Company have also performed at the festival, winning over Athenian audiences.

There is something magical, you'll discover, about sitting in a marble theater from Roman times (cushions are available for the sensitive), under a starlit sky, and listening to a Mahler symphony, say, or a jazz concert; at the sound of the first notes the chasm between the centuries seems to vanish and you become aware instead of the cultural link between the ancient world and the modern. The acoustics, by the way, are excellent (the area around the theater is closed to traffic during performances).

The festival runs from mid-June through September. Performances are given almost daily and are often sold out in advance. But you can buy tickets as early as 2 weeks before a performance at the **Athens Festival Box Office,** Odós Stadíou 4 (in a shopping mall off Odós Voukourestíou near Sýntagma Square); the box office is open daily from 8:30am to 2pm and from 5 to 7pm. Remaining tickets are also sold at the Herod Atticus Odeum box office on the day of the performance. For information about the current schedule, call the Greek Tourist Organization (EOT) or the Athens Festival at **322-1459,** or check *The Athenian* magazine or the *Athens News*. A program for the entire festival, containing also brief biographies of scheduled performers, may be purchased either at the Athens Festival Box Office or at the Herod Atticus Odeum box office.

Dora Stratou Dance Theater

The south side of the Acropolis can be a congested spot in summer. The crowd that's not heading for Pnyx Hill and the *son-et-lumière* (sound-and-light) show is probably on its way up Philopáppos Hill, following the sign for the Dora Stratou Dance Theater. The Dora Stratou Company is a group of folk dancers founded about 35 years ago; it has earned a lot of bravos since then, both in Greece and on tours around the world, including the United States. The show consists of a warm-up overture by the Zygia, a small orchestra made up of clarinet, violin, lute, *santoúri,* and drums. The players are dressed in typical Greek native costumes, which differ from region to region but include black waistcoats, miniskirts, blouses, white stockings, and snub-nosed shoes—like *évzones* in mufti. The songs and dances are songs and dances that Greeks have been performing for 2,500 years, and there's no finer place to hear and watch them than under the feathery trees on an Athenian hillside, a stone's throw from the Acropolis. You can almost see Pan and the nymphs dancing there. A typical program might include the Florina-Kratero from Macedonia, the Dodoni from Epirus (Ípiros), and the Ierissos from Chalkidikí.

You can get to the Dora Stratou Dance Theater by bus no. 9 from Sýntagma Square. The dances are performed every evening at 10:15pm, from May through September. On Wednesday and Sunday, there are "matinees" at 8:15pm. Admission prices range from

1,250 Drs to 2,500 Drs ($5 to $10); your ticket reserves a specific seat in the amphitheater (real seats, not bleachers). For information, call **324-6921.**

2   The Club & Music Scene

Bouzouki Clubs

Long before the movies *Never on Sunday* and *Zorba the Greek* there was bouzouki. This six-stringed lutelike instrument was popular with *rebétes,* men who scratched out a living on the fringes of society in places such as Piraeus, persecuted by the police for their crimes and drugs. Unsavory characters indeed, but their music had an appeal that reached out and touched Greeks everywhere. No one knows exactly when *rebétika*—the songs of the *rebétes*—began to be sung, but it was probably in the 1820s, around the time of Greek independence; they were played by the poor and the social outcasts in bitter but stoical protest against the injustices of their lives—much like the early blues songs. With the songs came the dances: the *zebékiko,* an intensely individualistic dance that the *rebétis* performs for himself and not for the people around him; the *chasápiko,* another traditional rebetic dance for two or three men, no more, and again a private, introverted dance. What you may recall from *Zorba the Greek* was the *syrtáki,* which is a modified and faster version of the *chasápiko.*

Over the years, bouzouki became fashionable with all strata of society, reaching its peak in the early 1950s. Then it declined, mainly because of commercialization; to make the instrument more versatile another pair of strings was added, then the instrument itself was electrified. Instead of just the traditional guitar for accompaniment, the sophisticated Athenians who went out for a night *stá bouzoúkia* (to the bouzouki haunts) came to expect guitars and drums and piano, and possibly double bass and electric organ, besides a couple of bouzoukia. This is basically what you'll hear today when you go *stá bouzoúkia;* the unamplified bouzouki has all but disappeared, and the districts where the *rebétes* themselves used to hang out have all been pulled down. However, you can still hear good modern bouzouki music in several tavernas in Pláka, in downtown clubs in the winter months, and in the seaside clubs in summer.

IN PLÁKA

Until recently, to take a few steps inside Pláka was to realize that pandemonium is indeed a Greek word. Before World War II, there was only one taverna in Pláka (it's still there), and the other buildings were private homes. Now every home seems to be a taverna, and every other sidewalk and rooftop is an extension of a taverna. Tavernas set up their tables in patios, on rooftops, even on the stepped streets climbing up to the base of the (Acropolis) rock. Most of the tavernas have music, which would be fine if they didn't also have amplifiers to blast out their sounds, reverberating through the alleyways and across the rooftops.

Fortunately, the government has cut down on the noise, banished cars from many of the narrow streets, and encouraged authorities and people to gut and restore the area's wonderful old buildings. When such restoration is completed, Pláka will once more be a unique experience. Meantime, if you're not in the mood for curling up with Aristotle, it can be a lot of fun. Tremendous fun. If you don't want to get yourself involved in the raucousness, you can still find an occasional taverna without music in a quiet (well, relatively quiet) terrace or courtyard, with the music arriving distantly across the rooftops.

Finding Your Way Around Pláka

Finding a particular club is not easy, since most of the streets are identified in Greek only. However, you'll get there if you follow these basic directions. First, go to Cathedral Square (Platía Mitropóleos). From the steps of the cathedral (facing out to the square), turn left and follow Venizélou Street until you come to a modern white marble building on the corner; bear right, past the Greek-art shops Stathis' and Zorba's, until you come to Odós Adrianoú, at a right angle to Venizélou. Now go left on Adrianoú, past a few gift shops, until you come to Milton's bar/restaurant on the left and a streetful of boutiques dead ahead. The street on your right is **Odós Fléssa,** and you'll know you're in Fléssa because on the right there's a building that looks something like a misfit from Kyoto, which is the Taverna Palia Athena. Continue up this street to the fork in the road and bear right. This puts you on **Odós Lysíou,** which is where most of the action is—here and on **Odós Mnisikléos,** which runs at a right angle to it.

If you're coming from the Acropolis, follow the path past the Areopagus and past the **Café-Bar Acropolis** (which has a magnificent view from its pathside terrace). There's an intersection on the left, but keep going along the path at the base of the hill, past an old church, and then follow a curve to the left and down to a white wall; now go right. From that point just follow the bustle; pretty soon you'll have to negotiate a series of steps cluttered with tourists just listening to the music, while tables nearby fill up every inch of flat surface and waiters try to get to the tables, jostling people trying to get to the Acropolis and one or two others trying to pinch a bottom.

Picking a Place in Pláka

Once you're in Pláka, how do you go about selecting a taverna?

On a busy weekend, the only valid piece of advice is to grab the first table you come to. There's really not so much difference in food or service between one restaurant and another; if you can, get to Pláka before you're likely to feel ravenous, wander around and look the places over until you see something you fancy—in a patio, on the sidewalk, on steps, or on a rooftop. Yes, a rooftop: In summer the warm and cozy tavernas become barren ghost rooms and everything moves onto roofs rimmed with potted plants and usually covered by a removable awning. The important thing here is the *view*—if you're going to sit outdoors on the roof you might as well be in a position to watch the Acropolis as you dine. As you walk through the streets of Pláka, you'll be importuned by countless waiters promising that their rooftop has the best view. Don't take their word for it—go up and have a look for yourself before committing your evening. Some tavernas are positioned in such a way that diners can look out on the Acropolis *and* Lykavittós Hill *and* the lights of Athens.

Check out the prices, too, as you go along. Tavernas with music cost more than tavernas without music; tavernas with shows cost more than tavernas with only music. Prices also depend on such variables as music tax, entertainment tax, show tax, and who is performing. Most tavernas are open 7 nights a week in the summer.

Some Suggestions

When you walk around Pláka looking for the places described below, you'll pass dozens of others. If you see one that looks interesting, just drop in; the list below doesn't claim to be the top 10 or so but simply a sampling to let you know what to expect.

Dionysus, Odós Lysíou 7. ☎ 322-7589.

Not to be confused with the restaurant of the same name mentioned in Chapter 5, this is another multicolored taverna with a roof garden located directly across the street from Mostrou (see below). It's more relaxed than Mostrou, prices are not too high, and here you have a chance to inspect what you're going to eat when you walk past the display case and kitchen at the entrance. Under its new management, it's been spiffed up, the waiters are courteous, and the atmosphere is much more welcoming than at Mostrou—but the breaking of plates is banned. Call for reservations.

Mostrou, Odós Mnisikléos 22. ☎ 322-5558.

The corner of Lysíou Street and Mnisikléos Street is where you'll find one of the liveliest concentrations of tavernas, one on each corner. I'll start with Mostrou. It's the only one around that has its name in large English characters on a sign above the door. It's your landmark, as well as a potential destination, if you don't mind spending an evening surrounded by other tourists. It's a big place with a roof garden for warm weather (the rest of the year there's a semirustic room with a ceiling that looks like a TV studio's complex of lights and spots for the floor show). The Mostrou show, indoors or outdoors, features a modern band and vocalists for dancing, six dancers (in folk costume), and the inevitable singer with hand-held microphone who always manages to sound like Barbra Streisand doing an imitation of Judy Garland. The show is at its best when the dancers and band cut out the jazz and get down to some serious Greek dancing. Then you can't even catch the waiter's attention. The Mostrou menu is probably one of the biggest in Pláka. It's more expensive than most—grilled swordfish at 1,900 Drs ($7) and chicken dishes at 1,330 Drs ($6)—but then it has a bigger floor show than most. The music begins at 9:30pm, and the show runs from 11pm to 12:30am, followed by more music. Mostrou is closed on Sunday and various weekdays in the winter.

Taverna Kalokerinoú, Odós Kékropos 10, off Odós Adrianoú. ☎ 323-2054.

This taverna has a very specific audience: tourists. The atmosphere is lively but has a slick, packaged quality to it. Main dishes (lamb chops and shrimp) are from 2,000 Drs to 3,300 Drs ($8 to $13); appetizers cost anywhere from 400 Drs to 1,000 Drs ($2 to $4); desserts are 500 Drs ($2); a bottle of local wine is 750 Drs ($3). Kalokerinoú is one of the most reliable of the tavernas with shows (folk dancing and belly dancing from 10 to 11:45pm and nonstop music from 9:30pm on for singing, dancing, or just plain finger-snapping and foot-tapping). However, be forewarned: It can get overcrowded with rowdy tourists who want to become part of the show. Like most other tavernas in these parts, the show is indoors in winter and on the roof in summer.

Admission: 2,000 Drs ($8).

Taverna Klimataria, at the corner of Odós Thrassyvoúlou and Odós Klopsýdras.

This taverna is located in a quiet corner on the outskirts of Pláka, just under the Acropolis. Climb the steps into the taverna and you are in what appears to be a very noisy, roughly decorated cellar with brick arches in the walls. The whole area is crammed with tables, except at the end, where the musicians stand in a niche beneath one of the brick arches. Klimataria has all the usual *mezédes* and a large selection of wines from all over Greece, from retsina to Robola; main courses are principally grills—shish kebab, veal chops, and beefsteak. In summer the roof comes off, and the music (a couple of guitars, piano, and bouzouki) fills the air until about 2am. A nice, friendly place, this one, where dinner for two should cost 8,000 Drs ($32) or less.

Taverna Kritikou, Odós Mnisikléos 24. ☎ 322-2809.

Across the street from Dionysus, this taverna, decorated in the simple, peasant style, is popular with Greek families (no tour groups) and consequently much cheaper. It's on the right as you face the steps that take you up the hill to the Acropolis, and you'll probably hear it before you see it. Its tables are spread over the steps and through the doors to the dance floor; and if the only free table is at the rear, allow yourself 3 or 4 minutes to squeeze through. This was the first taverna in Pláka, by the way. There's a minimum of decor here—a few murals in Pláka-primitive style and a less-than-classical arch of corrugated plastic above the band. The band is a four-piece combo—with electric organ, guitar, drums, and bouzouki—but it gets the place going, encouraging a steady stream of men getting up to dance, egged on by the audience to perform ever wilder and more contorted leaps. Its attractive menu is decorated with paintings of the beast, fowl, or fruit you're about to order—and the attractive prices include moussaká for 900 Drs ($4) and chicken or squid for 1,200 Drs ($5); house wine, from Crete, is from 1,500 Drs ($6) and up.

Nightclubs by the Sea

At midnight, when coaches turn into pumpkins, Athenians turn into swingers. Drop into any Athens nightclub just after dinner and you can almost certainly have a choice of ringside tables, overwhelming service, and a dance floor all to yourselves. At worst, you may have to dodge a few tangoing tourists (until midnight, all the bands sound like Guy Lombardo). Come midnight, the whole atmosphere changes: The local swingers start filing in, the bouzoukis are plugged into their amplifiers, and the air fills with bittersweet Greek melodies. Everything keeps blasting away until 3 or 4 in the morning or until the last plate has been thrown.

Before listing a few of the more popular clubs in Athens, here are some ground rules about nightclubbing in the city. You don't have to dress to the nines, but you'll find that most men wear jackets and ties. A new law makes cover charges mandatory for night clubs. The cover usually includes one drink and is somewhere in the region of 1,000 Drs to 3,000 Drs ($4 to $12). Subsequent drinks are usually a bit costly. If you have dinner to while away the evening until midnight, your drinks will cost less, but, of course, you'll still end up paying at least 10,000 Drs ($40) if you have Greek dishes, up to 15,000 Drs ($60) if you order steaks. It's expensive, but consider what you're getting in return—3 to 6 hours of entertainment, frequently with one of Greece's top singing stars, plus dancing.

Athens nightclubs set such a hot pace that the air conditioning can't keep up with them; so when the weather warms up, the nightclubs pack up for the shore and set up their music stands and stages all the way from Piraeus to Vouliagméni. The night owls of Athens then scan the newspapers to find out where their favorite stars are singing and follow them. The actual club is relatively unimportant—it's the performers who count. If you plan to follow suit, here are some of the names to watch for—Marinella, Dalaras, Bithikotsis, Zambetas, Voskopoulos, Dionyssiou, Tsitsanis, and Kokotas. They're the ones who get the plates flying.

Note: None of the seaside clubs is more than 2,500 Drs ($10) by taxi from downtown Athens, and you can always get a taxi to bring you home in the wee hours.

Boîtes

If you think the decor in a taverna is fairly basic, wait until you see a boîte. The typical Athenian boîte is small, crowded, smoky—and the seating may be stools, kindergarten chairs, or benches. The boîte is strictly for music—*rebétika*, folk, pop, variations on love, broken hearts, celebration, carousing, and protest, often original material. The songs' meanings will be lost on visitors, but the atmosphere is infectious and the tab exceedingly reasonable (about $10 for the first drink, admission, and cover all in one). A boîte is indeed a delightful way to wind up an evening in Pláka. Performers—on bouzouki, guitar, piano, accordion, whatever—are usually unknowns, but today's boîte artistes are often the stars of tomorrow. There are usually two shows nightly (the first never starts before 9pm, the second starts sometime after midnight).

One boîte that's particularly popular with Athenians—mostly young Athenians, many of them students from the university, but interspersed with a few dressy older folks—is **Boîte Esperides,** at Odós Thólou 6 (☎ **322-5482**) in the upper elevations of Pláka. It's run by two brothers—Yannis, who occasionally performs, and George, who is the congenial, welcoming host (and speaks excellent English). The decor of the 100-seat room consists of massed posters and pinups covering every available centimeter of walls and ceiling; in warm weather one wall folds back and Esperides expands into the small garden at the entrance. No reservations, no credit cards.

Another boîte worth mentioning is **Stoa Athanatos** (Immortal Arcade), at Odós Sophokléous 19 (☎ **321-4362**). It usually packs them in only between midnight and 6am. No reservations.

Discos/Dance Clubs

With all that lively Greek dancing going on around you, there's not much need for discos. However, if your feet start to itch for the big beat, here are a few suggestions.

Since discos tend to boom in and out of fashion in Athens as elsewhere, your best bet is to pick up a copy of *Athens News* or *The Athenian* and study the latest listings; alternatively, ask someone at your hotel to recommend something that fits your tastes. Generally speaking, discos have no entrance fee, but drinks will cost around 2,000 Drs ($8). That said, some of the current "in" spots are **Nine Plus Nine** (Enea syn Enea), at Odós Agrás 5 near the Olympic Stadium (☎ **722-2258**); **14,** right in Kolonáki Square; and **Papagayo,** at Odós Patriárchou Ioakím 37 in Kolonáki (☎ **723-0135**).

Another well-established favorite with Athenians is **Akrotiri,** on a promontory at Ághios Kosmás in Glyfáda, with dancing on a breeze-cooled patio beside a pool in summer. In winter the **Club** in the Athenaeum Inter-Continental Hotel has an enthusiastic following.

3 The Bar Scene

Late-Night Bars

"Late" is relative, of course, in a city where most people don't even get around to eating dinner until 9 or 10pm. There's no shortage of late-night spots in Athens, and you may have found your favorite on your first night in town. If not, here are two suggestions: **Montparnasse,** at Odós Cháritos in Kolonáki (☎ **729-0746**), is popular with the neighborhood's writers and artists and decorated with 1920s posters, glass-topped tables, and overstuffed cushions in the shape of fruit. **Balthazar,** at Odós Tsochá 27 (☎ **644-1215**), near the U.S. Embassy, is a fine restaurant, where the barflies may linger beyond the regular dining hours. Among the hotel lounges and bars, the **GB Corner** (☎ **323-0251**) in the Grande Bretagne and the rooftop **Galaxy** (☎ 722-0201) in the Hilton are especially popular with both locals and out-of-towners.

4 More Entertainment

Nighttime Tours

The simplest way to sample the nightlife of Athens is to take one of the special "Athens by Night" sightseeing tours. This kind of tour is more fun in Athens than in most cities because it usually includes a drive past the floodlit Acropolis, then along the edge of the sea to Castella in Piraeus, with refreshments in a typical taverna and dinner at a Greek nightclub, complete with floor show and folk dancing. **American Express, CHAT,** and **Key Tours** operate these "Athens by Night" tours, as well as "Theater Night" tours that take you to performances of the *son-et-lumière* (sound-and-light) spectacle and the Greek dances at the Dora Stratou Theater. The "Theater Night" tour costs 6,650 Drs ($27), including tickets but without dinner, and the "Athens by Night" tour costs 9,600 Drs ($38), with dinner.

Son-et-Lumière

If you arrive in Athens anytime between the beginning of April and the end of October, make a point of spending at least one evening watching the *son-et-lumière* (sound-and-light) spectacle at the Acropolis. *Son-et-lumière* involves batteries of lights—1,500 in all—that are flooded onto the Acropolis and the Parthenon in various combinations, to tie in with a commentary relating the history of the city. It's a stupendous show (with a pretentious commentary). It takes place every evening at 9pm in English, except on Good Friday.

To see the *son-et-lumière* show, you go to the small hill called Pnyx, which is on the south side of the Acropolis—the *far* side, if you're near Omónia Square or Sýntagma Square. If you don't want to walk, take bus no. 230, which goes along Dionysus Areopaghítou, past the Acropolis, and get off one stop past the Herod Atticus Odeum, where you'll find a sign that says SON-ET-LUMIÈRE. (Or take a taxi—it should cost less than $3—from either square.) From there, just follow the crowds. The 45-minute show costs 1,000 Drs ($4) (half price if you show a student card). If you don't want to spend even a couple of dollars, go to the Areopagus Hill; from that vantage point, you can see the show but won't hear the commentary or the music.

The *son-et-lumière* show is part of the Athens Festival (see "The Performing Arts" above).

Movies

You probably hadn't planned on taking in a movie on your trip to Athens, but if you're going to be in town for several days you may feel like seeing one some evening as a change of pace from Aristophanes and Euripides. In any case, movie-going in Greece is an experience in itself. Around the end of May, the indoor cinemas close up for the summer and take to the open air—wherever there's a space that's not currently a construction site or car park. If you go to the first showing, around 8:45 or 9pm, the sound is audible but the picture is faint; if you wait for the second show, after the sun has properly set, the picture may be clear but the sound may be almost inaudible so as not to antagonize the people living in nearby apartments (who have been known to show their resentment by turning their own radios and TVs up loud and switching on every available light). The films themselves are shown in their original language with Greek subtitles. Grab a Coke or beer and a bag of potato chips as you go in (everyone does). It may not be for the serious movie buff, but on a warm evening a visit to a movie can be fun and inexpensive—rarely more than 1,000 Drs ($4).

In case you want to call ahead for starting times, here are the telephone numbers of some of the leading *indoor* movie houses in Athens, open in winter only: **Asty,** Odós Koraí 4 (☎ **322-1925**); **Attikon,** Odós Stadíou 19A (☎ **322-8821**); **Embassy,** Odós Patriárchou Ioakím 5 (☎ **722-0903**); **Opera–Assos Odeon,** Odós Akadimías 57 (☎ **362-4269**); and **Radio City–Assos Odeon,** Odós Patissíon 240 at Odós Lissiatríon (☎ **862-4055**).

Casinos

If nightclubbing is too tame for you, try a casino. As of summer 1994, the closest gaming tables were on top of Mt. Parnes, an hour's drive north of Athens. Mt. Parnes has one of the largest casinos in Europe, with blackjack, roulette, punto banco, baccarat, chemin de fer, boule, and craps. All you need to get in is a jacket and tie (for men) and a passport; closed Wednesdays. For information, call **246-9111.**

The word is that the government will soon authorize the opening of new casinos in and around Athens, most notably at the Astir resort complex in Vouliagméni, about an hour south along the Apollo Coast. Since the Astir resort is a classier setup than Mt. Parnes, the opening of a casino there will be an exciting inducement for world-class players.

10

Easy Excursions from Athens

YOU'LL BE AMAZED AT HOW MANY TRIPS TO HOW MANY HISTORIC SITES YOU can make from Athens. Many of them can be completed in one day— there and back. To get some idea of the choices you have, skim through the catalog of the CHAT or Viking tour people: half-day tours to Cape Soúnio and the temple of Poseidon; half-day tours to Ancient Corinth and the Corinth Canal; half-day tours to Attica and Marathon; and 1-day tours to Mycenae, Náfplio, Epidaurus, Thebes, and Delphi. You can even make 1-day mini-odysseys to the Greek islands—and still be back in Athens in time for a night on Pláka.

You've already read about Cape Soúnio and the "Apollo Coast" in Chapter 6. Now here's a quick briefing on some of the other sights. Although I have grouped them here as day-trips, you may decide (wisely) to stay overnight, so I've included some comments, where appropriate, on accommodations.

1 Kaisarianí

5 miles from Downtown Athens

GETTING THERE • By Bus   Bus no. 234 runs every 20 minutes, more or less, from Polýgono, but there's also a stop on Káningos Street, near Omónia. It's a half-hour ride from downtown Athens and then a pleasant half-hour walk from the bus terminal (or a taxi ride).

Here you'll find the delightful 11th-century mini-monastery of Kaisarianí, or Caesariane. You can cheat and take a taxi for the last stage rather than walk, but then you won't appreciate the ice-cold water that gushes from the fountain in the monastery wall. In ancient times, these waters were believed to cure sterility, and they are still believed to have healthful if not magical qualities. It's quite safe to drink, and you will see many Greeks filling huge containers from the fountain.

You can visit the monastery's mill, bakery, bathhouse, refectory, and church, all in 20 minutes, if you wish; but it's much better to sit and relax in the peaceful surroundings for a spell before strolling back to the bus terminal. Kaisarianí lies almost at the base of Mt. Hymettus—so quiet and peaceful that it's difficult to believe you're just beyond the suburbs of Athens.

The monastery is open Tuesday to Sunday, 8:30am to 3pm; admission is 500 Drs ($2); telephone **723-6619.**

2 Delphi

110 miles NW of Athens

GETTING THERE • By Bus   The cheapest method of transportation is the regular bus service—only 3,900 Drs ($21) round-trip— which has a choice of five departures daily from the bus terminal at Odós Liossíon 260, a 3-hour trip.

Delphi Site Plan

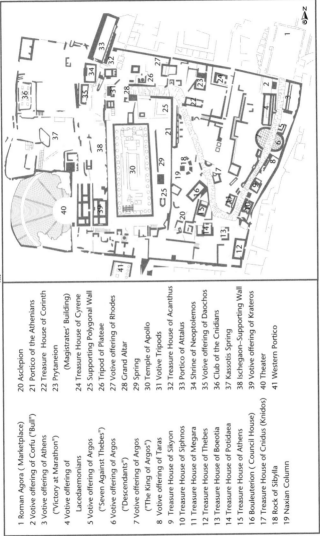

1 Roman Agora (Marketplace)
2 Votive offering of Corfu ("Bull")
3 Votive offering of Athens
   ("Victory at Marathon")
4 Votive offering of
   Lacedaemonians
5 Votive offering of Argos
   ("Seven Against Thebes")
6 Votive offering of Argos
   ("Descendants")
7 Votive offering of Argos
   ("The King of Argos")
8 Votive offering of Taras
9 Treasure House of Sikyon
10 Treasure House of Siphnos
11 Treasure House of Megara
12 Treasure House of Thebes
13 Treasure House of Boeotia
14 Treasure House of Potidaea
15 Treasure House of Athens
16 Bouleuterion (Council House)
17 Treasure House of Cnidus (Knidos)
18 Rock of Sibylla
19 Naxian Column

20 Asclepion
21 Portico of the Athenians
22 Treasure House of Corinth
23 Prytaneion
   (Magistrates' Building)
24 Treasure House of Cyrene
25 Supporting Polygonal Wall
26 Tripod of Plataea
27 Votive offering of Rhodes
28 Grand Altar
29 Spring
30 Temple of Apollo
31 Votive Tripods
32 Treasure House of Acanthus
33 Portico of Attalus
34 Shrine of Neoptolemos
35 Votive offering of Daochos
36 Club of the Cnidians
37 Kassotis Spring
38 Ischegaon–Supporting Wall
39 Votive offering of Krateros
40 Theater
41 Western Portico

• **By Car** The most convenient way to get to Delphi is to rent a car and drive. For the first third of the trip, drive on the relatively fast but tricky Athens-Thessaloníki National Highway; then, after an hour, turn off at the Delphi sign and start heading up into the mountains (where the roads are being improved enormously).

This is a tough trip, and you should either leave very early in the morning to get to the site before the museum closes for siesta or arrive in time for a leisurely lunch, an afternoon visit to the ruins and the museum, lingering there through sunset, then facing the after-dark drive back to Athens (allow 4 hours in this case). Better still, stay the night in Delphi and drive back the next day, stopping at the quaint hilltop town of Aráchova and the monastery of Óssios Loukás along the way.

• **By Organized Tour**   The simplest way to get to Delphi is to take a 1-day coach tour, in air-conditioned comfort, with a guide to explain the ruins and sights along the way. **Key Tours, American Express,** and **CHAT** operate 1-day tours (8:15am to 6:30pm), costing 14,900 Drs ($60) including lunch (12,900 Drs, or $52, without lunch) and a visit to the nearby monastery of Óssios Loukás. The 2-day tour is much better if you can afford the time, because you can spend more time among the magnificent ruins and see them (and photograph them) at sunrise or sunset; this full 34-hour tour costs 24,650 Drs ($99), with half board in air-conditioned hotels.

The famous city of the oracle is in that richly historical part of Greece known as Boeotia (*Viotía* in Greek). Thermopylae and Thebes are not far off. The combination of ruggedly grand scenery and the haunting quality of the ruins makes it one of the most dramatic sights in all of Greece.

What to See & Do

For centuries, the story of Delphi was the story of Mediterranean politics. Hardly a decision was reached without consulting the oracles at the Apollo temple. Evidently, the mountain exuded strange fumes (now considered water vapors or carbon monoxide) that put shepherds and peasant women into trances and led to prophetic pronouncements. In the magnificent setting of Mt. Parnassos, with eagles soaring from peak to peak, it was easy to believe that here you stood in the presence of the gods.

Initially, the name of the site was Pytho, and the Earth Mother known for her prophetic powers lived there. Later, seafarers from Knossós, in Crete, introduced the cult of Apollo Delphinius. The story starts with Apollo disguising himself as a dolphin. He jumps into the water and captures a Cretan ship, returning both booty and prisoners to Delphi. The prisoners become "priests" in his sanctuary, and Delphi's reputation for wisdom and prophecy is consolidated.

IMPRESSIONS

Delphi I should think the Greekest thing of all.
—Henry Adams, 1898

Above these mountains proud Olympus tow'rs.
The parliamental seat of heavenly pow'rs.
—Mary Wortley Montagu, *Verses Written in the Chiosk at Pera,*
Overlooking Constantinople, 1718

Nearby personages came to consult with the gods. And as was the custom, they brought gifts. From the 8th to the 4th century B.C., before an envious Nero looted the temples after Rome's conquest, the gift-giving and advice-seeking rose to such proportions that Delphi became a huge complex of treasures and temples, all laden with works of art and riches.

Today, Delphi consists mainly of a theater, a sanctuary, an athletic area surrounded by a wall, and an excellent museum. But it is more than a ruins-cum-museum site—it's a total environment. Start your exploration from the main road, which leads both to the town and to the ruins. Gaze toward the ruins, noting the distant views, the colors (especially at sunset and sunrise), and the sheer valley below. Then amble through the ruins, starting with the **Marmaria** and the **Castalian Spring,** both of which are located below the main road. The ancient Greeks regarded springs as gifts of the gods. Steps leading to the water can be seen carved into the solid rock surface. Then walk up the hill beyond the road, onto the main site.

The **Sacred Way** is a path leading from the entrance to the stadium. Follow it as it zigs and zags between half-columns, perches, stones, and the **Treasury of the Athenians.** The treasury is easy to recognize: it's almost completely reconstructed, using the original blocks of Parian marble. Look for the inscription on the marble:

> *The Athenians dedicate to Apollo*
> *the Persian spoils*
> *from the Battle of Marathon.*

At the top of the site is the **theater,** built for an audience of 5,000, a model of engineering and aesthetic brilliance. Farther up the hill is a 5th-century stadium almost 200 yards long.

Returning from the ruins to town, stop at the **museum** near the entrance to the site and go immediately to the *Charioteer,* the famous bronze sculpture from the 5th century B.C., one of the great masterpieces of Greek art. The museum's art pieces are mainly from the Mycenaean period (1600–1100 B.C.). Note particularly the Roman *Statue of Antinous,* a column of *Acanthus Dancing Girls,* and the *Wingless Sphinx of the Naxians,* a characteristic work of the 6th century B.C. The museum is open Monday from 11am to 5pm; Tuesday to Friday from 8am to 5pm; Saturday, Sunday, and holidays from 8:30am to 3pm. Admission is 1,000 Drs ($4).

For at least six centuries, Delphi's priests held most of the known world in thrall. Their ambiguous interpretations of the unintelligible ramblings from the "oracle" changed the course of history many times—and brought riches and incalculable power to a canny bunch of priests in a tiny mountainous village.

How it all began doesn't appear to be on record, but from the 7th century B.C. onward the god known as Phoebus Apollo was heard to be speaking through the mouth of an old woman known as the pythia, and her words, after being placed into neat hexameters by the priest-interpreters, made kings tremble and emperors lose their sleep.

Ordinary people consulted the oracle, too, of course; the gods were willing to answer the question of anybody who brought money. More often than not, important people brought silver, gold, precious stones, and other gifts, and Delphi soon built up considerable treasure.

There was a set routine for the pythia to follow on pronouncement days (which at first took place only during February, the month of Apollo's birthday). The routine was strictly adhered to by one pythia after another through the centuries.

First, the woman had to fast for three days and then, on the set day, bathe in the nearby Castalian Spring; then she burned laurel leaves at the altar, drank some water, and took up her place beside the copper-and-gold tripod set up over the fissure in the ground from which came "intoxicating vapors." Working her way into a trance, she would then mumble garbled replies to questions asked of her. Sometimes the questions concerned banal personal problems and sometimes they concerned matters of state. But all got answers, usually so cryptic that they could be construed to mean anything at all, and seekers invariably went away happy.

A king who was told that if he crossed a certain river a great empire would be destroyed was chagrined to discover that the empire was his own. A man who came to ask about his stammer was instructed to go live in another country. The Roman emperor Nero was warned to "beware 73"—and died well before he reached that age at the hands of Galvus, who was 73.

Naturally, there were some skeptics, among them Aesop, but the Delphi city fathers had providentially anticipated that by instituting formal trials for those they charged with sacrilege. The sentence was usually to toss the guilty off a high cliff onto the jagged rocks below.

That well-known heretic Socrates may well have been thinking about Delphi when he announced that "the augur should be under the authority of the general and not the general under the authority of the augur." His advice should have been taken to heart in 480 B.C., when Xerxes prepared to invade Greece with the combination of a massive army and fleet of ships. Athenians consulted the Delphic oracle to find out what to do. They were told the following:

Wretches, why sit ye here? Fly, fly to the ends of creation.
Nay, not alone shall ye suffer, full many a town shall be
*   leveled;*
Many a shrine of the gods will he give to fiery destruction
Get ye away from the Temple and brood on the doom that
*   awaits you.*

Athens, and most of Greece, were naturally in a panic. The message, for once, hardly seemed ambiguous, and some were ready to take it at face value and flee. But wiser counsels prevailed, and the Athenians and their Spartan allies held the northern passes until Themistocles built up the navy (here the Delphic oracle redeemed itself somewhat with a prediction that the city would be saved by its "wooden walls") and eventually repelled the invasion attempt.

Delphi, however, never entirely recovered from this erroneous taking of sides; and although the world rallied with contributions after an earthquake had almost destroyed the town in 373 B.C., the oracle's influence continued to decline. But worse was to come.

In 356 B.C. a band of Phocians from the west suddenly invaded the town and captured the shrine along with all its wealth. For a time, they terrorized their neighbors by raising an army of mercenaries paid with their newfound treasure, but eventually the shrine was restored to the priests, who continued their prognostications for three centuries more.

The coming of the Christian era was the beginning of the end. In A.D. 381, the emperor Theodosius outlawed "paganism," and Delphi passed into history.

Where to Stay

For a tiny town (population 800, more or less), Delphi certainly offers visitors a vast selection of accommodations, but then it has had a long time to practice being a host. The main street alone has over a dozen hotels, most of them inexpensive; those on the left side as you walk into the town are the most interesting, because they're perched on the edge of a cliff looking all the way across the plain to the Gulf of Corinth.

Among the finer hotels are the Amalia and the Xenia, both on Odós Apóllonos. **Amalia Hotel** (☎ **0265/82101**) has 185 rooms (rates, including half board, are 24,100 Drs or $96 double), with telephone and air conditioning; it offers a bar, a restaurant, room service, and free parking. The smaller **Xenia Hotel** (44 rooms, from about 18,500 Drs or $74 double) also has a bar and restaurant, as well as free parking.

Kastalia Hotel, Odós Vassiléos Pávlou 13 (☎ **0265/82205**), has only 22 rooms (10,800 Drs or $43 double) but offers a TV lounge, a bar and restaurant, as well as a roof garden, and free parking. **Acropole Hotel,** Odós Filellínon 13 (☎ **0265/82676**), which has 35 rooms with telephone (about 6,500 Drs or $26 double), offers a bar, a TV lounge, and a breakfast room, as well as free parking; it has partial air conditioning.

3   Marathon

26 miles from Downtown Athens

GETTING THERE • By Bus   Buses leave Athens (from the terminal at Odós Mavromatéon 29) for the Marathon battlefield approximately every half hour. The ride takes about 1 hour and costs 600 Drs ($2).

This, of course, is where the famous battle was fought in 490 B.C., when the Athenians trounced the Persians and the messenger Pheidippides ran the 26 miles back to the city, gasped out the news of victory—"*Nenikíkamen!*" ("We've won!")—and flopped down dead. The site of the battle is now marked by a tomb, in which the cremated remains of the Greek soldiers lie buried, and by a white marble column.

An **archeological museum** (☎ **0294/55155**) is at the site; it has displays of various finds unearthed at Marathon, from the Neolithic period to the Byzantine era. The museum is open Tuesday through Sunday from 8:30am to 3pm. The tomb of the Athenians is open during the same hours. Admission is 400 Drs ($2).

4 Eastern Peloponnese

The next batch of destinations are all on the peninsula known as the Peloponnese ("island of Pelops"), the almost-island chunk of land that makes up the southwestern corner of Greece. It's a region of mountain scenery highlighted by an incredible collection of ancient monuments and brightened by flashes of beach and sea.

Corinth

The first landmark you come to in the Peloponnese is the **Corinth Canal.** This channel, 3¹/₂ miles long and 75 feet wide, makes the peninsula an island, and chops 185 miles from the voyage between Italy and Piraeus. It was built between 1882 and 1893, but it was originally conceived way back in the days of Nero and Hadrian. In fact, Nero got so far as to dig the first shovelful—with a golden spade. But it didn't get much beyond Nero's first shovelful, and shipowners had to continue hauling their ships overland, over the *diolkos,* a stone-paved track, traces of which you can still see here and there.

This suited the Corinthians fine, because they supplied the hauling power and collected the fees. They also collected tolls on all cargos heading between the peninsula and the mainland and between the Gulf of Corinth and the Saronic Gulf. Their wealth made them self-indulgent, and at one point the city could boast 1,000 "sacred prostitutes," who plied their trade in the name and to the honor of Aphrodite. No wonder St. Paul came along and gave the Corinthians a tongue-lashing. The tribune where he delivered his sermon is still there in Ancient Corinth.

There are now two Corinths. The new city was destroyed by an earthquake in 1928, and an even newer one was built after that. Its main interest for visitors is as a base for excursions to the fascinating surroundings. The more fascinating of the two is **Ancient Corinth.** It, too, was completely destroyed—by the Romans in 146 B.C.; most of what you see today dates from 44 B.C., when Caesar set up a colony here. The principal sites are the 6th-century temple of Apollo, St. Paul's tribune, the agora, and the Pirene fountain.

Acrocorinth is a mighty citadel towering over the town. This was originally the site of the temple of Aphrodite. The citadel was built by the Byzantines and at various stages was subtracted from or added to by Crusaders, Venetians, and Turks. Today you get a great view from the top. You can drive to the entrance up a precipitous dirt road, and both the view and the citadel justify the effort. There's a coffee shop at the top of the hill.

The Peloponnese

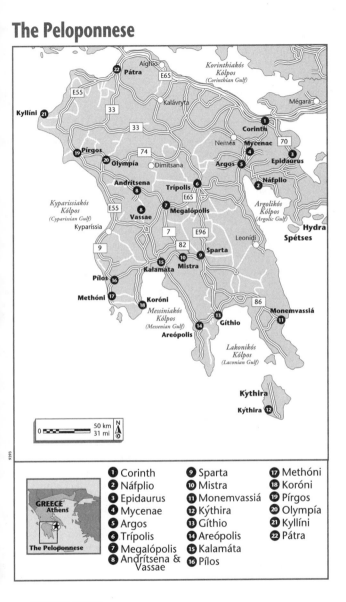

❶ Corinth	❾ Sparta	⓰ Methóni
❷ Náfplio	❿ Mistra	⓲ Koróni
❸ Epidaurus	⓫ Monemvassiá	⓳ Pírgos
❹ Mycenae	⓬ Kýthira	⓴ Olympía
❺ Argos	⓭ Gíthio	㉑ Kyllíni
❻ Trípolis	⓮ Areópolis	㉒ Pátra
❼ Megalópolis	⓯ Kalamáta	
❽ Andrítsena & Vassae	⓰ Pílos	

GETTING THERE

The full-day sightseeing tours leave Athens at 8:30am and return at
7pm, after stops also at Mycenae, Náfplio, and Epidaurus, and cost
13,900 Drs ($56) without lunch, 15,900 Drs ($64) with. You can
also get there by diesel train, rail, or bus from Athens (every half hour
from Kifissoú terminal; 2,000 Drs or $8 round-trip) or in roughly
1¹/₂ hours by car, on the National Highway.

Epidaurus

GETTING THERE

You can get to Epidaurus (Epídavros) by regular bus service from Athens via Náfplio, about 2,500 Drs ($10) one-way. During the festival, there's a special Pullman bus service from Athens directly to Epidaurus on days of the performance only (but you'd better have your hotel concierge make a reservation in advance).

WHAT TO SEE & DO

This town, 20 miles from Náfplio but on the Saronic Gulf, is famed for two things. In the 6th century B.C. it was a place of pilgrimage, a sort of Lourdes, where sick people journeyed to find a cure in the **sanctuary of Asclepius**, the god of healing. There was more than faith involved, however, and you can still see inscriptions of prescriptions in the sanctuary and in the nearby **museum,** as well as the votive offerings brought by the people who had been cured. (**Note:** There's a whole room of the National Archeological Museum in Athens devoted to friezes and statues on this subject—always with an oversize god-doctor seated nonchalantly at his desk, while Hygeia, his nurse, collects the loot from the patients, who are usually depicted as small and humble. Sound familiar?)

Other sights at Epidaurus include the **Greek Bath** (where the sick washed themselves); the **Abaton** (the so-called portico of incubation), where the sick slept on beds waiting for an apparition of the god who would cure them in their sleep; the **Roman bath;** the **stadium;** and the **museum.** The museum is open from 8am to 5pm during the week; Saturday, Sunday, and holidays from 8:30am to 3pm. Admission is 1,000 Drs ($4).

The other great sight of Epidaurus is the **ancient theater** with its circular "orchestra" and 50 tiers for 14,000 spectators. It was built in the 4th century B.C. by Polycleitus the Younger, who ought to be around today to teach acoustics to his successors; despite the theater's size and age, its acoustics are so perfect that you can hear the performers' gowns trailing across the stage. Fortunately, you can still enjoy the benefits of these acoustics, because performances are given here every summer during the **Epidaurus Festival** (in June and July). Contact the Greek Tourist Organization (EOT) for details of dates and plays.

Mycenae

Mycenae, identified on some maps, signposts, and guides as Mikínes (its modern Greek name), is the mountain palace/fortress of Agamemnon, "lord of the many islands and all of Argos." (This part of the Peloponnese, including Náfplio and Epidaurus, is in a region known as the Argolia.) This is the place that gave its name to an entire civilization that was cock-of-the-walk in the 14th century B.C., although some of the archeological digs have uncovered evidence that the area was inhabited as early as 3000 B.C. What you see there today are the impressive entrance to the royal palace (the **Lion Gate**) and the remains of granaries, reservoirs, and the **shaft graves** that sheltered the golden treasures of Mycenaean art (Homer's "Golden Mycenae") for all those thousands of years, before they were carted off to the National Archeological Museum in Athens. Just outside the fortress walls, you can see nine **beehive tombs,** one of which is thought to be the tomb of Clytemnestra (who, you'll remember, bumped off her husband, Agamemnon, before she in turn was disposed of by her son, Orestes); one of the others is probably the tomb of Agamemnon himself. Admission to the site is 1,000 Drs ($4). Open Wednesday through Monday from 8:30am to 3pm.

GETTING THERE

Take the regular bus from Athens to Náfplio (see next page) and get off at Argos, where you catch a local bus to Mycenae; there's also a train service from Athens to Fichtiá, a couple of miles by bus from the ruins.

Corinth, Mycenae, Náfplio, and Epidaurus are included in 1-day (one-crowded-day) sightseeing tours from Athens. The tours leave at 8:15am and return at 6:30pm, and cost 14,900 Drs ($60), including lunch at Náfplio.

Náfplio

I've kept this one to the end of the eastern Peloponnese group because although Náfplio (also Náfplion and Nauplion) is an easy day-trip from Athens, it also makes an ideal tour center if you want to stay overnight (or over nights) and do a series of morning and afternoon excursions to Mycenae, Epidaurus, and other attractions, such as the ruins of ancient Tiryns; you can also take longer trips to Porto Heli and the island of Spétses (also Spétsai).

Depending on your first impression, Náfplio is a holiday resort, a medieval fortress town, or a picturesque little port. A walk around town tells you it's all three. Náfplio was also at one time the capital of Greece, right after its liberation from the Turks. The tiny island fortress, **Bourtzi,** out in the bay, was built by Venetians; the **Akronáfplio** citadel towering over the town's south side was built on the site of an even more ancient acropolis; and the town's third fortress, **Palamidi,** is actually seven fortresses in one, built by the Franks and added to by several later conquerors. Náfplio is now a pleasant resort, its waterfront lined with cafés and tavernas and with steep stairways that lead to narrow streets lined with more tavernas, some boutiques, and a few boîtes. If you walk past the cafés, you'll find a narrow pathway by the sea running around the base of the Akronáfplio; at the opposite end, it leads up to the fortress itself, where you can take the elevator of the deluxe Xenia Palace Hotel back down to town.

GETTING THERE

You can get to Náfplio by regular hourly bus service from Athens. Buses leave every hour on the half hour from the Kifissoú terminal; round-trip fare is 3,400 Drs ($14) for the 2^{1}/$_{2}$-hour ride. It's also included on most of the 1-day and 2-day coach tours to the Peloponnese.

WHERE TO STAY

If you decide to stay overnight, there's a wider selection of hotels here than in other towns in the region. However, since it's also one of the most popular spots in Greece at any time of the year, you must always make reservations in advance. You may have to pay a half-board rate; and the attitude of the hotel personnel, especially in the two Xenias, tends to be off-hand.

Xenia Palace, Akronáfplio. ☎ **0752/28981.** Telex 298154 XENI GR. 48 rms, 54 bungalows. A/C TEL

> **Rates** (including half board): 25,000–30,000 Drs ($100–$120) single or double. AE, DC, MC, V. **Parking:** Available.

This is the most interesting hotel in town, built right on top of the Akronáfplio, with all its rooms overlooking the bay and the fortress of Bourtzi. There's room service—and a swimming pool in the garden.

Amalia Hotel, 21100 Néa Tirýnthia. ☎ **0752/24401.** Fax 0752/24400. Telex 215161 AMAL GR.

> **Rates** (including half board): From 24,100 Drs ($97) double. AE, DC, MC, V. **Parking:** Available.

The Amalia is located near the waterfront but on the edge of town. Built in neoclassical style, it has comfortable rooms, a pool, and a stylish restaurant. It also has room service.

Xenia Hotel, Akronáfplio. ☎ **0752/28990.** Telex 298154 XENI GR. 58 rms.

> **Rates** (including half board): From 17,350 Drs ($70) double. AE, DC, MC, V. **Parking:** Available.

The down-scale brother of the Palace stands on the shoulder of the acropolis. Half of its rooms face the bay, and half face the gulf and the fortress of Palimida (which is not necessarily the less interesting view of the two).

5 Mini-Odyssey

Everybody wants to see the Greek islands, but not everyone has the time to be away from Athens for a few days. No problem. You just take the subway down to Piraeus, hop on a ferry, and sail across to an island with pine-clad hills, valleys of vineyards and pistachio trees, and a ruined temple overlooking a bay; or an island with a harbor ringed by restaurants and surrounded by a hillside of small palazzos; or an island with no cars where the only way to get around is by horse-drawn carriage or donkey. If you want to explore these Saronic Gulf islands independently, read on. If you're pressed for time, or want to sample more than one island, call CHAT, Viking Tours, Key Tours, American Express, or some other tour operator. Have them pick you up at your hotel and drive you to Paleó Phálero—and leave everything else to them.

"Everything else" will add up to a memorable day that's part Mediterranean cruise exploration, part sightseeing, part sunning, and wholly relaxing. Say that you decide to take the cruise: A bus will collect you; transfer you to a second bus; and drive you down to Paleó Phálero, a marina at the end of Leofóros Syngroú; there, you'll board your cruise ship and head out of the harbor past the private yachts and the three-masted schooners waiting patiently for busy shipping tycoons to come and take them out for a sail.

There are currently half a dozen ships operating this three-island cruise of the Saronic Gulf—some as big as 3,000 tons, some with cabins that you can rent by the day. All of them have swimming pools, plenty of deck space for sunning, as well as dining salons, lounges, bars, hostesses, and boutiques for souvenirs and film. Mini-odyssey fares are around $65.

Your first port of call, 1¼ hours out, is the island of **Aegina.** This is the closest island to Athens and consequently one of the busiest on weekends. Aegina is a hilly little island, with a precipitous town perched above the dock, with a few cafés, a bakery shop, a souvenir shop or two, and a movie house.

You can go to the beach or can join a tour up through the pistachio plantations and vineyards to the almost mystical **Temple of Aphaea,** "a very ancient local deity," with a hexastyle Doric temple built of local limestone. (See below for more on Aegina.) Back on board, you then have lunch (a simple tray lunch). An hour later, you come to one of the most interesting parts of the cruise as the ship squeezes through the Strait of Póros.

Póros is a conical island with a tiny village (also called Póros) that's a classic of its kind—a jumble of whitewashed buildings piled above the harbor, which also constitutes the roadway, the sidewalk, and the plaza and is totally hidden under a mass of awnings and café tables that come right down to the edge of the water. Unfortunately, some of the ships don't stop here, so you may want to mark Póros down in your diary as one of those places that you have to come back to some day.

The next stop is **Hydra,** a bleak, rocky, undulating island, until you get into the harbor, which you immediately recognize from a thousand photographs. It's unique. The ship sails right into this small bowl-like haven, almost right into the nearest café, next to the fishing boats and the tiny ferries that shuttle cargo and people back and forth to the Peloponnese. (See below for more on Hydra.) You have 1½ hours there, so you can either flop into one of the cafés and admire the harbor or wander around to the rocky cove on the other side of the bay and join the artists, writers, and jet-setters in the unbelievably clear rockbound sea. (**Note:** Some of the ships reverse this itinerary, giving you a longer stay on Hydra; for details on voyaging to the island on your own, see below.)

By the time you sail for home, the sun is low in the sky and glistening on the sea, and you can enjoy a comfortable cocktail on deck; by the time you get to Piraeus and the waiting buses, the sun has settled behind the mountains of the Peloponnese. You've cruised on the Mediterranean, you've seen three islands, and you've probably had a swim in the "Med." Not a bad day for 7,500 Drs ($30) or thereabouts.

Independent Trips

If you don't feel like following an organized itinerary, you can easily get to any of these islands by ferryboat or hydrofoil. That way you get to go ashore at Póros, too, and you'll also be able to visit the fourth and farthest island of the group, Spétses (the one with no cars), and maybe catch a glimpse of Spetsopoúla, the private island of Stavros Niarchos, the shipping tycoon. There's plenty to see on all of these islands—ruined temples, monasteries, and picturesque fishing villages with almost as many tavernas as houses—but most people come over to find a secluded stretch of beach (and there are hundreds of those).

AEGINA

Perhaps the most interesting (and, at 20 miles southwest of Piraeus, the most accessible) of these islands for a one-day excursion is Aegina (Aíghina). To get there independently, you go down to the docks at Piraeus as early as possible in the morning and take the first available regular ferry, express ferry, or hydrofoil (the hydrofoil takes only 35 minutes; the ferry, 75 minutes). When you arrive at the main town of Aegina, find out when the next bus leaves for Aghía Marína; while you're waiting, stroll along the front and have an ouzo with a small platter of freshly grilled octopus.

You arrive in a typical Greek isle waterfront—a tiny whitewashed chapel guarding the entrance to a harbor that has been used by fisherfolk since classical times, a curving waterfront lined with terrace cafés, tavernas, and shops, as well as colorful caïques moored against the quay and piled with fruits and vegetables and fish. Horse-drawn carriages are waiting to trot you along the waterfront, but at $11 for 20 minutes you're better taking a leisurely stroll, stopping off for coffee and pastry at Eakion. When it's time to head off for some sightseeing, walk to the end of the quay, past the ferry dock, to the bus stop and board a bus marked AGHIA MARINA.

The bus takes you right across the island through fig and pistachio plantations, past fields of olives and almonds, and across the mountains to your first stop, the **Temple of Aphaea,** a 5th-century B.C. marvel in limestone perched at the top of a steep hill above Aghía Marína, a temple that some people rate alongside those at Delphi and Soúnio. Pause and admire. Have a coffee or soft drink at Taki's gift shop (opposite the entrance) while you decide on your next move. If you opt for sunbathing and swimming, take the bus on down to Aghía Marína (or follow the path down through the fields and vineyards, a 20-minute hike). During the summer months, incidentally, you can catch the boat back to the mainland from Aghía Marína.

If, instead, you opt for more sightseeing, get on a bus heading back to the town of Aegina and ask the conductor to put you off at Paleochóra (if the bus is crowded, sit near the driver and keep reminding him). At Paleochóra (Old Town—it was once the ancient capital), leave the bus and strike off right, up the hillside, until you come to a hill dotted with numerous tiny churches and monasteries. Right at the top of this hill there's also a ruined castle. Peek inside some of the churches along the way to admire the Byzantine frescoes, some of them barely visible. You should allow yourself a good two hours for this visit (and wear sturdy walking shoes). In springtime the hillside is a riot of red and yellow flowers; in midsummer it's a good idea to take a bottle of water with you as the nearest café is opposite the bus stop, back down by the main road.

You can also get around the island by taxi (for less than 5,000 Drs or $20, with a little negotiating, from Aegina town to Aghía Marína and Paleochóra and back) or by renting a motor scooter, about 4,000 Drs ($16) from one of the stores on the waterfront.

One of the pleasures of the Aegina waterfront, or *paralía,* is the array of terrace cafés, pastry shops, and tavernas. Try lunch or dinner under the canvas awnings at Costas Besis or Economou, where you can make a meal of fish soup (which consists of broth and a side dish piled with, say, cod), Greek salad, and a small carafe of wine for around 2,500 Drs ($10).

A word of advice: Before setting off into the hinterland of Aegina, check the times of the last ferries back to Piraeus. Don't wait for the last one, and buy your ticket in advance. All Athens, it seems, heads for Aegina on weekends in summer.

HYDRA

Whether you sail to Hydra (Ýdra) by ferryboat or hydrofoil, you enter a picturesque little harbor that is one of Greece's prettiest, despite the prominent DISCO HEAVEN sign on one side.

Caïques, fishing boats, fishing nets, and fishermen abound. There are hundreds of cats on the prowl, waiting dockside to snatch the stray fish head before it hits the ground. (You can even buy small food packets for them at 250 Drs or $1 each.) Burros are lined up, patiently waiting to be laden down with groceries, bags of cement, or tourists—this is an island with no cars.

Hydra had its heyday in the time of Napoleon, when more than 30,000 people lived there; now the population is down to a little more than 2,000, and many of them are artists or writers, or gallivanting jet-setters. The town is different from any other in these parts because it's terraced with a type of house known as the Hydriot palazzo, dating from the 19th century. Hydra's own color, *lomuláki* blue, outlines door frames, windows, and shutters.

Right in the harbor, you'll hear the clocktower ringing in the hours; behind its green-grilled gates lies the clocktower courtyard, once a monastery, now the town hall. The harbor road is lined with the ubiquitous Greek souvenir and jewelry shops, but walk farther along that same road and you'll come to the Merchant Navy Training School, with its mounted cannons at the harbor entrance. Or you may want to visit some of Hydra's famous *archontiká,* or mansions: Most impressive are those of the Kountouriotis family, now a museum dedicated to memorabilia from the War of Independence, and the Voulgaris and Tombazis families.

But there's a whole island behind that charming little harbor that many of the day-trippers never get to. Hike up Odós Miaoúli, the pretty little cobbled street that curves uphill away from the harbor. Along the way are beautiful homes built right into the rock croppings. Citrus trees, geranium and ivy vines, and huge cacti fill up every inch of garden and terrace space. Cats hang out in trees like squirrels, dogs doze on garden walls, olive trees shade the steep steps up to some lucky soul's villa.

If you start your walk early in the morning, the first thing that lets you know you've left town is the sounds: cheeping birds, loud chickens and even louder geese, raucous roosters and unbridled burros, buzzing bees.

There are some terrific choices for hikes in Hydra. All Souls Church, with its white campanile and terra-cotta roof, offers a cool respite and a great view of the harbor, neighboring mainland, and the monastery below. The monastery itself also has a harbor view, an eternal blessing, since, judging from the number of anchors on the tombstones, there must be many a sailor buried here.

The goat path beyond the monastery leads to the island's other side. In and up a steep ravine, the only sounds are birds and sheep bells; the only sights are green gorse, gray stone, blue skies, and the occasional peek at the harbor. Keep going until the path stops between the ruins of two windmills, where there's a truly panoramic view of the Peloponnese and the choice of two monasteries (Aghía Matróni and Ághios Mamás), should you wish to continue your walk.

Back at the harbor, **Laiko** taverna offers comfy seats to rest weary feet. Indoors, the cream-colored walls are lined with 19th-century oil paintings, and you can check out what's doing in the kitchen. There's a pleasant outdoor seating area; though if you pick the right seat, it looks as if all the boats entering the harbor are headed straight for your table. Laiko's fish dishes run around 1,900 Drs ($8); other à la carte items from 1,000 to 1,200 Drs ($4 to $5).

Ferry Services from Piraeus*

	No. of Departures	
To	Weekdays	Weekends
Aegina	32	48
Póros	12	12
Hydra	4	4
Spétses	4	4

* Fares are around 5,000 Drs ($20), round-trip. But because they are subject to change, they may be slightly higher when you visit. Call **451-1311** for further information.

HYDROFOILS

During the summer months (and on calm days in spring and fall), you also have the choice of a **hydrofoil** trip to these islands aboard the Flying Dolphins of Ceres Flying Hydroways or the Ilios Line's Iliodolphins. They're Soviet-built hydrofoils, and they tend to be noisy; there's very little deck space on top. The fares are almost double those of the regular ferryboat, and the ride can be unpleasant on choppy seas. Nevertheless, the hydrofoils do get you to the islands quickly (just 2 hours all the way to Spétses), so they're popular with Athenians. The Flying Dolphins now also serve locations on the Peloponnese coast, getting you there more quickly than a car (but if the sea is rough, you may prefer the traffic jams), as well as select Greek islands.

For full details of all schedules to these islands, check with the reception desk of your hotel or with the Greek Tourist Organization (EOT) information services at Sýntagma Square in Athens; don't be discouraged if they hedge their answers, because the published schedules don't always tally with reality. In addition, *double-check your ticket* as soon as you pay for it, to make sure that it's for the correct shipping company and correct vessel and correct destination; mistakes have been made, and it's usually impossible to have your money refunded. But don't let these words of caution dissuade you—your trip to the Saronic islands can be one of the highlights of your vacation.

Fares may be higher in summer and subject to change without notice. For further information, call the Flying Dolphins at **428-0001,** or the Iliodolphins at **322-5139.**

Sample Hydrofoil Fares from Piraeus & Zéa Marina

Piraeus to Aegina	1,407 Drs ($6)
Zéa to Hydra	3,386 Drs ($14)
Zéa to Spétses	3,761 Drs ($15)
Zéa to Monemvassiá	6,187 Drs ($25)

6 Western Peloponnese, Central Greece & Northern Greece

There's now an efficient network of bus routes fanning out from Athens through the country to 66 cities and towns. The buses are big, comfortable, and mostly Pullman-type, and the fares are remarkably low. The fare from Athens to Thessaloníki in the north is about 11,000 Drs ($44) round-trip. Athens to Delphi is around 3,900 Drs ($16) round-trip. The services operate several times a day—for example, 13 departures daily to Messolónghi, 8 a day to Pýrgos (for Olympia), and 6 a day to four different towns in Thessaly.

Greek State Railways operates 195 diesel trains to the Peloponnese and the north and supplement them with Pullman coaches into the smaller towns. There are five trains daily to Pýrgos (4,320 Drs or $17 round-trip) and Pátra (3,610 Drs or $13 round-trip), as well as to Thessaloníki (6,880 Drs or $27 round-trip). These are the least expensive ways of getting around in Greece.

Sightseeing Tours by Coach

Most of the tour companies in Athens also offer a choice of conducted tours of the hinterlands lasting for from 3 to 9 days. Some are seasonal, roughly March through October. Check with your hotel concierge for details of tours by CHAT, American Express, and Key Tours. Meantime, here are some samples of the range of tours and typical prices available.

FOUR-DAY CLASSICAL TOUR

This includes Corinth, Mycenae (lunch), Epidaurus, Náfplio (overnight), Trípolis, Vytína, Olympia (lunch, dinner, overnight), Pátra, ferry ride from Río to Antírio, and Delphi (lunch, dinner, overnight). The cost is 84,000 Drs ($336), with half board.

FIVE-DAY ARCHEOLOGICAL TOUR

This includes Corinth, Mycenae (lunch), Epidaurus, Náfplio (dinner, overnight), Trípolis, Sparta (lunch), Mystrá, Sparta or Trípolis (dinner, overnight), Vytína, Olympia (lunch, dinner, overnight), Pátra, ferry ride from Río to Antírio, and Delphi (lunch, dinner, overnight). The cost is 108,000 Drs ($432), with half board (CHAT only).

SIX-DAY NORTHERN GREECE TOUR

This includes Thebes, Aráchova, Delphi (lunch, dinner, overnight), Amphíssa, Lamía, Tríkkala, Kalambáka (dinner, overnight), Metéora, Lárissa, Valley of Tempi, Plátamo, Thessaloníki (dinner, overnight), Amphípolis, Philippi, Kavála (dinner, overnight), Thássos (lunch), Kavála, Thessaloníki (dinner, overnight), Pélla, Lárissa (lunch), Thermopylae, and Kamména Voúrla. The cost is 120,000 Drs ($480), with half board (CHAT only).

Again: Not all these tours leave every day of the week, and not all operate year-round; your travel agent can find the tour and operator that best suit your schedule.

Touring Greece by Car

In the end, if you have the time, the cash, and the inclination, the best way to tour Greece is by car. The Greek government has been forging ahead with its road-building program; and although there are only limited stretches of expressway, there are now good, comfortable roads linking all the major tourist areas.

There's an expressway, National Highway 1, all the way from Athens, along the eastern shores of Attica, through Lamía, Lárissa, and Katería to Thessaloníki—a distance of just over 300 miles. And there's another one from Athens, around the Saronic Gulf to Corinth and along the northern shore of the Peloponnese to Pátra (where you can catch a ferryboat to Italy). There's also a new extension of the expressway that goes from Corinth south to the city of Epidaurus.

Central Greece

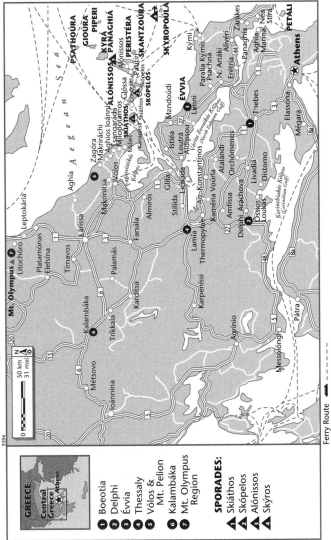

N

50 km
31 mi
0

9394

Ferry Route

GREECE

Central
Greece

1 Boeotia
2 Delphi
3 Évvia
4 Thessaly
5 Vólos & Mt. Pelion
6 Kalambáka
7 Mt. Olympus Region

SPORADES:
1 Skiáthos
2 Skópelos
3 Alónissos
4 Skýros

These highways are considered expressways in Greece, and you have to pay tolls (trifling amounts) on some stretches, but don't zoom onto them expecting an interstate highway or you'll be disappointed—in addition to which you'll have your timetable thrown for a loop. The stretch of National Highway 1 from Athens to Thebes (the turnoff for Delphi) is a four-lane highway, without dividers and with an unmarked shoulder on the right, so that most drivers seem to position themselves halfway between the right lane and the passing lane. Also, the standard of driving in Greece is probably the most immature this side of the Middle East. This doesn't mean that you shouldn't drive in Greece—it's simply a warning to drive with extra care and not to plan on averaging more than 40 m.p.h.

But you don't need an expressway to enjoy some pleasurable driving. The coastal road from Athens to Soúnio, for example, is a well-engineered corniche-type highway with many bends but no tricky corners, and there are some fine, scenic roads in the mountains of Arcadia and around Olympia.

Distances in Greece are manageable, and you can cover a lot of territory even with leisurely driving. The table below will give you an idea of the distances involved in traveling to some of the larger cities.

Distances from Athens

To	Kilometers
Corinth	84
Ioánnina	444
Kalamáta	283
Kardítsa	302
Katerína	440
Lamía	215
Lárissa	356
Messolónghi	248
Náfplio	145
Náoussa	533
Pátra	217
Thessaloníki	539

7 Seeing the Islands

Olympic Airways, its subsidiary, Olympic Aviation, and Greek shipping companies operate "bus" services by plane or ferry to many of the islands, and between them they cover most of the islands tourists are likely to visit. However, some of the islands cannot be reached directly, either by sea or by air, from Athens; if you have an urge to visit any of those spots, check out possible transportation with the Greek Tourist Organization (EOT).

By Sea

In an area of the world where so much history was written by seafarers for so many centuries, you'll probably want to sail from the mainland to the islands. There are plenty of boats, lots of departures, and accommodations to suit every budget. An island such as Mýkonos, for example, is only 6 or 7 hours away by sea, and you can get to the farthest islands, such as Rhodes, within 24 hours. Mýkonos and

Western Greece & the Ionian Islands

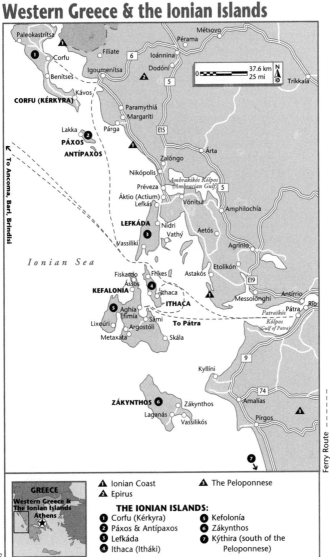

Paleokastrítsa · Métsovo · Pérama
Filiate · Ioánnina · Tríkkala
Corfu · Igoumenítsa · Dodóni
Benítses · Kávos
CORFU (KÉRKYRA)
Paramythiá · Margariti
Lakka · Párga · Zalóngo · Arta
PÁXOS
ANTÍPAXOS
Nikópolis
Préveza · *Ambrakikós Kólpos* · Amphilochía
Áktio (Actium) · *(Ambracian Gulf)*
Lefkás · Vónitsa
LEFKÁDA · Nidri · Aetós
Vathý · Agrínio
Vassilikí
Ionian Sea · Etolikón
Fiskardo · Fríkes · Astakós
Ássos
KEFALONÍA · Ithaca · Messolónghi · Antírrio
Aghía · **ITHACA** · Pátra · Río
Efimía · Sámi · *Patraikós*
Lixoúri · Argostóli · **To Pátra** · *Kólpos*
Metaxáta · Skála · *(Gulf of Patra)*
Kyllíni
ZÁKYNTHOS · Amalías
Laganás · Zákynthos · Pírgos
Vassilikós

0 — 37.6 km / 25 mi   N

To Ancoma, Barí, Brindisi

Ferry Route

GREECE
Western Greece &
The Ionian Islands
Athens ★

△ Ionian Coast   ▲ The Peloponnese
▲ Epirus

THE IONIAN ISLANDS:
❶ Corfu (Kérkyra)   ❺ Kefolonía
❷ Páxos & Antípaxos   ❻ Zákynthos
❸ Lefkáda   ❼ Kýthira (south of the
❹ Ithaca (Itháki)   Peloponnese)

neighboring Cyclades islands, as well as Rhodes and its neighbors, are now linked by regular hydrofoil service.

The ferryboats and ships that carry passengers from Piraeus to the islands vary considerably (some of them have been around for a long time), and it's not possible in these few pages to give you a listing of the best craft—you'll have to get that information from your travel agent, the Greek Tourist Organization, or someone standing in line at the American Express office on Sýntagma Square in Athens. Generally, you'll be able to choose between private cabins, shared cabins, bunks, lounges, and deck class (which may be rugged but in some ways is the most fun). Most ferryboats have some kind of snack bar on board, but to be on the safe side take along a simple picnic.

Theoretically, the boats operate on a fixed schedule; but since so many indirect factors may affect their performance (weather and cargo, to name two), you should never rely on precise timing. Getting around *between* the islands is strictly for people with time to spare.

There's a more reliable (and more comfortable) way of seeing the islands by boat, and that's by taking one of the dozens of cruise ships on 3-day, 4-day, or longer voyages (see the section "Island Cruises" below). But the great advantages of ferryboats and interisland boats are frequency of schedules and *economy.*

Here are examples of economical fares: A "deluxe" cabin (about the equivalent of an average outside cabin on a cruise ship, with private bathroom and wobbly TV) costs only $52 on the trip from Piraeus to Crete; a "deck" ticket—that is, with seating in lounges or on deck—costs only $20. And that's on a 9- to 10-hour voyage (by air the 1-hour Athens-to-Crete trip is $51). To magical Mýkonos—a 5- to 7-hour trip—the cheapest ferryboat fare is around $13. Always check the details on your ticket—name of shipping company, name of vessel, and destination—before leaving your travel agent or ticket office.

The logistics of getting to the islands is now simpler and more pleasant with the completion of a new terminal just outside the dock area at Piraeus, complete with spacious waiting room, café, and sidewalk tables shaded by sun umbrellas.

By Air

Air service within Greece is operated by Olympic Airways and a subsidiary, Olympic Aviation S.A., the latter handling those domestic services that involve light aircraft. However, all the services are listed together in the Olympic timetable, individual flights use Olympic codes, and all reservations are handled by Olympic Airways offices throughout the world.

On its domestic routes, Olympic Airways flies Boeing 737s, Boeing 727s, and a few commuter aircraft such as ATRs and Dorniers; Olympic Aviation now has a versatile fleet of Piper Aztecs, Britten-Norman Islanders, and Alouette helicopters for rich Swiss who can't get to their yachts fast enough. For island-hopping vacationers, the best news is that this augmented fleet offers service within the islands, so that travelers no longer have to double back to Athens to get from one island to the other. Olympic Aviation operates several times a week between Rhodes, Santoríni (Thíra), and Crete; between Rhodes

IMPRESSIONS

The isles of Greece, the isles of Greece!
—Byron, *Don Juan,* 1819–24

The Cyclades

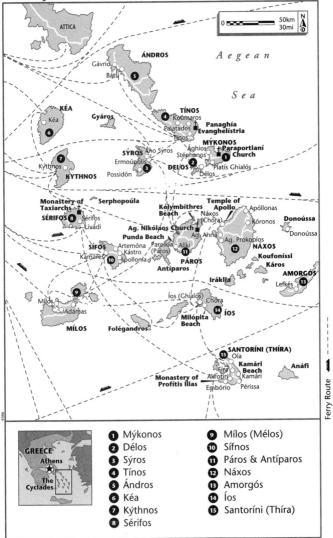

1 Mýkonos	**9** Mílos (Mélos)
2 Délos	**10** Sífnos
3 Sýros	**11** Páros & Antíparos
4 Tínos	**12** Náxos
5 Ándros	**13** Amorgós
6 Kéa	**14** Íos
7 Kýthnos	**15** Santoríni (Thíra)
8 Sérifos	

and Kos; and between Rhodes and Mýkonos. There are also services to and from Skiáthos, Límnos, Mytilíni (Lésvos), and Kastoriá, and between Athens and Vólos, to name just a few. These services make life simpler for travelers with limited time; when it's time to plan your trip, ask your travel agent for the latest details of these and other new domestic services. You can also pick up an Olympic Airways schedule at the Greek Tourist Organization.

8 Island Cruises

There are two other ways of seeing these gleaming sunny islands—
by cruise ship or by charter yacht. You board a luxury cruise ship in
Piraeus and set off for a few days of relaxed island-hopping—without having to pack and unpack more than once, without having to
dash out to airports to catch flights. These island cruises are a happy
combination of touring and vacationing—you have a chance to see
the sights, but you also get to lounge around the pool or sunbathe
on the deck between ports of call.

Usually, the longer stretches between islands are covered during
the night, when you can't really do much sightseeing anyway, and
the time you do have to spend on shore varies, depending on all sorts
of factors—time of departure from Piraeus, availability of berths on
tenders, and arrangement of itinerary.

Some stops you'll find too short—obviously on a three-day cruise,
for example, you can't include everything. However, a stop on Crete
will always allow you time at least to visit the Minoan ruins at
Knossós, and in Rhodes you'll be able to visit the old walled city and
its museums, and you'll probably have time also to take the four-hour
coach tour to Líndos.

There are half a dozen shipping companies operating cruises
through the Greek islands on a regular basis, and one in six visitors
to Greece takes a cruise—or, put another way, a total of more than
a dozen ships transport a million passengers every year. The leading
cruise lines with dependable track records are Sun, Epirotikí, and
Dolphin Hellas. In addition, you can also board other cruise ships
making stops in Piraeus on longer voyages through the eastern or
western Mediterranean—ships such as one of the luxurious *Sea
Goddess* liner/yachts (from the French or Italian Riviera), or even su-
perliners such as the *QE2* or *Vistafjord* of Cunard Line or the *Royal
Viking Sun.*

Many of the cruise ships operating short cruises through the Greek
islands, such as the five-star *Stella Solaris* and the *Triton,* are full-scale
ocean liners; all of them are equipped with the full range of facilities
that you would expect to find in a resort hotel—swimming pool, air
conditioning, nightclub, disco, bars, mini-casinos, and beauty
salon—everything except a beach (and even there they invariably put
you ashore near one.) Most of their cabins are equipped with
wall-to-wall carpeting, private toilet and shower (in larger cabins, full
bathtub), telephone, and two-channel radio. Stewards, cruise directors, tour guides, and most other members of the crew who come
into contact with passengers speak fluent English.

Rates vary enormously, of course, depending on the duration of
the cruise, the size and facilities of the ship, and the type of cabin
accommodations. An *average* cost runs something like $300 to $380
per day per person. Your travel agent will be able to show you deck
plans when you get around to choosing a specific cruise and a

The Dodecanese

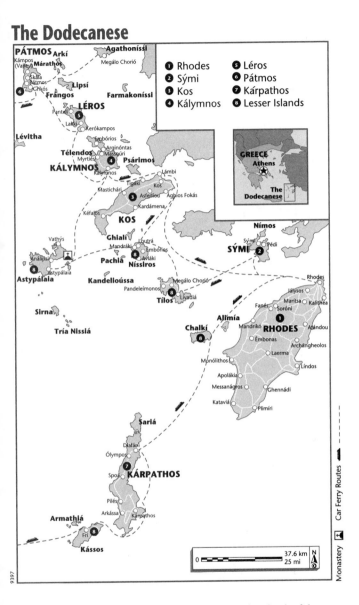

specific ship, at the same time giving you up-to-date details of the fares.

Remember that fares include all your meals for three or four days—a total of 15 meals, for example, on a three-day cruise. The food is usually international fare, with a touch of Greek at most meals; at least one poolside buffet; and usually one Greek evening when the entire meal is Greek and the crew entertains you with folk music and dancing.

Rhodes

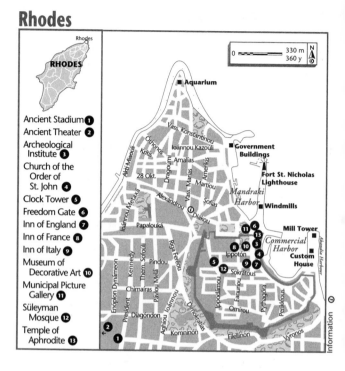

Ancient Stadium **1**
Ancient Theater **2**
Archeological
  Institute **3**
Church of the
  Order of
  St. John **4**
Clock Tower **5**
Freedom Gate **6**
Inn of England **7**
Inn of France **8**
Inn of Italy **9**
Museum of
  Decorative Art **10**
Municipal Picture
  Gallery **11**
Süleyman
  Mosque **12**
Temple of
  Aphrodite **13**

Think about it. A cruise is a great way to see several islands on a short vacation. It's a great way to get some sun. The sea is usually calm—*usually*. You see the sights. You make new friends. You eat heartily. Chances are that you'll probably find the three-day cruise too short and wish you had opted for four days, at least.

Shore excursions are extra, but if keeping costs down is a prime consideration, check the prices: You may be able to arrange a better deal with a local taxi driver or tour operator, but, of course, you may lose valuable time ashore if you have to negotiate a trip or find someone who can take you.

The other extra on cruises is tipping—another $10 per day per person. The crew usually has a system for reminding passengers about tips, suggesting appropriate figures and collecting the currency—but tipping is, of course, optional.

Crete

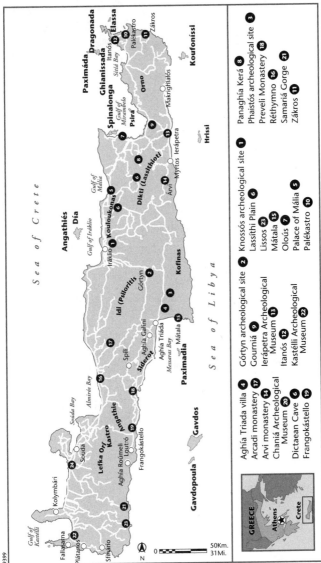

Aghía Triáda villa **4**
Arcadi monastery **17**
Arvi monastery **14**
Chaniá Archeological Museum **20**
Dictaean Cave **6**
Frangokástello **19**

Górtyn archeological site **2**
Gourniá **9**
Ierápetra Archeological Museum **13**
Itanós **12**
Kastélli Archeological Museum **22**

Knossós archeological site **1**
Lassíthi Plain **6**
Lissós **23**
Mátala **15**
Oloús **7**
Palékastro **10**

Panaghía Kerá **8**
Phaistós archeological site **18**
Preveli Monastery **16**
Réthymno **16**
Samariá Gorge **11**
Zákros **21**

Appendix

Basic Greek Vocabulary

Greek is relatively easy to pronounce. Every syllable in a word is uttered as written, and words of more than one syllable almost always have a stress accent. The pronunciation guide below is intended to aid you as you go over the basic words and phrases listed in this appendix. While your pronunciation may not be perfect, you'll find that people in Greece will quickly warm to you if you try to speak to them in their own language.

The transliteration of Greek into English presents a special problem, because there is no recognized standard system to go by. Thus, for example, the island of ΑΙΓΙΝΑ is variously spelled Aegina, Aiyina, and Egina, while the name ΓΕΩΡΓΙΟΣ shows up in English as Georgios, Gheorghios, and Yeoryios, to cite only some of the variants. So, don't be surprised if you see a street or a town spelled differently on your map or on a signpost. (If you can read the Greek, you have the game won!)

GREEK ALPHABET	NAME	TRANSLITERATION	PRONUNCIATION
A, α	álfa	a	f*a*ther
B, β	víta	v	e*v*ade
Γ, γ	gámma	gh or y	*y*es
Δ, δ	délta	d or dh	*th*en
E, ε	épsilon	e	e*gg*
Z, ζ	zíta	z	*z*one
H, η	íta	i	mach*i*ne
Θ, θ	thíta	th	*th*in
I, ι	yóta	i y (semi-consonantal)	*is* nat*i*on
K, κ	káppa	k	*k*ey
Λ, λ	lámbda	l	*l*amb
M, μ	mí	m	*m*other
N, ν	ní	n	*n*et
Ξ, ξ	xí	x	a*x*e
O, o	ómikron	o	*o*ver
Π, π	pí	p	*p*et
P, ρ	ró	r	bu*rr*o (with a slight trill)
Σ, σ, ς*	sígma	s	*s*ee
T, τ	táf	t	*t*op
Y, υ	ípsilon	y or i	p*y*ramid
Φ, φ	fí	f or ph	*ph*ilosophy
X, χ	chí	ch or h	Scottish lo*ch* or German *ich*
Ψ, ψ	psí	ps	la*ps*e
Ω, ω	oméga	o	*o*ver (but slightly longer)

*The letter ς occurs only at the end of a word; σ occurs elsewhere in a word. For example: σεισμός, "earthquake."

DIPHTHONGS	TRANSLITERATION	PRONUNCIATION
AI, αι	ai, ae, *or* e	like *e* above
EI, ει OI, οι	i	like *i* above
OY, ου	ou	L*ou*vre
AY, αυ	av before vowels and some consonants af before other consonants	a*v*ert *af*firm
EY, ευ	ev before vowels and some consonants ef before other consonants	le*v*el l*ef*t

DOUBLE CONSONANTS	TRANSLITERATION	PRONUNCIATION
ΓΓ, γγ ΓΚ, γκ	ng nasalised	a*ng*le
ΜΠ, μπ	b	*b*ar
ΝΤ, ντ	d (at the beginning of a word) nd (in the middle of a word)	*d*andy da*nd*y
ΤΣ, τσ	ts	hi*ts*

WORDS & PHRASES

Airport	**Aerodrómio**
Automobile	**Aftokínito**
Avenue	**Leofóros**
Bad	**Kakós, -kí, -kó***
Bank	**Trápeza**
The bill, please.	**Tón logaryazmó(n), parakaló.**
Breakfast	**Proinó**
Bus	**Leoforío**
Can you tell me?	**Boríte ná moú píte?**
Car	**Amáxi**
Cheap	**Ft(h)inó**
Church	**Ekklissía**
Closed	**Klistós, -stí, stó***
Coast	**Aktí**
Coffeehouse	**Kafenío**
Cold	**Kríos, -a, -o***
Dinner	**Vradinó**
Does anyone speak English?	**Milái kanís angliká?**
Excuse me.	**Signómi(n).**
Expensive	**Akrivó**
Farewell!	**Stó ka-ló! (to person leaving)**
Glad to meet you.	**Chéro polí.****
Good	**Kalós, -lí, -ló***
Good-bye	**Adío or chérete**
Good evening	**Kalispéra**
Good health (cheers)!	**Stín (i)yá sas or Yá-mas!**
Good morning	**Kaliméra**
Good night	**Kaliníchta**
Hello!	**Yássas or chérete!**
Here	**Edó**
Hot	**Zestós, -stí, -stó***
Hotel	**Xenodochío**
How are you?	**Tí kánete or Pós íst(h)e?**
How far?	**Pósso makriá?**
How long?	**Póssi óra or Pósso(n) keró?**
How much is it?	**Pósso káni?**
I am from New York.	**Íme apó tí(n) Néa(n) Iórki.**
I am lost or I have lost the way.	**Écho chathí or Écho chási tón drómo(n).**
I'm sorry, but I don't speak Greek (well).	**Lipoúme, allá dén miláo elliniká (kalá).**

I don't understand, please repeat it.	**Dén katalavéno, péste to páli, sás parakaló.**
I want to go to the airport.	**Thélo ná páo stó aerodrómio.**
I want a glass of beer.	**Thélo éna potíri bíra.**
It's (not) all right.	**(Dén) íne én dáxi.**
Left (direction)	**Aristerá**
Ladies' room	**Ghinekón**
Lunch	**Messimerianó**
Map	**Chártis**
Market(place)	**Agorá**
Men's room	**Andrón**
Mr.	**Kýrios**
Mrs.	**Kyría**
Miss	**Despinís**
My name is . . .	**Onomázome . . .**
New	**Kenoúryos, -ya, -yo***
No	**Óchi**
Old	**Palyós, -lyá, -lyó***
Open	**Anichtós, -chtí, -chtó***
Pâtisserie	**Zacharoplastí-o**
Pharmacy	**Farmakío**
Please	**Parakaló**
Please call a taxi (for me).	**Parakaló, fonáxte éna taxí (yá ména).**
Post office	**Tachidromío**
Restaurant	**Estiatório**
Restroom	**Tó méros** *or* **I toualétta**
Right (direction)	**Dexiá**
Saint	**Ághios, aghía, (*plural*) ághi-i (*abbrevlated* ag.)**
Shore	**Paralía**
Square	**Platía**
Street	**Odós**
Show me on the map.	**Díxte mou stó(n) chárti.**
Station (bus, train)	**Stathmós (leoforíou, trénou)**
Stop (bus)	**Stási(s) (leoforíou)**
Telephone	**Tiléfono**
Temple (of Athena, Zeus)	**Naós (Athinás, Diós)**
Thank you (very much).	**Efcharistó (polí).**
Today	**Símera**
Tomorrow	**Ávrio**

Very nice	**Polí oréos, -a, -o***
Very well	**Polí kalá** or **En dáxi**
What?	**Tí?**
What time is it?	**Tí óra íne?**
What's your name?	**Pós onomázest(h)e?**
Where is . . . ?	**Poú íne . . . ?**
Why?	**Yatí?**

*Masculine ending -os, feminine ending -a or -i, neuter ending -o.
**Remember, ch should be pronounced as in Scottish loch or German ich, not as in the word church.

NUMBERS

0 **Midén**	18 **Dekaoktó**	152 **Ekatón penínda dío**
1 **Éna**	19 **Dekaenyá**	200 **Diakóssya**
2 **Dío**	20 **Íkossi**	300 **Triakóssya**
3 **Tría**	21 **Íkossi éna**	400 **Tetrakóssya**
4 **Téssera**	22 **Íkossi dío**	500 **Pendakóssya**
5 **Pénde**	30 **Triánda**	600 **Exakóssya**
6 **Éxi**	40 **Saránda**	700 **Eftakóssya**
7 **Eftá**	50 **Penínda**	800 **Oktakóssya**
8 **Októ**	60 **Exínda**	900 **Enyakóssya**
9 **Enyá**	70 **Evdomínda**	1,000 **Chílya**
10 **Déka**	80 **Ogdónda**	2,000 **Dío chilyádes**
11 **Éndeka**	90 **Enenínda**	3,000 **Trís chilyádes**
12 **Dódeka**	100 **Ekató(n)**	4,000 **Tésseris chilyádes**
13 **Dekatría**	101 **Ekatón éna**	5,000 **Pénde chilyádes**
14 **Dekatéssera**	102 **Ekatón dío**	
15 **Dekapénde**	150 **Ekatón penínda**	
16 **Dekaéxi**	151 **Ekatón penínda éna**	
17 **Dekaeftá**		

CALENDAR

Monday **Deftéra**	Friday **Paraskeví**
Tuesday **Tríti**	Saturday **Sávvato**
Wednesday **Tetárti**	Sunday **Kiriakí**
Thursday **Pémpti**	

January **Ianouários**	July **Ioúlios**
February **Fevrouários**	August **Ávgoustos**
March **Mártios**	September **Septémvrios**
April **Aprílios**	October **Októvrios**
May **Máios**	November **Noémvrios**
June **Ioúnios**	December **Dekémvrios**

MENU TERMS
Hors d'Oeuvres—Orektiká

Taramosaláta Fish roe with mayonnaise
Tirópita Cheese pie
Spanokópita Spinach pie
Melitzanosaláta Eggplant salad
Domátes yemistés mé rízi Tomatoes stuffed with rice

Chórta Dandelion salad
Piperiés yemistés Stuffed green peppers
Tzatzíki Yogurt-cucumber-garlic dip

Fish—Psári

Astakós (ladolémono) Lobster (with oil-and-lemon sauce)
Bakaliáro (skordaliá) Cod (with garlic)
Barboúnia (skáras) Red mullet (grilled)
Karavídes Crayfish
Garídes Shrimp

Glóssa (tiganití) Sole (fried)
Kalamarákia (tiganitá) Squid (fried)
Kalamarákia (yemistá) Squid (stuffed)
Oktapódi Octopus
Soupiés yemistés Stuffed cuttlefish
Tsípoura Dorado

Meats—Kréas

Arní soúvlas Spit-roasted lamb
Arní yiouvétsi Baked lamb with orzo
Arní avgolémono Lamb with lemon sauce
Brizóla moscharísia Beef or veal steak
Brizóla chiriní Pork steak or chop
Dolmadákia Stuffed vine leaves
Keftédes Fried meatballs

Kotópoulo soúvlas Spit-roasted chicken
Kotópoulo yemistó Stuffed chicken
Loukánika Spiced sausages
Moussaká Meat and eggplant
Païdákia Lamb chops
Piláfi rízi Rice pilaf
Souvláki Lamb (sometimes veal) on the skewer
Youvarlákia Boiled meatballs with rice

B   The Metric System

Length

1 millimeter (mm)	=	.04 inches (*or* less than $1/16$ in.)
1 centimeter (cm)	=	.39 inches (*or* just under $1/2$ in.)
1 meter (m)	=	39 inches (*or* about 1.1 yards)
1 kilometer (km)	=	.62 miles (*or* about $2/3$ of a mile)

To convert kilometers to miles, multiply the number of kilometers by .62. Also use to convert kilometers per hour (kmph) to miles per hour (m.p.h.).

To convert miles to kilometers, multiply the number of miles by 1.61. Also use to convert from m.p.h. to kmph.

Capacity

1 liter (l)	=	33.92 fluid ounces	=	2.1 pints
	=	1.06 quarts	=	.26 U.S. gallons
1 Imperial gallon	=	1.2 U.S. gallons		

To convert liters to U.S. gallons, multiply the number of liters by .26.

To convert U.S. gallons to liters, multiply the number of gallons by 3.79.

To convert Imperial gallons to U.S. gallons, multiply the number of Imperial gallons by 1.2.

To convert U.S. gallons to Imperial gallons, multiply the number of U.S. gallons by .83.

Weight

1 gram (g)	=	.035 ounces (*or* about a paperclip's weight)		
1 kilogram (kg)	=	35.2 ounces		
	=	2.2 pounds		
1 metric ton	=	2,205 pounds	=	1.1 short ton

To convert kilograms to pounds, multiply the number of kilograms by 2.2.

To convert pounds to kilograms, multiply the number of pounds by .45.

Temperature

To convert degrees Celsius to degrees Fahrenheit,
multiply °C by 9, divided by 5, and add 32
(example: 20°C $\times\, ^9/_5 + 32 = 68°F$).

To convert degrees Fahrenheit to degrees Celsius,
subtract 32 from °F, multiply by 5, then divide by 9
(example: 85°F $- 32 \times\, ^5/_9 = 29.4°C$).

INDEX

204

Accommodations in Athens

Accommodations in Excursion Areas ————————

Restaurants in Athens ————————————

Restaurants in Excursion Areas

Now Save Money On All Your Travels By Joining
FROMMER'S™ TRAVEL BOOK CLUB
The World's Best Travel Guides
At Membership Prices!

Frommer's Travel Book Club is your ticket to successful travel! Open up a world of travel information and simplify your travel planning when you join ranks with thousands of value-conscious travelers who are members of the Frommer's *Travel Book Club.* Join today and you'll be entitled to all the privileges that come from belonging to the club that offers you travel guides for less to more than 100 destinations worldwide. **Annual membership is only $25.00 (U.S.) or $35.00 (Canada/Foreign).**

The Advantages of Membership:

1. Your choice of **three free** books (any **two** Frommer's Comprehensive Guides, Frommer's $-A-Day Guides, Frommer's Walking Tours or Frommer's Family Guides—plus **one** Frommer's City Guide, Frommer's City $-A-Day Guide or Frommer's Touring Guide).

2. Your own subscription to the **TRIPS & TRAVEL** quarterly newsletter.

3. You're entitled to a **30% discount** on your order of any additional books offered by the club.

4. You're offered (at a small additional fee) our **Domestic Trip-Routing Kits.**

Our **Trips & Travel** quarterly newsletter offers practical information on the best buys in travel, the "hottest" vacation spots, the latest travel trends, world-class events and much, much more.

Our **Domestic Trip-Routing Kits** are available for any North American destination. We'll send you a detailed map highlighting the best route to take to your destination—you can request direct or scenic routes.

Here's all you have to do to join:

Send in your membership fee of $25.00 ($35.00 Canada/Foreign) with your name and address on the form below along with your selections as part of your membership package to the address listed below. Remember to check off your three free books.

If you would like to order additional books, please select the books you would like and send a check for the total amount (please add sales tax in the states noted below), plus $2.00 per book for shipping and handling ($3.00 Canada/Foreign) to the address listed below.

FROMMER'S TRAVEL BOOK CLUB
P.O. Box 473
Mt. Morris, IL 61054-0473
(815) 734-1104

[ ] **YES!** I want to take advantage of this opportunity to join Frommer's Travel Book Club.

[ ] My check is enclosed. Dollar amount enclosed_____ *
(all payments in U.S. funds only)

Name _____

Address _____

City _____ State _____ Zip _____

Phone ( ) _____ (In case we have a question regarding your order).

All orders must be prepaid.

To ensure that all orders are processed efficiently, please apply sales tax in the following areas: CA, CT, FL, IL, IN, NJ, NY, PA, TN, WA and CANADA.

*With membership, shipping & handling will be paid by Frommer's Travel Book Club for the three FREE books you select as part of your membership. Please add $2.00 per book for shipping & handling for any additional books purchased ($3.00 Canada/Foreign).

Allow 4-6 weeks for delivery for all items. Prices of books, membership fee, and publication dates are subject to change without notice. All orders are subject to acceptance and availability.

Please send me the books checked below:

FROMMER'S COMPREHENSIVE GUIDES

*(Guides listing facilities from budget to deluxe,
with emphasis on the medium-priced)*

	Retail Price	Code		Retail Price	Code
☐ Acapulco/Ixtapa/Taxco, 2nd Edition	$13.95	C157	☐ Jamaica/Barbados, 2nd Edition	$15.00	C149
☐ Alaska '94-'95	$17.00	C131	☐ Japan '94-'95	$19.00	C144
☐ Arizona '95 (Avail. 3/95)	$14.95	C166	☐ Maui, 1st Edition	$14.00	C153
☐ Australia '94'-'95	$18.00	C147	☐ Nepal, 2nd Edition	$18.00	C126
☐ Austria, 6th Edition	$16.95	C162	☐ New England '95	$16.95	C165
☐ Bahamas '94-'95	$17.00	C121	☐ New Mexico, 3rd Edition (Avail. 3/95)	$14.95	C167
☐ Belgium/Holland/ Luxembourg '93-'94	$18.00	C106	☐ New York State '94-'95	$19.00	C133
☐ Bermuda '94-'95	$15.00	C122	☐ Northwest, 5th Edition	$17.00	C140
☐ Brazil, 3rd Edition	$20.00	C111	☐ Portugal '94-'95	$17.00	C141
☐ California '95	$16.95	C164	☐ Puerto Rico '95-'96	$14.00	C151
☐ Canada '94-'95	$19.00	C145	☐ Puerto Vallarta/ Manzanillo/Guadalajara '94-'95	$14.00	C135
☐ Caribbean '95	$18.00	C148			
☐ Carolinas/Georgia, 2nd Edition	$17.00	C128	☐ Scandinavia, 16th Edition (Avail. 3/95)	$19.95	C169
☐ Colorado, 2nd Edition	$16.00	C143	☐ Scotland '94-'95	$17.00	C146
☐ Costa Rica '95	$13.95	C161	☐ South Pacific '94-'95	$20.00	C138
☐ Cruises '95-'96	$19.00	C150	☐ Spain, 16th Edition	$16.95	C163
☐ Delaware/Maryland '94-'95	$15.00	C136	☐ Switzerland/ Liechtenstein '94-'95	$19.00	C139
☐ England '95	$17.95	C159	☐ Thailand, 2nd Edition	$17.95	C154
☐ Florida '95	$18.00	C152	☐ U.S.A., 4th Edition	$18.95	C156
☐ France '94-'95	$20.00	C132	☐ Virgin Islands '94-'95	$13.00	C127
☐ Germany '95	$18.95	C158	☐ Virginia '94-'95	$14.00	C142
☐ Ireland, 1st Edition (Avail. 3/95)	$16.95	C168	☐ Yucatan, 2nd Edition	$13.95	C155
☐ Italy '95	$18.95	C160			

FROMMER'S $-A-DAY GUIDES

(Guides to low-cost tourist accommodations and facilities)

	Retail Price	Code		Retail Price	Code
☐ Australia on $45 '95-'96	$18.00	D122	☐ Israel on $45, 15th Edition	$16.95	D130
☐ Costa Rica/Guatemala/ Belize on $35, 3rd Edition	$15.95	D126	☐ Mexico on $45 '95	$16.95	D125
			☐ New York on $70 '94-'95	$16.00	D121
☐ Eastern Europe on $30, 5th Edition	$16.95	D129	☐ New Zealand on $45 '93-'94	$18.00	D103
☐ England on $60 '95	$17.95	D128	☐ South America on $40, 16th Edition	$18.95	D123
☐ Europe on $50 '95	$17.95	D127			
☐ Greece on $45 '93-'94	$19.00	D100	☐ Washington, D.C. on $50 '94-'95	$17.00	D120
☐ Hawaii on $75 '95	$16.95	D124			
☐ Ireland on $45 '94-'95	$17.00	D118			

FROMMER'S CITY $-A-DAY GUIDES

	Retail Price	Code		Retail Price	Code
☐ Berlin on $40 '94-'95	$12.00	D111	☐ Madrid on $50 '94-'95	$13.00	D119
☐ London on $45 '94-'95	$12.00	D114	☐ Paris on $50 '94-'95	$12.00	D117

FROMMER'S FAMILY GUIDES

*(Guides listing information on kid-friendly
hotels, restaurants, activities and attractions)*

	Retail Price	Code		Retail Price	Code
☐ California with Kids	$18.00	F100	☐ San Francisco with Kids	$17.00	F104
☐ Los Angeles with Kids	$17.00	F103	☐ Washington, D.C.		
☐ New York City			with Kids	$17.00	F102
with Kids	$18.00	F101			

FROMMER'S CITY GUIDES

*(Pocket-size guides to sightseeing and tourist
accommodations and facilities in all price ranges)*

	Retail Price	Code		Retail Price	Code
☐ Amsterdam '93-'94	$13.00	S110	☐ Montreal/Quebec City '95	$11.95	S166
☐ Athens, 10th Edition			☐ Nashville/Memphis,		
(Avail. 3/95)	$12.95	S174	1st Edition	$13.00	S141
☐ Atlanta '95	$12.95	S161	☐ New Orleans '95	$12.95	S148
☐ Atlantic City/Cape May,			☐ New York '95	$13.00	S145
5th Edition	$13.00	S130	☐ Orlando '95	$13.00	S145
☐ Bangkok, 2nd Edition	$12.95	S147	☐ Paris '95	$12.95	S150
☐ Barcelona '93-'94	$13.00	S115	☐ Philadelphia, 8th Edition	$12.95	S167
☐ Berlin, 3rd Edition	$12.95	S162	☐ Prague '94-'95	$13.00	S143
☐ Boston '95	$12.95	S160	☐ Rome, 10th Edition	$12.95	S168
☐ Budapest, 1st Edition	$13.00	S139	☐ St. Louis/Kansas City,		
☐ Chicago '95	$12.95	S169	2nd Edition	$13.00	S127
☐ Denver/Boulder/Colorado			☐ San Diego '95	$12.95	S158
Springs, 3rd Edition	$12.95	S154	☐ San Francisco '95	$12.95	S155
☐ Dublin, 2nd Edition	$12.95	S157	☐ Santa Fe/Taos/		
☐ Hong Kong '94-'95	$13.00	S140	Albuquerque '95		
☐ Honolulu/Oahu '95	$12.95	S151	(Avail. 2/95)	$12.95	S172
☐ Las Vegas '95	$12.95	S163	☐ Seattle/Portland '94-'95	$13.00	S137
☐ London '95	$12.95	S156	☐ Sydney, 4th Edition	$12.95	S171
☐ Los Angeles '95	$12.95	S164	☐ Tampa/St. Petersburg,		
☐ Madrid/Costa del Sol,			3rd Edition	$13.00	S146
2nd Edition	$12.95	S165	☐ Tokyo '94-'95	$13.00	S144
☐ Mexico City, 1st Edition	$12.95	S170	☐ Toronto '95 (Avail. 3/95)	$12.95	S173
☐ Miami '95-'96	$12.95	S149	☐ Vancouver/Victoria '94-'95	$13.00	S142
☐ Minneapolis/St. Paul,			☐ Washington, D.C. '95	$12.95	S153
4th Edition	$12.95	S159			

FROMMER'S WALKING TOURS

*(Companion guides that point out the places
and pleasures that make a city unique)*

	Retail Price	Code		Retail Price	Code
☐ Berlin	$12.00	W100	☐ New York	$12.00	W102
☐ Chicago	$12.00	W107	☐ Paris	$12.00	W103
☐ England's Favorite Cities	$12.00	W108	☐ San Francisco	$12.00	W104
☐ London	$12.00	W101	☐ Washington, D.C.	$12.00	W105
☐ Montreal/Quebec City	$12.00	W106			

SPECIAL EDITIONS

	Retail Price	Code		Retail Price	Code
☐ Bed & Breakfast Southwest	$16.00	P100	☐ National Park Guide, 29th Edition	$17.00	P106
☐ Bed & Breakfast Great American Cities	$16.00	P104	☐ Where to Stay U.S.A., 11th Edition	$15.00	P102
☐ Caribbean Hideaways	$16.00	P103			

FROMMER'S TOURING GUIDES

*(Color-illustrated guides that include walking tours,
cultural and historic sites, and practical information)*

	Retail Price	Code		Retail Price	Code
☐ Amsterdam	$11.00	T001	☐ New York	$11.00	T008
☐ Barcelona	$14.00	T015	☐ Rome	$11.00	T010
☐ Brazil	$11.00	T003	☐ Tokyo	$15.00	T016
☐ Hong Kong/Singapore/ Macau	$11.00	T006	☐ Turkey	$11.00	T013
☐ London	$13.00	T007	☐ Venice	$ 9.00	T014

*Please note: If the availability of a book is several months away, we may
have back issues of guides to that particular destination.
Call customer service at (815) 734-1104.*